Microsoft®

Windows® 2000
Professional

Built on **NT** Technology

At a
Glance

Jerry Joyce and
Marianne Moon

PUBLISHED BY
Microsoft Press
A Division of Microsoft Corporation
One Microsoft Way
Redmond, Washington 98052-6399

Library of Congress Cataloging-in-Publication Data
Joyce, Jerry, 1950-
    Microsoft Windows 2000 Professional At a Glance / Jerry Joyce and Marianne Moon.
        p. cm.
    ISBN 1-57231-839-2
    1. Microsoft windows (Computer file)   2. Operating systems (Computers)   I. Title.   II.
Moon, Marianne.
QA76.76.O63 .J6935   1999
005.4'4769 21--dc21   99-045527

Printed and bound in the United States of America.

1 2 3 4 5 6 7 8 9   QEQE   5 4 3 2 1 0

Distributed in Canada by Penguin Books Canada Limited.

A CIP catalogue record for this book is available from the British Library.

Microsoft Press books are available through booksellers and distributors worldwide. For further information about international editions, contact your local Microsoft Corporation office or contact Microsoft Press International directly at fax (425) 936-7329. Visit our Web site at mspress.microsoft.com.

Acquisitions Editor: Christey Bahn
Project Editor: Kim Fryer
Technical Editor: Moon Joyce Resources
Manuscript Editor: Marianne Moon

Contents

Acknowledgments . . . . *x*

*A quick
overview*

See page 2.

*Windows 2000
is your working
headquarters.*

See page 6.

Explore your network.
See pages 22–23.

1 **About This Book** **1**
 No Computerese! 1
 A Quick Overview 2
 A Few Assumptions 3
 A Final Word (or Two) 4

2 **Jump Right In** **5**
 Windows 2000 at a Glance 6
 Starting Up 8
 Shutting Down 9
 Managing a Program Window 10
 Folders and the File Structure 12
 Using Shortcut Menus for Quick Results 13
 Getting Help 14
 Mouse Maneuvers 16
 Wheeling Around with the Mouse 18

3 **Accessing** **19**
 Exploring Your Documents 20
 Exploring Your Computer 21
 Exploring Your Network. 22
 Different Ways of Networking 24
 Reconnecting to a Network Folder 26
 Assigning a Drive Letter to a Network Folder. 27
 Opening a Document 28
 Opening a Document You Used Recently. 30
 Creating Quick Access to a Document. 31
 Opening a Document You Used Previously 32
 File Associations, File Extensions, and Registered Programs. 34
 Finding a Document 36

Create your own
toolbars.
See page 41.

Organize your files.
See page 58.

Finding a Document Based on Its Properties 38
Checking the Details About a File or Folder. 39
Navigating with Toolbars. 40
Creating Your Own Toolbars 41
Finding Someone 42
Exploring the Internet 43
Finding Something on the Internet 44
Going to a Specific Web Site 45
Changing Links 46
Returning to Your Favorite Sites. 48
Adding Links to the Desktop 49
Creating Quick Access to a Web Site 50
Accessing Folders from the Command Prompt. 51

④ Organizing   53

Arranging the File Listings. 54
Organizing Your Folders. 56
Reorganizing Your Folders 57
Organizing Your Files. 58
Renaming or Deleting a File or Folder 59
Recovering a Deleted Item 60
Renaming Multiple Files 61
Copying an Item to a Special Location 62
Adding Documents and Folders to the Desktop. 64
Arranging Windows on the Desktop 66
Tidying Up the Desktop. 67
Organizing the Start Menu 68
Reorganizing the Start Menu 70
Organizing Your Favorite Items 72
Cleaning Up Your Lists of Activities. 74
Displaying File and Folder Locations and Types. 75

Publish your own
web pages.
See page 92.

"Look, Ma, I'm multitasking!"

See page 97.

£ ¥

☎ ⇨

Insert special characters.
See page 105.

5 Sharing   **77**

Sharing Your Computer 78
Groups, Permissions, and Security 79
Sharing Documents and Folders 80
Limiting Access to a Shared Folder 82
Monitoring Who's Connected 84
Making Shared Documents Always Available 86
Sharing Programs On Line 88
Sharing a Printer 90
Publishing Your Own Web Pages 92

6 Running Programs   **93**

Starting a Program 94
Starting a Program When Windows 2000 Starts 95
Changing the Way a Program Starts 96
Managing Multiple Programs 97
Copying Material Between Documents 98
Linking to Information That Changes 100
Editing Inserted Material 101
Editing a Document in WordPad 102
Dialog Box Decisions 104
Inserting Special Characters 105
Creating a Picture 106
Editing a Picture 108
Modifying an Image 110
Creating Your Own Font Characters 111
Crunching Numbers 112
Running Commands 114
Exploring the Command Prompt Commands 116
Copying Text at the Command Prompt 117
Sending Command Prompt Output to a File 118
Modifying the Way an MS-DOS Program Runs 119
Quitting When You're Stuck 120

"I want my print job to jump the queue!"

See pages 128–129.

7 Printing — 121

- Installing a Local Printer 122
- Printing from a Program 123
- Printing Documents. 124
- Specifying a Default Printer 125
- Connecting to a Network Printer 126
- Separating Print Jobs 127
- Controlling Your Printing 128
- Printing a Document to a File 130
- Printing Without a Printer 132
- Printing from the Command Prompt to a Network Printer 133

8 Working with Multimedia — 135

- Playing an Audio File 136
- Playing a Music CD 138
- Listening to the Radio 140
- Playing a Video Clip. 141
- Playing Media from the Net 142
- Associating a Sound with an Event 144
- Multimedia Formats and CODECs 145
- Creating a Sound File. 146
- Controlling the Volume 148

9 Connecting — 149

- Adding E-Mail and News Accounts. 150
- Sending E-Mail. 152
- Reading E-Mail 154
- Sending and Receiving Attachments. 156
- Replying to or Forwarding a Message 157
- Managing Messages 158
- Subscribing to Newsgroups 160
- Reading the News. 161
- Downloading the News 162

View streaming media from the net.
See page 142.

Conduct a meeting
on the net.
See pages 184–185.

*Take network
files with you
when you travel.*

See pages 190–193.

Adding to the News 163
Mail Messages, Formats, and Servers 164
Adding a Signature to a Message 165
Adding a Contact to the Contacts List. 166
Defining Identities in Outlook Express. 168
Customizing Outlook Express 170
Sending a Business Card. 171
Sending and Receiving Secure Messages. 172
Setting Up to Send Faxes 174
Setting Up to Receive Faxes 176
Sending a Fax. 178
Receiving a Fax 180
Annotating a Fax 182
Creating a Fax Cover Page 183
Conferring on the Net 184
Making a Phone Call 186

10 Traveling   **189**
Tracking Copied Files. 190
Taking Along Network Files 192
Securing Files with Encryption 194
Connecting from Different Locations 195
Calling to Your Computer 196
Connecting to a Network by Modem. 198
Logging On to a Network from a Remote Location 199
Connecting to a Computer or a Network over the Internet 200
Controlling Your Computer Remotely 202
Connecting with a Terminal 204
Transferring Files by Modem 206
Connecting Two Computers with a Cable 208
Storing Information on a Removable Disk 210
Downloading Files over the Internet 212

Change the look of
your Desktop.
See pages 220–221.

Add a picture to
a folder window.
See page 227.

*"How do I back
up my files?"*

See pages 250–252.

11 **Customizing** **213**

Customize Your Environment 214

Rearranging the Taskbar and the Toolbars 216

Hiding the Taskbar or a Toolbar 218

Changing the Look of the Desktop 220

Creating a Custom Desktop Background 222

Hiding the Desktop Icons 223

Customizing Toolbars 224

Opening a Folder in Its Own Window 225

Adding a Comment to a Folder Window 226

Adding a Background Picture to a Folder Window 227

Customizing a Folder Window for Pictures 228

Displaying Classic Folder Windows 229

Using a Screen Saver 230

Changing Your Click 231

Changing the Mouse Pointers 232

Adjusting Mouse Actions 234

Changing Your Input 236

Changing Your Output 238

Enlarging the View 240

Improving the Look of Your Screen 242

Fitting More Items onto the Desktop 243

Changing Screen Colors 244

Making Everything More Colorful 245

Using Two Monitors 246

12 **Managing Windows 2000** **249**

Backing Up Your Files 250

Restoring Backed-Up Files 252

Securing Your Computer 253

Managing Your Computer's Power 254

Changing the Date and Time Format 256

Adjusting International Settings 258

Adjusting the Date and Time 260

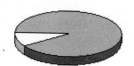

Maintain your
hard drive.
See page 267.

Add or remove
Windows 2000
components.
See pages 276–277.

*"How do I share
my Internet
connection?"*

See pages 294–295.

Changing Your Password 261
Adding Fonts to Your System 262
Hooked on Fonts 264
Updating Your System 266
Maintaining the Drives 267
Diagnosing Problems 268
Documenting the System Configuration 270
Creating an Emergency Repair Disk 271
Starting Up When There's a Problem 272

13 Taking Control   275

Adding or Removing Windows 2000 Components. 276
Installing a Software Program 278
Modifying a Program's Installation 279
Removing a Software Program 280
Starting a Program with Full Access Rights 281
Protecting Individual Files and Folders 282
Adding New Users 284
Defining Custom Access. 286
Defining Access Rights 287
Hosting a Web Site 288
Scheduling Programs 290
Creating Custom Management Tools 292
Editing Windows 2000 Settings. 293
Sharing an Internet Connection 294
Joining a Domain or a Workgroup 296
Creating a New Hardware Profile 297
Changing a Hardware Profile 298
Changing Your Disk Format. 299
Controlling the Startup 300
Creating More Disk Space 302
Allocating Disk Space. 304

Index   305

Acknowledgments

This book was produced by a team of people whose work we trust and admire and whose friendship we value highly. Ken Sánchez meticulously laid out the complex design; no detail was too small to escape his eagle-eyed scrutiny. Alice Copp Smith does much more than proofread and copyedit: her gentle and witty chiding on countless yellow sticky notes makes us groan but teaches us to write better. We welcome two more old friends to our book team: Jan Wright, indexer *par excellence*, whose index reveals in microcosm the soul of the book; and Sue Cook, who produced and polished the interior graphics until they shone, and then cheerfully reworked them as the inevitable interface changes occurred. Sue Bishop once again provided hand-drawn art. We thank them all for their exceptional work and their good-humored patience under shifting deadlines.

At Microsoft Press, we thank Lucinda Rowley for making it possible for us to write this book and our previous five books in the *At a Glance* series. Thanks also to Kim Fryer, Christey Bahn, and Susanne Forderer for editorial and scheduling assistance; to Kevin Coomes, Jim Kramer, and Kurt Meyer for advice and production tools; and to Donnie Cameron and Robert Lyon for help in testing the VPN configurations. Thanks also to Jay Lowe of Parallel Technologies, Inc., for information about the direct-cable connection; to Steve Dunn for the registry-editing example; and to the Microsoft Windows 2000 Beta Support Team for their rapid responses to questions about the software throughout its development.

Roberta, Rick, and Zuzu Abeni Krause provided love and laughter, and allowed their puppies, Baiser and Pierre, to grace some of our pages with their furry little images.

About This Book

IN THIS SECTION

No Computerese!

A Quick Overview

A Few Assumptions

A Final Word (or Two)

If you want to get the most from your computer and your software with the least amount of time and effort—and who doesn't?—this book is for you. You'll find *Microsoft Windows 2000 Professional At a Glance* to be a straightforward, easy-to-read reference tool. With the premise that your computer should work for you, not you for it, this book's purpose is to help you get your work done quickly and efficiently so that you can get away from the computer and live your life.

No Computerese!

Let's face it—when there's a task you don't know how to do but you need to get it done in a hurry, or when you're stuck in the middle of a task and can't figure out what to do next, there's nothing more frustrating than having to read page after page of technical background material. You want the information that you need—nothing more, nothing less—and you want it now! *And* it should be easy to find and understand.

That's what this book is all about. It's written in plain English—no technical jargon and no computerese. There's no single task in the book that takes more than two pages. Just look the task up in the index or the table of contents, turn to the page, and there's the information you need, laid out step by step and accompanied by graphics that add visual clarity. You don't get bogged down by the whys and wherefores: just follow the steps, look at the illustrations, and get your work done with a minimum of hassle.

Occasionally you might have to turn to another page if the procedure you're working on has a "See Also" in the left column. That's because there's a lot of overlap among tasks, and we didn't want to keep repeating ourselves. We've also scattered some useful tips here and there, and thrown in a "Try This" once in a while, but by and large we've tried to remain true to the heart and soul of the book, which is that the information you need should be available to you at a glance.

Useful Tasks...

Whether you use Windows 2000 in the office, at home, or on the road, we've tried to pack this book with procedures for everything we could think of that you might want to do, from the simplest tasks to some of the more esoteric ones.

...And the Easiest Way to Do Them

Another thing we've tried to do in *Microsoft Windows 2000 Professional At a Glance* is to find and document the easiest way to accomplish a task. Windows 2000 often provides a multitude of methods to accomplish a single end result—which can be daunting or delightful, depending on the way you like to work. If you tend to stick with one favorite and familiar approach, we think the methods described in this book are the way to go. If you like trying out alternative techniques, go ahead! The intuitiveness of Windows 2000 invites exploration, and you're likely to discover ways of doing things that you think are easier or that you like better than ours. If you do, that's great! It's exactly what the developers

of Windows 2000 had in mind when they provided so many alternatives.

A Quick Overview

First—because the installation of an operating system within a corporate environment is usually handled over the network by an administrator, and because outside the corporate environment most computers come with Windows 2000 Professional preinstalled—we're going to assume that Windows 2000 is already installed on your computer. If it's not, the Setup Wizard makes installation so simple that you won't need our help anyway. So, unlike many computer books, this one doesn't start with installation instructions and a list of system requirements. You've already got that under control.

Next, you don't have to read this book in any particular order. It's designed so that you can jump in, get the information you need, and then close the book and keep it near your computer until the next time you need to know how to get something done. But that doesn't mean we scattered the information about with wild abandon. We've organized the book so that the tasks you want to accomplish are arranged in two levels—that is, you'll find the overall type of task you're looking for under a main section title such as "Accessing," "Organizing," "Printing," "Running Programs," and so on. Then, in each of those sections, the smaller tasks within the main task are arranged in a loose progression from the simplest to the more complex.

Sections 2 through 4 of the book cover the basics: starting Windows 2000, managing program windows, and learning about the file structure; using shortcut menus, and getting help if you need it; accessing and organizing your documents, files, and folders; using the toolbars and creating your own custom toolbars; rearranging the Start menu; and reaching out and exploring your network and the Internet—searching for people, finding specific web sites, putting a web page on your Desktop, and so on. There's also an introduction to networking—the different types of networks you're likely to encounter, how to find what you need on your network, and how to use the power of a network to your best advantage.

Sections 5 through 8 describe tasks that are a little more technical but are really useful: everything you need to know about sharing your files and folders—and even your printer—with your colleagues and coworkers, and how to control the type of access you'll allow individuals or groups; working with programs, including some of the programs that come with Windows 2000; working painlessly with printers and their idiosyncrasies; and an introduction to working with multimedia, including sound and video files.

Sections 9 and 10 are about communicating with coworkers and friends and using Windows 2000 as your window on the world at large: sending and receiving e-mail and faxes, perusing and taking part in newsgroup discussions, and using some of the tools that go along with working and playing in cyberspace, including telecommuting and videoconferencing directly from your computer whether you're at home, in the office, or on the road. If you think these tasks sound complex, rest assured that they're not—Windows 2000 makes them so easy that you'll sail right through them.

The final sections, 11 through 13, deal with more advanced topics: customizing your Desktop, your folder windows, your mouse, the toolbars, and even the way you enter information, so that everything on your computer looks and works exactly the way you want it to;

backing up your files and securing your computer; updating your system and maintaining the drives; diagnosing and taking care of problems; adding and removing software or hardware components; protecting your files and folders by specifying which individuals or groups are allowed to access them; hosting your own web site; sharing an Internet connection with others in your workgroup; and creating hardware profiles, changing your disk format, and creating more disk space by compressing files, folders, or drives.

A Few Assumptions

Microsoft Windows 2000 Professional sets the standard for a new generation of operating systems. It's designed for ease of use and efficiency whether you're using it on a stand-alone computer, in a small workgroup, or on a large client-server network. It's also an extremely flexible system, which can be configured in so many ways that we can't possibly detail all of them within the scope of this book. To standardize our descriptions, we've used the default settings that Windows 2000 uses—double-clicking a mouse button to open a folder or a document, for example, and having a subfolder open in the same window as its "parent" folder.

When we talk about a workgroup, we assume that all the computers in the group are running Windows 2000 Professional. For a client-server network, we assume that the servers are running Windows 2000 Server with the Active Directory installed. What if your computer's configuration doesn't match any of those we describe? Don't worry. Throughout the book we show you how to modify the ways in which Windows 2000 works and what results you can expect from those customizations. In addition, Windows 2000 is designed to work with different operating systems and network protocols. If you're not sure how to work with those systems or protocols, you'll need to check their documentation.

A Final Word (or Two)

We had three goals in writing this book:

◆ Whatever you want to do, we want the book to help you get it done.

◆ We want the book to help you discover how to do things you *didn't* know you wanted to do.

◆ And, finally, if we've achieved the first two goals, we'll be well on the way to the third, which is for our book to help you *enjoy* doing your work with Windows 2000. We think that's the best gift we could give you to thank you for buying our book.

We hope you'll have as much fun using *Microsoft Windows 2000 Professional At a Glance* as we've had writing it. The best way to learn is by doing, and that's how we hope you'll use this book.

Jump right in!

Jump Right In

IN THIS SECTION

Windows 2000 at a Glance

Starting Up

Shutting Down

Managing a Program Window

Folders and the File Structure

Using Shortcut Menus for Quick Results

Getting Help

Mouse Maneuvers

Wheeling Around with the Mouse

Microsoft Windows 2000 Professional is designed to work for you, not you for it. Don't be afraid to jump right in and try out some features. You'll find that there are often several ways to accomplish one task. Why? Because people work differently. Because different tasks have different requirements. And because you want to find the way that works best for you, get your work done quickly, and get away from the computer!

You'll find that the procedures are simple and straightforward and that you can often use automated methods to get the more complex tasks done easily. This doesn't mean that you can't get stuck or get into trouble, but there are so many safeguards built into Windows 2000 and so many places to get help that you'll have to work pretty hard to get into *real* trouble.

This section of the book covers the basics, from starting Windows 2000 through shutting it down. There's also a handy visual glossary on the following two pages that will help you become familiar with the various parts of the Windows 2000 environment.

Don't change or delete anything just yet—you want to feel comfortable with the basics before you do any customizing. The best way to learn about running programs, managing windows, and getting help if you *do* get into trouble is to jump right in and try things out.

Windows 2000 at a Glance

Windows 2000 is your working headquarters—the *operating system* that lets you run different programs simultaneously and share information between programs if you need to. Most of the programs you'll use have common characteristics that were designed to work together in the Windows 2000 environment so that once you learn how to do something in one program, you know how to do it in other programs.

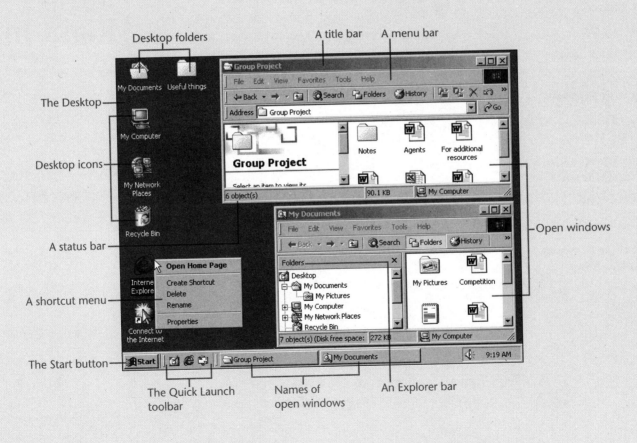

Take a look at the different parts of the Windows 2000 environment displayed on these two pages—what they do and what they're called—and you'll be on the road to complete mastery. As you use Windows 2000,

you might change the way some of these items look and work, but the basic concepts are the same. And if you need to, you can always come back to this visual glossary for a quick refresher on Windows 2000 terminology.

2

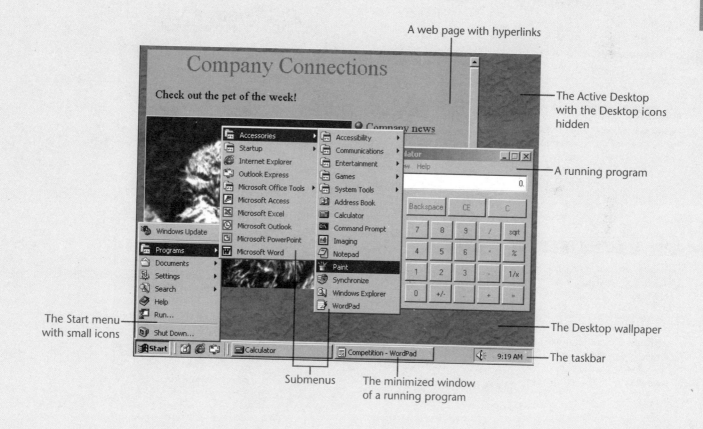

A web page with hyperlinks

The Active Desktop with the Desktop icons hidden

A running program

The Desktop wallpaper

The taskbar

The Start menu with small icons

Submenus

The minimized window of a running program

Starting Up

When you turn on your computer, you're also starting Windows 2000. Startup time depends on your computer's speed, configuration, and connections, and on the programs that are set up to start automatically. Depending on the security settings, you might have to press a key combination before you enter your password.

TIP

Choices. *If your computer has more than one operating system or more than one hardware profile, you'll be prompted to select a system or a profile as Windows 2000 loads.*

SEE ALSO

For information about passwords, see "Changing Your Password" on page 261.

For information about modifying the logon process, see "Creating a New Hardware Profile" on page 297 and "Controlling the Startup" on page 300.

Start Windows 2000

1 Turn on your computer, your monitor, and any peripheral devices—your printer, for example.

2 Wait for Windows 2000 Professional to load. If you see a message telling you to press the Ctrl, Alt, and Delete keys, press the keys simultaneously and then release them.

3 In the Log On To Windows dialog box, type the name you've been assigned in the User Name text box (if it's not already there), and press the Tab key.

4 Type your password in the Password text box. Be sure to use the correct capitalization!

5 If you need to change the way you log on, click Options, and do any of the following:

◆ Enter or select the domain name.

◆ Select the computer name to log on locally.

◆ Turn on the check box to log on using a dial-up connection.

6 Click OK.

The logon when the computer is connected to a network with a domain

The logon for a stand-alone computer or a computer that's part of a workgroup

Shutting Down

Don't just turn off the computer when you've finished your work! Windows 2000 needs a little time to close any open programs or connections and to save your current settings.

TIP

Time to restart. *You'll probably want to restart Windows 2000 after you've made changes to the computer's configuration or if you're having any software problems.*

SEE ALSO

For information about what to do if you're having problems when you try to quit Windows 2000, see "Quitting When You're Stuck" on page 120.

For information about enabling hibernation, see "Managing Your Computer's Power" on page 254.

Shut Down and Turn Off Your Computer

1 Click the Start button, and choose Shut Down.

2 Click to turn on the appropriate option. The options available depend on the configuration of your computer.

3 Click OK. If you chose to shut down, and if the computer has advanced power-management capabilities that are enabled, the computer will probably shut itself off. If it doesn't, wait for the message that tells you it's safe to turn off your computer, and then turn it off.

Exits Windows 2000 and prepares the computer to be turned off.

Unloads your settings and suspends Windows 2000 until a new user logs on. Any shared folders on the computer are still accessible over a network.

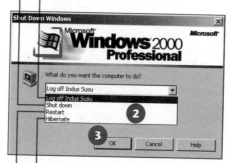

Records all the items contained in the computer's memory onto the hard disk and then shuts down the computer. All the items are restored when the computer is restarted.

Exits and then restarts the computer.

Managing a Program Window

"Managing" a window means bossing it around: you can move it, change its size, and open and close it. Most programs are contained in windows. Although these windows might have some different features, most program windows have more similarities than differences.

TIP

Quick close. *Clicking the Close button on the title bar usually closes the program and the program window, but you'll often find more options when you use the program's menu commands to quit the program.*

Use the Buttons to Switch Between Sizes

1. Click the Maximize button, and the window enlarges and fills the screen. (If the window is already maximized, you won't see the Maximize button.)

2. Click the Restore Down button, and the window gets smaller. (If the window is already restored, you won't see the Restore Down button.)

3. Click the Minimize button, and the window disappears but you see its name on a button on the taskbar.

4. Click the window's name on the taskbar, and the window zooms back to the size it was before you minimized it.

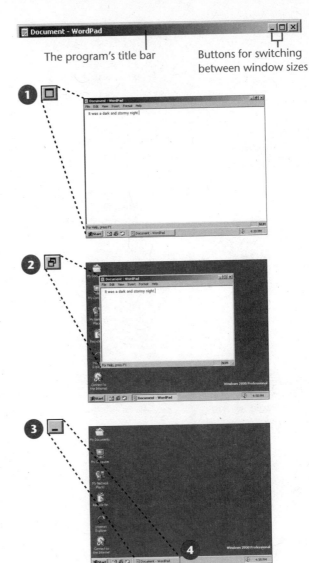

The program's title bar

Buttons for switching between window sizes

Use the Mouse to Resize a Window

1. Click the Restore Down button if the window is currently maximized. (You can't manually size a maximized window.)

2. Move the mouse over one of the borders of the window until the mouse pointer changes into a two-headed arrow. The directions of the arrow-heads show you the directions in which you can move the window border.

3. Drag the window border until the window is the size you want.

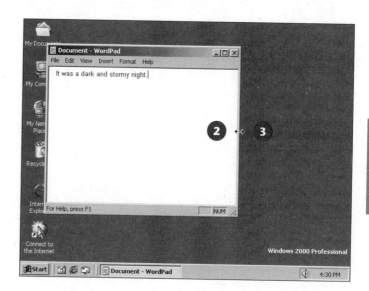

Move a Window

1. Point to the title bar.

2. Drag the window to a new location.

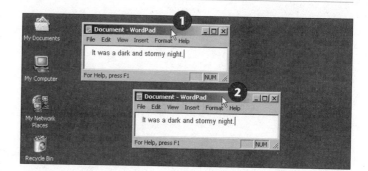

Folders and the File Structure

The filing system in Windows 2000 is structured very much like a paper-filing system: My Computer is the filing cabinet; the drives are the drawers of the filing cabinet; the folders in the drives are the folders in the drawers; and sometimes, in each system, there are folders inside folders. And, just as with the paper-filing system, you store your documents, or files, inside the folders.

Windows 2000 maintains the basic structure for you—My Computer, the drives, and the folders for your programs—but it also does a lot of other behind-the-scenes work. For example, it creates personal folders for you, such as the My Documents folder, and it locks up any critical files, such as program files, so that no one can make any changes to those files without the appropriate permission. You can, of course, customize the filing system by adding, moving, and deleting files and folders, but the more work you let Windows 2000 do, the less you'll have to do!

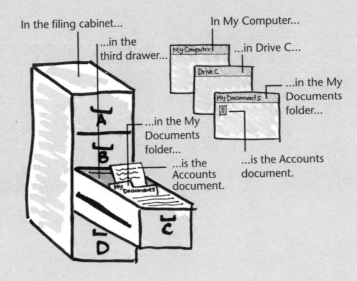

In the filing cabinet...

...in the third drawer...

...in the My Documents folder...

...is the Accounts document.

In My Computer...

...in Drive C...

...in the My Documents folder...

...is the Accounts document.

Using Shortcut Menus for Quick Results

Windows 2000 and the programs that work with it were designed to be intuitive—that is, they anticipate what you're likely to want to do when you're working on a particular task, and they place the appropriate commands on a shortcut menu that you open by clicking the *right* mouse button. These shortcut menus are *dynamic,* which means that they change depending on the task in progress.

Use a Shortcut Menu Command

1. Right-click an item.

2. Choose a command from the shortcut menu to accomplish the task at hand. (A few items and the shortcut menus they produce when right-clicked are shown here.)

3. If the item or action you want isn't on the shortcut menu, do any of the following:

   ◆ Choose from the shortcut menu the items whose names have arrows next to them to see whether the item or action you want is on one of the shortcut menu's submenus.

   ◆ Check to be sure that you right-clicked the proper item.

   ◆ Verify that what you want to do can be accomplished from the item you right-clicked.

Right-click My Computer.

Right-click the Desktop.

Right-click a disk drive.

2

Getting Help

What are big and colorful; packed with information, procedures, shortcuts, and interactive troubleshooters; and sadly underutilized? The Help programs! Of course, they couldn't possibly replace this book, but you can use them to find concise step-by-step procedures for diagnosing and overcoming problems, and to learn how to accomplish your tasks faster and more easily than you ever imagined.

Get Basic Information

1. Click the Start button, and choose Help.

2. On the Contents tab, click the main topic of interest. Click a subtopic, if necessary.

3. Click the item of interest.

4. Read the information about the topic.

5. Repeat steps 2 through 4 to review other topics.

6. Use the Back or Forward button to return to topics you've already reviewed.

7. Do either of the following to save a helpful reference:

   ◆ Click Options, and choose Print to print a hard copy of the information.

   ◆ Click the Favorites tab, and click Add to add the topic to your personal list of Help topics.

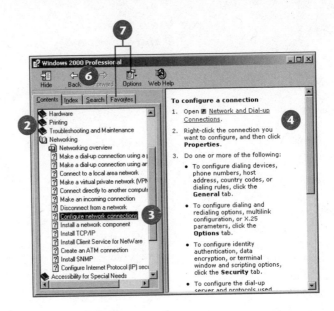

TIP

Small view. *To read the Help information while you're working with a window, click the Hide button to see only the topic information; click the Show button to return to the list of topics.*

TIP

Save the information. *To copy or print the Help information from a popup window, right-click in the popup window, and choose Copy or Print Topic from the shortcut menu.*

TIP

Fast learner. *The first time you run Help, it has to compile a list of topics and index words, so you'll have to wait for a few moments while it gets itself ready—but it's worth the wait! After that, Help is the place to go for quick answers to any problems.*

Get Specific Help

1. Click the Index tab.

2. Type a word (or part of a word) that describes what you want to do.

3. Double-click the related word or phrase in the list box.

4. Read the information about the topic.

5. Click the Close button when you've finished.

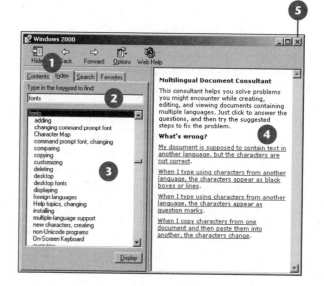

Use Dialog Box Help

1. In any Windows 2000 dialog box, click the Help button.

2. Click the item you want more information about.

3. Read the Help information, and then click anywhere to close Help.

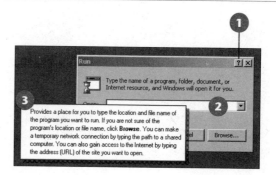

Mouse Maneuvers

Navigating with a mouse is like traveling in a helicopter: you can lift off from any spot, fly a straight line over hills and canyons, and set down wherever you want. Using the keyboard to navigate is like taking the scenic route: you'll run into detours in a program's topography, and you might need a good map to navigate through menus and shortcut keys to reach your destination. You might prefer the longer keyboard route—you get to explore the road less traveled, and you might even come across features and techniques that are new to you. But to finish your tasks as quickly as possible—and to take advantage of some of the best features of Windows 2000—give your mouse the job!

Before you fly off on your mouse wings, though, you might need some Mouse Basics. At Mouse School, we believe there are no bad mice (okay, mouse devices)—only bad mouse operators. Here you'll learn to point, click, double-click, right-click, select, multiple-select, and drag with your mouse. Don't be too surprised if the mouse acts a bit differently from the way you expect it to. Windows 2000 gives you numerous options for customizing the way your mouse works, so be patient, experiment a bit, and read pages 231 through 235 for information about setting up Windows 2000 so that your mouse works the way you want it to.

Point: Move the mouse until the mouse pointer (either a small arrow-shaped pointer or a tiny hand) is pointing to the item you want.

Depending on your mouse-click settings, either you click an item to select it...

...or the item becomes selected when you simply point to it.

Click: Point to the item you want, and then quickly press down and release the left mouse button.

Double-click: Point to the item you want, and then quickly press down and release the left mouse button twice, being careful not to move the mouse between clicks.

Right-click: Point to the item you want, and then quickly press down and release the right mouse button.

Select: Point to an item, and click to select it. To select a web-style icon, point to it but don't click. A selected item is usually a different color from other similar items or is surrounded by a frame.

Multiple-select: Point above and to the left of the first item, hold down the left mouse button, move the mouse pointer below and to the right of the last item to be selected, and release the mouse button. To select a long list of sequential items, click the first item, hold down the Shift key, and click the last item. To select or deselect nonsequential items, hold down the Ctrl key and click each item you want. Only certain windows and dialog boxes permit multiple selection.

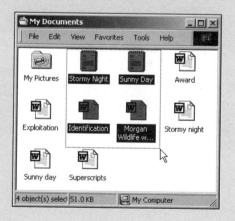

Drag: Select the item you want. Keeping the mouse pointer on the selected item, hold down the left mouse button and move the mouse until you've "dragged" the item to the desired location; then release the left mouse button.

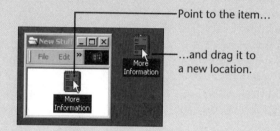

You can customize the way your mouse works, including switching the roles of the left and right mouse buttons (but you'll have to remember to reverse left and right in the previous instructions). If you're using a mouse that has a wheel, you'll want to read "Wheeling Around with the Mouse" on page 18.

Wheeling Around with the Mouse

With a mouse that has a wheel, the functionality of both the wheel and the wheel button is determined by the individual program. The wheel button functions in the same manner as a third mouse button, so if the program you're using has features that work with a third mouse button, those features will work with the wheel button. Rotating the wheel, however, works only in a program that's designed to work with a wheel mouse.

TIP

Change the wheel click. *With Microsoft IntelliPoint software installed, you can change what happens when you click the wheel button. To do so, click the Start button, point to Settings, and choose Control Panel from the submenu. Double-click the Mouse icon, and adjust the setting on the Wheel tab.*

Find Out What the Wheel Does

1. Read the program's documentation and online help.

2. If the information is inadequate, experiment! Try any of the methods described in the table at the right, and see how your program responds to the wheel action.

EXAMPLES OF USING THE WHEEL	
Action	What it does
Rotate the wheel.	In a folder window and in most applications: scrolls up or down.
Shift+rotate the wheel.	In a folder window set to display web content, or in Internet Explorer, Windows Help, and other HTML viewers: acts like the Back and Forward buttons to browse through windows. The function varies depending on the program.
Ctrl+rotate the wheel.	In Internet Explorer, Windows Help, and other HTML viewers: changes the font size. In WordPad and some other applications: changes the Zoom setting.
Click the wheel button and move the mouse.	In Internet Explorer, Windows Help, and some other applications: scrolls in the direction in which the mouse is moved. Click again to turn off scrolling.

Accessing

IN THIS SECTION

Exploring Your Documents, Your Computer, and Your Network

Working with Network Folders

Working with Documents

Navigating with Toolbars

Exploring the Internet

Going to a Specific Web Site

Returning to Your Favorite Sites

Adding Links to the Desktop

Creating Quick Access to a Web Site

Accessing Folders from the Command Prompt

The Microsoft Windows 2000 Professional Desktop is a "gateway" through which you can access your files and folders, your computer's drives, all the computers that are part of your network or workgroup, and, of course, the Internet itself. Among the items on your Desktop are the My Documents folder, where you can store and access all your documents; the My Computer icon, from which you can explore as deep into your computer's drives as you want to go; the My Network Places folder, where you can find items that are stored on other computers; and, of course, Internet Explorer, through which you connect to the Internet.

This section shows you simple ways to create links and shortcuts to the documents and folders that you use frequently, and how you can tell Windows 2000 to search for a document whose name or location you can't remember. You'll navigate quickly and easily through documents, folders, and networks using the toolbars that Windows 2000 provides, and you'll even learn how to create toolbars for your own special requirements. You'll find out how to use hyperlinks to speed up your access to web sites, whether you're looking for information or returning to a favorite site, and we'll show you how you can put your favorite web-page links right on your Desktop. Go ahead—explore!

Exploring Your Documents

Sitting on your Desktop is the My Documents folder—a personal storage area where you can store and access all your documents. If more than one person uses your computer, each user has a separate My Documents folder.

TIP

My Documents location.
The My Documents folder on the Desktop is a shortcut to the folder itself, which is buried deep in the file structure of your hard drive. To determine the folder's location, right-click the My Documents folder on the Desktop, choose Properties from the shortcut menu, and note the location listed on the Target tab of the My Documents Properties dialog box.

SEE ALSO

For information about displaying or hiding the web content in a folder see "Adding a Comment to a Folder Window" on page 226.

Open My Documents

1. Double-click the My Documents folder on the Windows 2000 Desktop.

2. Use the scroll bars, if necessary, to view all the documents. Click the scroll arrows to scroll a small increment at a time, or drag the scroll box to scroll a greater distance.

3. Click a file or folder to select it.

4. Read the description of the selected document or folder. If you can't see all the information, increase the size of the window until the information is visible.

5. Repeat steps 2 through 4 to look at the descriptions of the documents or folders you want to review.

6. Double-click a document or folder to open it.

7. Click the Close button when you've finished.

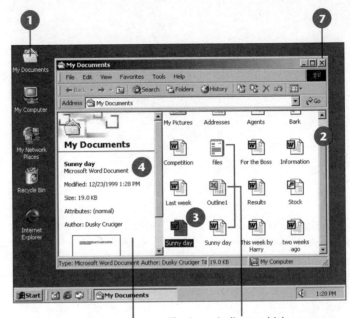

The icons indicate which programs the documents are associated with.

Web content provides information about the selected document or folder.

Exploring Your Computer

Sitting on your Desktop is the My Computer folder—the gateway to everything on your computer. The My Computer folder contains icons for all your local storage areas: removable disk drives, hard disks, CD drives, and so on. From here you can venture as deep into the folder structure of your computer as you dare.

SEE ALSO

For information about changing the way information is displayed in the folder window, see "Arranging the File Listings" on page 54 and "Adding a Comment to a Folder Window" on page 226.

For information about displaying the drives and folders in a traditional tree structure, see "Reorganizing Your Folders" on page 57.

For information about opening each folder in a separate window, see "Opening a Folder in Its Own Window" on page 225.

Open a Folder

1. Double-click My Computer on the Windows 2000 Desktop.

2. Click a drive icon to select it.

3. Read the information about the drive.

4. Double-click a drive icon to open a window for that drive.

5. Click a document or folder to select it, and read the information about the selected document or folder. To move back to the previous window, press the Backspace key or click the Back button on the Standard Buttons toolbar.

6. Double-click a document or folder to open it.

7. Click the Close button when you've finished.

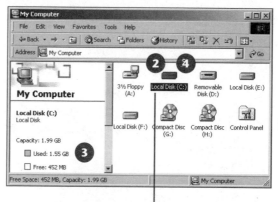

When you open the window for a drive...

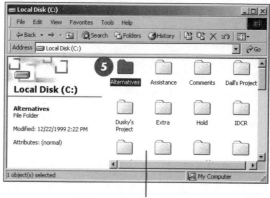

...the contents of the drive appear in the same window.

3

Exploring Your Network

Networks come in many different sizes and forms. Fortunately, Windows 2000 doesn't force you to use the arcane naming conventions of the past to find a folder you need to access. Whether your network consists of a few computers joined together as a workgroup, a larger grouping of computers in a domain, or a giant assemblage of multiple domains, you can easily connect to another computer and find what you need with just a few clicks of the mouse.

TIP

Direct connection. *If you know the name of the computer you want to connect to, display the Address toolbar on the taskbar and type the name of the computer in the form \\computername.*

Browse Your Workgroup

1. Double-click the Network Neighborhood icon on the Windows 2000 Desktop.

2. Double-click Computers Near Me. (This icon is present only if your computer is part of a workgroup and is not a member of a domain.)

3. Double-click the name of a computer.

4. Double-click the shared folder you want to access.

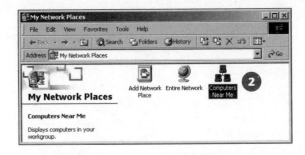

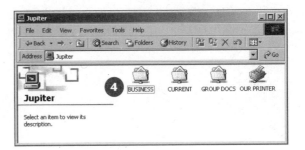

Search the Network

1. Open the My Network Places window if it's not already open.

2. Click the Search button on the Standard Buttons toolbar.

3. Enter the name of the computer you're looking for.

4. Click Search Now.

5. Double-click the computer in the search results.

6. Double-click the shared folder you want to access.

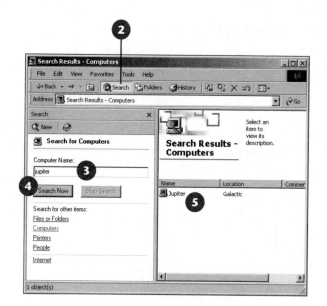

3

Different Ways of Networking

Working with networks means that you could be dealing with a *client-server network* system, a *peer-to-peer network* system, or both. What's the difference?

A client-server network is the conventional corporate-type network in which one or more computers (the server or servers) *hosts,* or provides network services to, other computers (the clients). Almost everything on the network has to pass through the servers, which are the center of this networking universe. The servers are managed by a tyrannical overlord known as the *network administrator,* who dictates what each client is allowed to do on the network and often prescribes how each client computer is set up.

The management unit of a client-server network is the *domain.* In a small network, there might be only a single domain. In a large network, there are usually many domains, grouping clients and servers into logical associations. For example, there might be one domain for the accounting department, another domain for the advertising department, and so on.

When you log on, you're usually logging on to a domain, which gives you access to all the servers and computers that are part of that domain. Because so many different programs are used to run networks, and because the network administrator can customize the system, you need to refer to your company's networking guidelines for the technical details about using your network.

A peer-to-peer network, as its name implies, is a more democratic structure than a client-server network. In this kind of network, all computers are created equal and the users of the computers decide whether and what they will share with others. Any computer in the group can act as a server (sharing its printer or its files, for example), as a client (using someone else's printer), or as both. When you connect to another computer in a workgroup, you're using peer-to-peer networking.

Why the different systems? It's mostly a matter of scale. A peer-to-peer system is the easiest to use but can quickly become overloaded as more and more computers are added to the workgroup. A client-server system with one or more powerful server computers and sophisticated management software is designed to handle very large volumes of network traffic and to provide more complex services, such as an intranet and full directory services.

A Client-Server Network

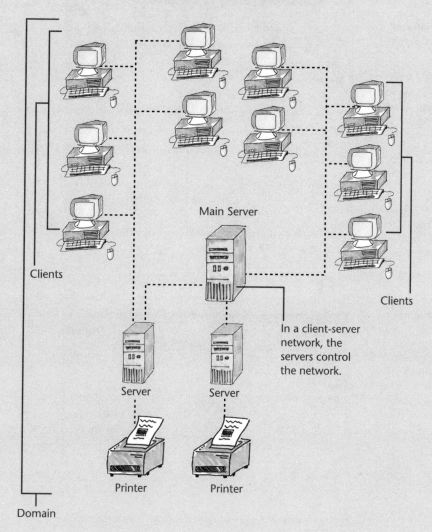

Clients

Main Server

Server

Server

Printer

Printer

Clients

In a client-server network, the servers control the network.

Domain

A Peer-to-Peer Network

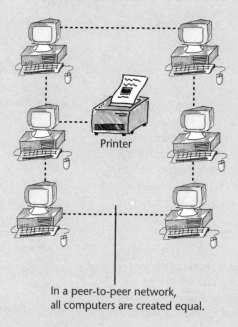

Printer

In a peer-to-peer network, all computers are created equal.

3

Reconnecting to a Network Folder

If you need to frequently access a folder on another computer, you can use a link that Windows 2000 creates for you instead of searching for the folder each time you need it. When you open a folder on another computer and use the files in the folder, Windows 2000 creates a link to the folder. That link then appears in the My Network Places window and in many of the standard Windows 2000 dialog boxes, such as the Open and the Save As dialog boxes. If you don't want the connection cluttering up the window, you can delete it.

TIP

Manual link. *If Windows 2000 hasn't automatically created a link to a network source, you can create the link manually. Double-click Add Network Place in the My Network Places window, and step through the wizard.*

Add a Network Location

1. Open the My Network Places window if it's not already open.

2. Navigate to a folder on a different computer, and open a document. Work with the document if you want to, and then close it.

3. Use the Back button to move back to My Network Places.

4. Double-click the network connection to the folder you just worked on to reconnect to the folder.

5. Work with any of the documents.

6. If you decide that you don't want the link, return to My Network Places, right-click the link, and choose Delete from the shortcut menu.

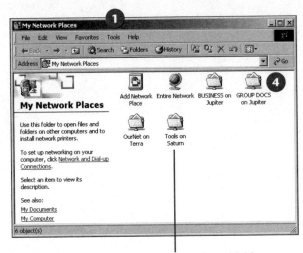

When you access documents in a shared folder, Windows 2000 creates a link to the folder for you.

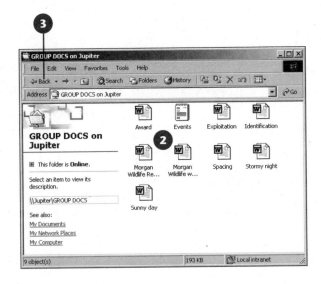

Assigning a Drive Letter to a Network Folder

If you need frequent access to a network folder, or if you're using a program that doesn't allow you to specify a network location using the computer name and folder name, you can make the network location into a "virtual" drive. Then, when you need to access the network folder, you simply specify the drive letter.

> **TIP**
>
> **Drive to my computer.**
> *When a network location has a drive assigned to it, the drive appears in the My Computer window.*

Assign the Drive

1 Open the My Network Places window if it's not already open.

2 Use the Computers Near Me window or the Entire Network window to locate the shared folder to which you'll assign the drive letter.

3 Right-click the folder, and choose Map Network Drive from the shortcut menu. If the command doesn't appear on the shortcut menu, verify that you're in the shared folder and not in one of the subfolders of the shared folder.

4 Verify that the correct drive letter and folder are specified.

5 If you want to connect to this folder every time you log on, verify that the Reconnect At Logon check box is turned on.

6 Click Finish to assign the drive letter.

7 Use the mapped network drive as you would use any other drive.

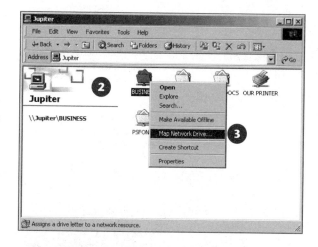

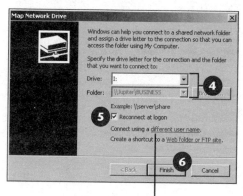

Click if you need to log on to the shared folder as a different user.

Opening a Document

Documents are the files that contain your data—formatted or plain text, numbers, pictures, even complex databases—and they work within specific programs. When you open a document, Windows 2000 starts the associated program (if it's not already running) and opens the document in that program. You can also tell Windows 2000 to open the document in a different program.

SEE ALSO

For information about the way Windows 2000 determines which program to use to open a document, see "File Associations, File Extensions, and Registered Programs" on page 34.

Open a Document

1. Open the folder (My Documents or My Computer, for example) that contains the document.

2. Double-click the document to open it.

3. Wait for the program to start and the document to load.

4. Work on the document.

5. Use the program's File menu commands to save (if necessary) and close the document, and open any other documents you want to work on in that program.

6. Repeat steps 4 and 5, and close the program when you've finished your work.

The type of icon that's displayed indicates which program will open the document.

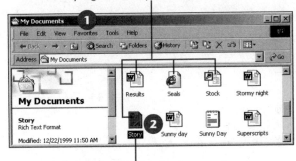

When you double-click the document...

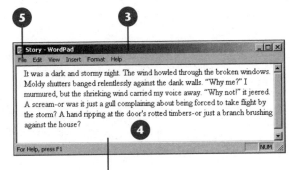

...it opens in its associated program.

Programs remembered.
Locate the text document you want, right-click it, and choose Open With. Find WordPad in the list, and click OK. Close WordPad, right-click the document again, and point to Open With. Notice that there is now a submenu listing the default program (Notepad) and the program you chose to use (WordPad). From the submenu, click Choose Program, select Internet Explorer, and click OK. Close the program when you've finished. Note that from now on, all you need to do is choose the program from the Open With submenu.

Open a Document in a Different Program

① Open the folder that contains the document.

② Right-click the document, and point to Open With on the shortcut menu.

③ If the Open With command doesn't display a submenu, click the Open With command. If a submenu appears, do either of the following:

◆ Click the program name to open the document this time only in this program. Skip steps 5 and 6 below.

◆ Click Choose Program to select a different program or to always open the document in the selected program.

④ Select the program in which you want to open the document.

⑤ Turn on the Always Use This Program To Open These Files check box to always open all documents of this type using the program you specify.

⑥ Click OK, and wait for the document to load into the program.

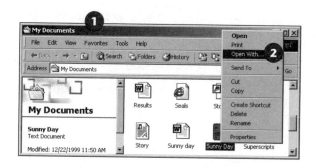

Sometimes the Open With command has a submenu.

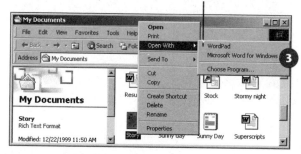

Leave this option unchecked to use this program this time only.

Opening a Document You Used Recently

Have you ever wanted to open a document that you recently worked on but whose name or location you just couldn't remember? Or perhaps your memory is working fine but you don't want to take the time to locate the document. In either case, Windows 2000 can do the work for you. It keeps track of the documents that you recently worked on, including their location, so all you need to do is review the list and choose the document you want.

SEE ALSO

For information about removing the items that are listed on the Documents menu, see "Cleaning Up Your Lists of Activities" on page 74.

Open the Document

1 Click the Start button on the Windows 2000 taskbar.

2 Point to Documents.

3 Choose the document you want to open from the submenu.

4 The document opens in the default program it is associated with. Work with the document, and close it when you've finished.

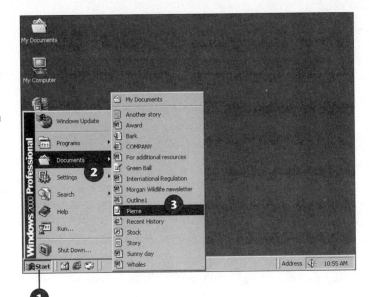

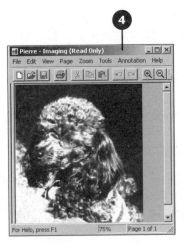

Creating Quick Access to a Document

Sometimes you need to open a document frequently—whether the document is a report, a database, or a picture of your grandchild. You can create a shortcut to the document, thereby creating a permanent link to it so that you don't need to remember in which folder, or on which computer on the network, the document resides. To return to it, all you need to do is double-click the shortcut.

SEE ALSO

For information about displaying the Quick Launch toolbar, see "Navigating with Toolbars" on page 40.

For information about adding items to the Start menu, see "Organizing the Start Menu" on page 68.

Create a Shortcut

1 Use any folder window (My Computer or My Network Places, for example) to locate the document.

2 Right-click the document.

3 Point to Send To on the shortcut menu, and choose Desktop (Create Shortcut) from the submenu.

4 Click the Show Desktop button on the Quick Launch toolbar.

5 Do any of the following:

◆ Leave the shortcut on the Desktop.

◆ Drag the shortcut onto the Start button to place it on the Start menu.

◆ Drag the shortcut onto the Quick Launch toolbar.

6 Double-click the shortcut to confirm that it loads the document into its program.

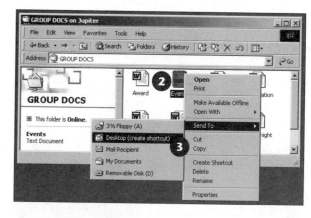

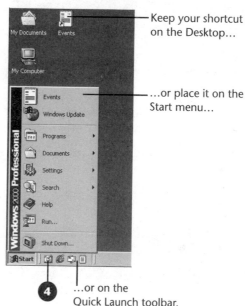

Keep your shortcut on the Desktop...

...or place it on the Start menu...

...or on the Quick Launch toolbar.

Opening a Document You Used Previously

When you want to return to a document that you used earlier today or a week ago—whether it's a text document, a web page, or any other type of document—you can review a categorized list that contains all the documents you've been using.

TIP

A different view. *To sort the history by different categories—By Site, By Most Visited, or By Order Visited Today—click the View button and specify how you want the items sorted.*

SEE ALSO

For information about opening one of the last 15 documents you used, see "Opening a Document You Used Recently" on page 30.

View the History

1. In any folder window (My Documents, for example), click History on the Standard Buttons toolbar to display the History Explorer Bar.

2. Point to and then click the time period during which you last worked on the document.

3. If necessary, click the name of the computer that contains the document. The category expands to show all the documents opened in that period and at that location.

4. Click the document you want to use. If the document isn't listed, click a different time period and locate the document.

The History Explorer Bar

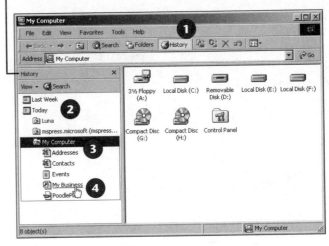

Some documents open differently from others.
Certain documents—Microsoft Word 2000 documents, for example—will open in a window that is a combination of Internet Explorer and the program (Word, for example). You'll be able to use the program's capabilities, but you might find that the Internet Explorer features clutter up the window. To use the program without the Internet Explorer features, open the document directly in its program.

Use the address. *In the History Explorer Bar, locate the document you want to open. Right-click it, and choose Copy from the shortcut menu. Choose Run from the Start menu, and press Ctrl+V to paste the document's address into the Open box. Press Enter to open the document in its default program.*

View by date. *To redisplay the documents you visited in a selected time period instead of the search results, click the View button, and choose By Date from the menu.*

Search the History

1 If you still can't find the document, click the Search button.

2 Type a keyword—a word in the document's name, for example, or the name of the folder that contains the document.

3 Click Search Now.

4 Point to a file, and read the tooltip to verify that this is the correct document.

5 Click the document you want to open.

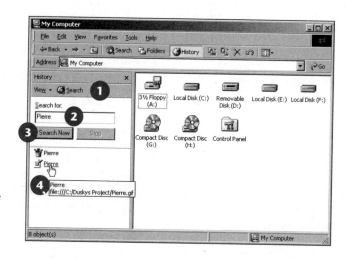

File Associations, File Extensions, and Registered Programs

Windows 2000 tries very hard to let your work be *docucentric*—that is, you concentrate on keeping your *documents* organized and Windows 2000 will do the work of figuring out which *programs* your documents need to run in. To do this, Windows 2000 needs three main pieces of information:

- ◆ The programs you have installed
- ◆ The types of documents that are to be opened in each program
- ◆ The file type of the document you want to use

Windows 2000 keeps track of all this information in a special database called the *registry*. Whenever you install a software program, information about that program is added to the registry, including the name and location of the program and the types of documents and files the program will open.

To link a document with a program, Windows 2000 uses the file's *extension*—the three-character code that follows the period after the document's name—to identify the document as a specific file type. The file's extension, which is usually added automatically when you save a document in a program, might or might not be visible, depending on your settings, but Windows 2000 is always aware of it. (See "Displaying File and Folder Locations and Types" on page 75 for information

about displaying a file's extension.) By recognizing the file extension, Windows 2000 knows the file type of the document and its associated program.

You can identify the file type of a document by its icon and, when you're in Details view, by the description in the Type column. Because a document is identified by its extension, you shouldn't change the extension when you create a document or when you're conducting any file management.

Sometimes, alas, things just don't work out as they're supposed to. Some programs are installed without being properly registered. Other programs can grab a file extension that "belongs to" another program.

When a program isn't properly registered, whatever the reason, you can generally solve the problem by reinstalling the program or by changing which program is associated with a document, as described in "Open a Document in a Different Program" on page 29. If neither of these methods works, contact the people who sold you the software. They might be able to supply you with updated software that properly registers the program, or they might tell you how to fix the problem with a workaround. But remember—if anyone suggests that you edit the registry (and if you have permission to do so), proceed with extreme caution or you could make your computer inoperable. You'll also want to read the section "Editing Windows 2000 Settings" on page 293.

EXAMPLES OF FILES AND THEIR EXTENSIONS			
Document type	**Icon**	**Filename with extension**	**Typical associated program**
Text document	My Stories	My Stories.txt	Notepad
Bitmap image	Island	Island.bmp	Microsoft Paint
TIFF image	PILOT1	Pilot1.tif	Imaging Preview
Rich Text Format document	Story	Story.rtf	WordPad
Internet document (HTML)	Seals	Seals.htm	Internet Explorer
Wave sound	Bark	Bark.wav	Windows Media Player

3

Finding a Document

If you don't remember the exact name or location of a document, tell Windows 2000 what you do remember—part of the name, the type of document, the drive or the computer where the document resides, for example—and then let Windows 2000 do the searching for you.

SEE ALSO

For information about opening a document you used recently or one you used some time ago, see "Opening a Document You Used Recently" on page 30 or "Opening a Document You Used Previously" on page 32.

TIP

Use the Search button.
You can also search for a document by clicking the Search button in any folder window. Verify that Files Or Folders is selected in the Search For Other Items section of the Search Explorer Bar.

Find a Document Based on Its Name

1. Click the Start button, point to Search, and choose For Files Or Folders from the submenu.

2. Type the name, or as much of it as you can remember.

3. Specify where you want to search. Click the Browse item in the list if the location you want to search isn't listed.

4. Click Search Now.

5. Click the document you're looking for.

6. Review the information about the document to confirm that it's the document you want.

7. Either double-click the document to open it or right-click the document and choose the action you want from the shortcut menu.

The Search Explorer Bar

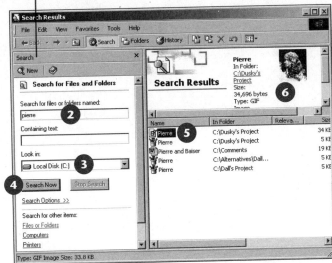

Narrow the Search

1. Type as much information as you can about the document's name and location.

2. Type any text contained in the document that you want use as a search parameter.

3. Click Search Options.

4. To specify additional information, check

   ◆ Date to specify whether the document you want was modified, created, or last accessed within a specific time period. Use the drop-down calendar to specify dates.

   ◆ Type to select the type of document.

   ◆ Size to specify any file size restrictions.

   ◆ Advanced Options to choose not to search subfolders or to make the text search match the upper- and lowercase characters you typed.

5. Click Search Now, and examine the results.

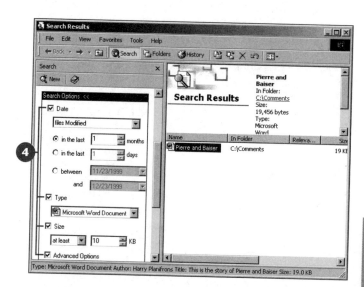

Finding a Document Based on Its Properties

If your computer is running Indexing Service, you can search for a document, or for a group of documents, based on the document's *properties*—the author, the keywords, or the subject of the document, for example. Of course, the documents must support these types of properties, and the properties must have been recorded for the document.

TIP

Indexing Service. *To see whether Indexing Service is being used, open the Search Options list and note the status. For additional information about Indexing Service, about the types of documents that can be indexed, and about searching file properties, click the Indexing Service link, and search the associated Help.*

Search by Property

1. Click the Start button, point to Search, and choose For Files Or Folders from the submenu.

2. To find a specific document, type the name, or as much of it as you can remember. To find a group of documents that have the same property but dissimilar names, do not enter a name.

3. In the Containing Text box, type a query for the property, as shown in the table at the right. You can use wildcard characters to find variations of the property text, or you can use quotation marks to clarify the property text.

4. Specify where you want to search.

5. Specify any other parameters under Search Options.

6. Click Search Now.

7. Review the search results for the document.

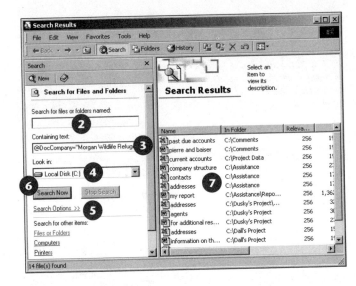

COMMON DOCUMENT PROPERTY QUERIES

Property	Query Example
Author	@DocAuthor=Dusky Cruciger
Company	@DocCompany=Morgan Wildlife Refuge
Category	@DocCategory=Newsletters
Keywords	@DocKeywords=Fundraising
Subject	@DocSubject=Building Fund
Title	@DocTitle=November Newsletter

Checking the Details About a File or Folder

If you're not absolutely sure that you've located the correct file or folder, or if you simply need more information about it, you can check its *properties*. Windows 2000 Professional records specific information and statistics about every file and folder. In some types of documents, depending on the type of file or what's contained in the folder, the user can also enter additional information.

SEE ALSO

For information about locating a document, see "Finding a Document" on page 36.

Review the Properties of a File or Folder

1. Find the file or folder you want to examine.

2. Right-click it.

3. Choose Properties from the shortcut menu.

4. Review the information in the Properties dialog box.

5. Click OK.

Different types of documents have different tabs.

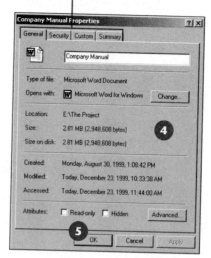

Folders have different tabs and options, depending on the file system you're using.

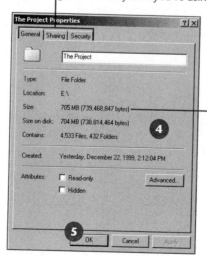

Shows the size taken up by all files, including those in subfolders.

3

Navigating with Toolbars

There are four toolbars associated with the taskbar in Windows 2000, and they provide access to programs, folders, and documents, as well as Internet and intranet sites.

SEE ALSO

For information about creating toolbars, see "Creating Your Own Toolbars" on the facing page.

For information about modifying the toolbars in folder windows, see "Customizing Toolbars" on page 224.

TRY THIS

Get to know the toolbars. *Right-click a blank spot on the taskbar, and use the Toolbars command on the shortcut menu to display several toolbars. Double-click the "raised" bar on a toolbar to maximize its length. Double-click the bar again to restore the toolbar's original size. Drag the bar to create a custom-size toolbar.*

Display a Toolbar

1. Right-click a blank spot on the taskbar or on any of the taskbar's toolbars.

2. Point to Toolbars on the shortcut menu, and choose the toolbar you want to display. (A toolbar with a check mark next to its name is one that's already displayed.)

See All the Buttons

1. If an entire toolbar or taskbar isn't displayed, double-click the small "raised" bar on the toolbar.

2. If any of the buttons on the Links or the Desktop toolbar are still not visible, click the right-facing chevrons to display the hidden items.

3. If all the buttons on the taskbar are still not visible, use the up or down arrow to scroll through all the items.

THE TASKBAR'S TOOLBARS	
Toolbar	**Function**
Address	Opens the item when you specify its address.
Links	Links you to the same locations that are shown on the Internet Explorer Links toolbar.
Desktop	Provides quick access to the Desktop icons, files, folders, and shortcuts on your Windows 2000 Desktop.
Quick Launch	Launches Internet Explorer and Outlook Express, or minimizes all the windows on your Windows 2000 Desktop.

Creating Your Own Toolbars

The toolbars that come with Windows 2000 are invaluable, but if they don't precisely meet your needs you can easily create your own custom toolbars by connecting to a folder in which you've placed all the items you want to appear on your toolbar.

TIP

Delete a toolbar. *If you no longer need a custom toolbar and want to delete it permanently, right-click it, and choose Close from its shortcut menu. The toolbar will go away, but the contents of the folder to which it was connected will be unchanged.*

Create a Toolbar

1. Create a folder containing the documents, folders, and shortcuts that you want to appear on the toolbar.

2. Right-click a blank spot on a toolbar or on the taskbar, point to Toolbars on the shortcut menu, and choose New Toolbar.

3. In the New Toolbar dialog box, navigate to the folder you created, and select it.

4. Click OK.

5. Drag any documents, folders, or programs from other windows onto the toolbar to add a shortcut to each of the items. The shortcut to each item is added to the folder that the toolbar is based on.

6. Use the new toolbar just as you use any of the other toolbars on the taskbar, or drag the toolbar onto the Desktop to use it as a floating toolbar (as shown in the illustration at the right).

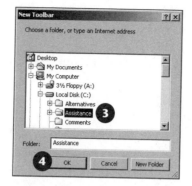

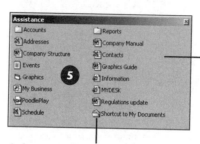

The folders and documents in the Our Project folder

A shortcut created by dragging folders and documents from other folders onto the new toolbar

3

Finding Someone

Whether you need to find someone in your Address Book, on your network, or on the Internet, Windows 2000 will take whatever information you have and will try to locate the person you want to connect to.

TIP

Active Directory. *To directly locate someone on the network, the network needs to have Active Directory—a component of Windows 2000 Server—installed. If your system doesn't have Active Directory, use your Address Book or your e-mail system's Address Book.*

TIP

Try again. *The Internet address services use different methods to acquire e-mail addresses, so if you don't find the person you're looking for, try a different service.*

Search for a Person

1. Click the Start button, point to Search, and choose For People from the submenu.

2. Select the service that contains the listing for the person.

3. Type the person's name and/or e-mail address.

4. If you can, complete any other information that's requested.

5. Click Find Now.

6. Right-click the name you're looking for, point to Action on the shortcut menu, and choose the action you want to take.

7. Click Add To Address Book if you want the information added to your Address Book.

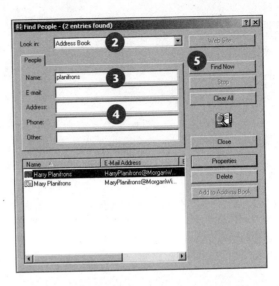

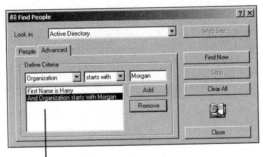

You can use a variety of search parameters to search Active Directory.

Exploring the Internet

Most of your navigation on the Internet uses links (also called *hyperlinks* or *jumps*) that are located on web pages. When you click a link, an Internet address is sent to your web browser, which looks for the web site and displays the requested page. Once you've located a web page, you can continue to explore.

TIP

Exploring. *If you start Internet Explorer from your Desktop, the Quick Launch toolbar, or the Start menu, Internet Explorer goes to the page you've designated as your start page. If you start Internet Explorer by clicking a link or a menu command, or by using an Internet address, Internet Explorer goes to that specific page, bypassing your start page.*

SEE ALSO

For information about changing your start page, see "Set a New Start Page" on page 46.

Explore

1. Start Internet Explorer if it's not already running. If you're using a dial-in connection and aren't already connected to the Internet, connect to your service provider.

2. From your current page, do any of the following:

   ◆ Click the Search button, and use a service to locate a site by name or location.

   ◆ Click a relevant jump on the page to go to a new site.

   ◆ Click the Back button to return to a previously visited site.

   ◆ Click the Forward button to return to a site you left using the Back button.

   ◆ Open the Address Bar drop-down list to select and jump to a previously visited site.

   ◆ Click the Stop button to stop downloading a page, and then jump to a different location.

3. If you get lost, click the Home button to return to your start page.

The Stop button

The Home button

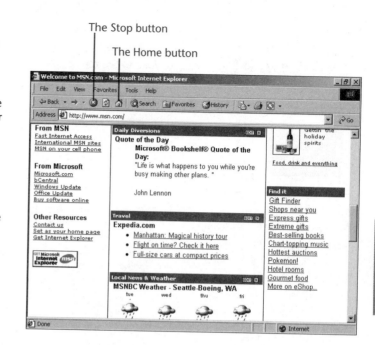

Finding Something on the Internet

To search for a specific item on the Internet—sources where you can buy other *At a Glance* books, for example, or the menu and locator map for that new restaurant you want to try—you can jump right to a search page and set up your query. Once the results are displayed, you can jump to the page that contains the information you're looking for, and, if it's not what you want, you can try another page.

TIP

A step ahead. *If Internet Explorer is already running, just click the Search button on the Standard Buttons toolbar to display the Search pane.*

Search for an Item

1 Click the Start button, point to Search, and choose On The Internet from the submenu. Connect to the Internet if you're not already connected.

2 Select a category. Click More to see additional categories.

3 Type the information you want. Drag the border between the Search Explorer Bar and the main window if you need more room.

4 Click Search.

5 Click a link and view the item.

6 If you want to see other results, click a relevant link and view the item.

7 Close the Search Explorer Bar when you've finished with the search results.

Click to change your default search settings.

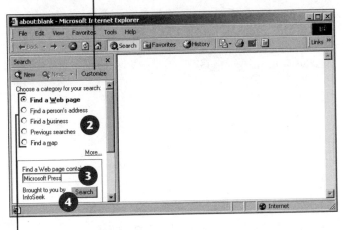

Click to use a different search service.

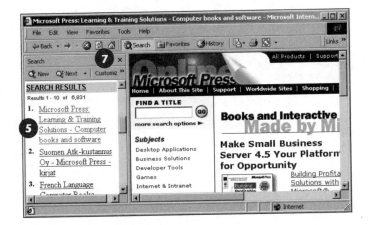

Going to a Specific Web Site

To Internet Explorer, there's no difference between the Internet and a company intranet except that the former is public and the latter is private. In either case, you can go directly to a specific site or page, provided you have its address, a shortcut, or a link to it.

TIP

Copy an address. *If you have a web page address in a document but the address doesn't work as a link, select and copy it. Then click in the Address Bar, press Ctrl+V to paste the address there, and press Enter to go to the site.*

TIP

Type an address. *You can type the address of a web page in the Address toolbar on the taskbar, in the Run dialog box from the Start menu's Run command, or in the Address Bar in any folder window.*

Jump to a Web Site

1. If you have a link or a shortcut to a web site in a document, an e-mail message, or some other source, click the link. Internet Explorer starts (if it's not already running).

2. Connect to the Internet if necessary, and wait for the site to load.

Specify a Web Page

1. If the Address Bar isn't already displayed in the Internet Explorer window, point to Toolbars on the View menu, and choose Address Bar from the submenu.

2. In the Address Bar, select the current address, and replace it with the address of the web page you want, or select a previously visited page from the Address Bar drop-down list. Press Enter.

For additional resources, check out http://mspress.microsoft.com/ or go to the Microsoft Windows 2000 Professional At a Glance page.

Click a link...

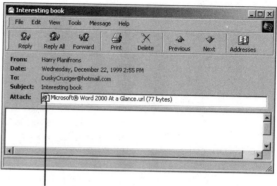

...or a shortcut to go to a web page.

When you type an address, Internet Explorer offers you available addresses. (You don't need to include the *http://* part of the address.)

Changing Links

When you first start Microsoft Internet Explorer, it opens a preinstalled start page that already contains some links to other pages. Depending on your needs, you might want a different Internet start page. If you're using an intranet, you might want to set the start page to the main intranet page. And by customizing the other links, you can create quick and easy access to other pages with a click of a button.

TIP

Returning home. *When you set up a new Internet service provider on your computer, the installation often sets its own web page as your start page. You can quickly navigate to your previous start page by using the Address Bar or the History Explorer bar.*

Set a New Start Page

1. Go to the page you want to use as your start page.

2. Choose Internet Options from the Tools menu, and click the General tab in the Internet Options dialog box.

3. Click the Use Current button.

4. Click OK.

5. After you've navigated to other web sites, click the Home button on the Standard Buttons toolbar to verify that you've specified the correct start page.

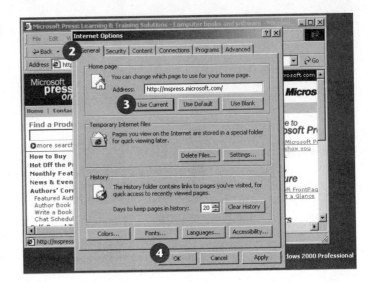

Add a Link

1. Go to the page you want to use as a link.

2. If either the Address Bar or the Links toolbar isn't displayed, point to Toolbars on the View menu, and choose Address Bar or Links from the submenu.

3. Drag the address of the current site from the Address Bar toolbar into an empty spot on the Links toolbar.

4. Rearrange items on the Links toolbar by doing either of the following:

   ◆ Drag a button into a new location on the Links toolbar.

   ◆ Right-click a button, and choose Delete from the shortcut menu to remove that button from the Links toolbar.

5. If the button text is too long, right-click the button, choose Rename from the shortcut menu, type a new name, and click OK.

Drag an address...   ...to the Links toolbar...

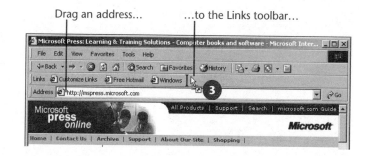

...to create a new link.

Add, delete, and move links to customize a toolbar.

Returning to Your Favorite Sites

When you find a good source of information or entertainment, you don't need to waste a lot of time searching for that site the next time you want to visit it. You can simply add the site to your Favorites list, and Internet Explorer will obligingly create a short-cut to the site for you.

TIP

Organize your favorites. *If you'll be storing many different favorite locations, click the Create In button in the Add Favorite dialog box, and create a file structure for your pages.*

SEE ALSO

For information about returning to a site that you didn't save, see "Opening a Document You Used Previously" on page 32.

Save a Location

1. Go to the site whose location you want to save.

2. Choose Add To Favorites from the Favorites menu.

3. Specify whether you want to store the site for offline viewing.

4. Type a name for the site, or use the proposed name.

5. Click OK.

Return to a Location

1. Click the Favorites button on the Standard Buttons toolbar.

2. In the Favorites Explorer Bar, click the name of the site you want to return to. If the site is contained in a subfolder, click the folder and then click the site.

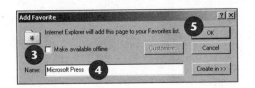

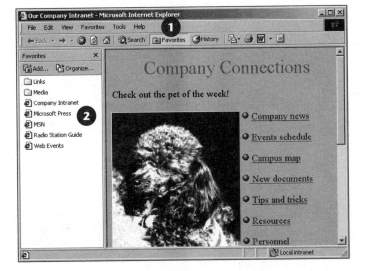

Adding Links to the Desktop

For easy and quick access to web pages or other documents, you can put a web page containing links right on your Desktop. The page can be one you create yourself, an intranet page, or even a page from the Internet.

Put a Web Page on the Desktop

1. Use Internet Explorer to go to the page you want to put on your Desktop.

2. Click in the Address Bar to select the entire address, and press the key combination Ctrl+C to copy the address.

3. Right-click a blank spot on the Desktop, point to Active Desktop on the shortcut menu, and choose Customize My Desktop.

4. Turn on the check box for web content.

5. Click New.

6. Click in the Location box, and press the key combination Ctrl+V to paste in the address.

7. Click OK.

8. Point to the page on your Desktop, and drag a border to resize the page, or drag the title bar to move the page.

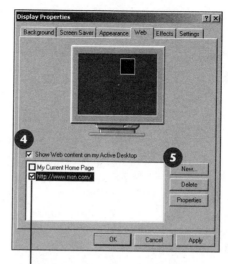

Only the items that are checked will be displayed.

Creating Quick Access to a Web Site

When you've found a particularly useful or interesting web site that you use frequently or want to share with others, you can create a shortcut to that site. For your personal use, you need only double-click the shortcut to start Internet Explorer and go to the web site. To share the site, you can include the shortcut in a document or in an e-mail message.

TIP

Offline viewing. *To reread a page off line instead of reconnecting, either save the page (choose Save As from the File menu) or set the page up for offline viewing.*

SEE ALSO

For information about setting up a page for offline viewing, see "Save a Location" on page 48.

Create a Shortcut

1. Use Internet Explorer to go to the web site.

2. On the File menu, point to Send.

3. From the submenu, choose Shortcut To Desktop.

4. Close Internet Explorer and minimize any other open windows.

5. Locate the shortcut on the Desktop.

6. Do any of the following:
   - Double-click the shortcut to go to the site.
   - Open a folder window (My Documents, for example), and drag the shortcut into that window.
   - Create an e-mail message, and drag the shortcut into the message to send to someone else.
   - Drag the shortcut into a document.

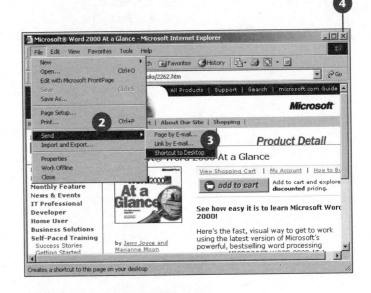

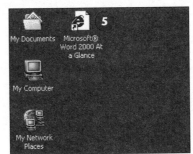

Accessing Folders from the Command Prompt

The command prompt is a throwback to the early days before Windows, but sometimes it's useful. If you want or need to work with the command prompt, you can either use standard MS-DOS commands or get a little help from a folder window.

TIP

Switch folders. *To switch to a folder on a different drive, first switch to that drive by typing the drive letter followed by a colon at the command prompt, and press Enter. Then use the cd command to switch to the folder.*

Switch Between Folders

1. If the command prompt isn't already running, click the Start button, point to Programs and then Accessories, and choose Command Prompt from the submenu.

2. Use any of the Change Directory (cd) commands shown in the table. (Type *cd* and a space, followed by the required number of periods.) Substitute the actual paths and folder names for those shown here, and include the quotation marks where indicated.

Use a Folder Window

1. Type *cd* and a space.

2. Switch to the folder window.

3. Drag the folder to the command prompt.

4. Click in the Command Prompt window.

5. Press Enter.

MS-DOS COMMANDS FOR CHANGING FOLDERS	
Command	**Result**
cd ..	Moves up one folder (to parent folder).
cd ...	Moves up two folders.
cd	Moves up three folders.
cd *ms-dos directory name*	Moves to specified subfolder.
cd *path**ms-dos directory name*	Moves to specified folder.
cd *"long folder name"*	Moves to specified subfolder.
cd *"\path\long folder name"*	Moves to specified folder.

3

The dropped folder shows the full MS-DOS path.

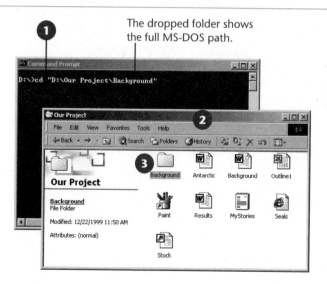

4

Organizing

IN THIS SECTION

**Arranging the
File Listings**

**Organizing, Renaming,
and Deleting Files
and Folders**

**Recovering a
Deleted Item**

**Adding Documents and
Folders to the Desktop**

**Arranging Windows
on the Desktop**

**Organizing the
Start Menu**

**Organizing Your
Favorite Items**

**Cleaning Up Your
Lists of Activities**

**Displaying File
and Folder Locations
and Types**

We all know that to work productively and efficiently, with minimal stress and frustration, we must *get organized!* But organizing the files, folders, and other items that live in your computer is a highly selective and personal process that doesn't lend itself to a one-size-fits-all solution. That's where Microsoft Windows 2000 Professional comes in. It gives you the flexibility to organize anything and everything in exactly the way that suits you best. Then, if you change your mind, you can reorganize with a few mouse clicks.

Windows 2000 supplies the framework—a basic file structure of drives and folders, which you can leave as is if it's compatible with the way you work. Otherwise, customize! Create your own system of folders and subfolders. Organize the files within those folders—alphabetically, or by size, type, or date—and view them with large or small icons, as detailed lists, and so on. Organize your Desktop—specify the way you want your windows to be arranged; put frequently used documents, folders, and scraps of text on the Desktop so that they're quite literally at your fingertips. Organize the Start menu—it's quick and easy to add or delete programs and other items according to your needs. Organize the Favorites menu. Clean up the Documents menu when you start a new project. In other words, get organized!

Arranging the File Listings

Microsoft Windows 2000, by default, displays all your files as large icons, arranged alphabetically. If you'd prefer to group your files differently, you can change the way they're displayed and ordered.

TIP

Thumbnails. *Thumbnails view displays an icon instead of a preview if Windows 2000 doesn't have the filters installed to create a preview of the file contents, or if a preview of a document wasn't saved with the document. Thumbnails are particularly useful for displaying documents in different graphical formats.*

TIP

Refreshing. *To update, or refresh, the file list manually, click in the folder window, and press the F5 key.*

Change the Display

1. Click the View menu.

2. Choose one of the following views:

   ◆ Large Icons to see files or folders with large representative icons

   ◆ Small Icons to see small representative icons arranged from left to right

   ◆ List to see small representative icons arranged from top to bottom

   ◆ Details to see small representative icons and detailed file information

   ◆ Thumbnails to see a small picture of the file (for file types that are supported by this feature)

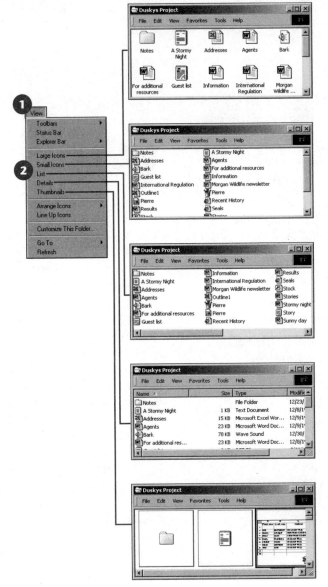

TRY THIS

Save a preview. *If you have a Microsoft Word or Microsoft Excel document that doesn't show a preview in Thumbnails view, open the document, and choose Properties from the File menu. On the Summary tab, turn on the Save Preview Picture check box. Save and close the document. Now take a look at the thumbnail image.*

TIP

Quick sort or re-sort. *To quickly sort the listings in Details view, click the category name at the top of the list. To reverse the sort order, click the name a second time.*

TIP

Folders first. *Folders are always sorted before files, so unless you reverse the sort order based on any field other than Name, folders will appear at the beginning of the list.*

Sort the Files

1 Open the folder you want to examine.

2 Click the View menu, and point to Arrange Icons.

3 From the submenu, choose the type of sorting you want:

◆ By Name to order the files by their filenames

◆ By Type to order the files by their type— Word, Excel, Paint, and so on

◆ By Size to order the files by their size in kilobytes

◆ By Date to order the files by the date they were created or most recently modified

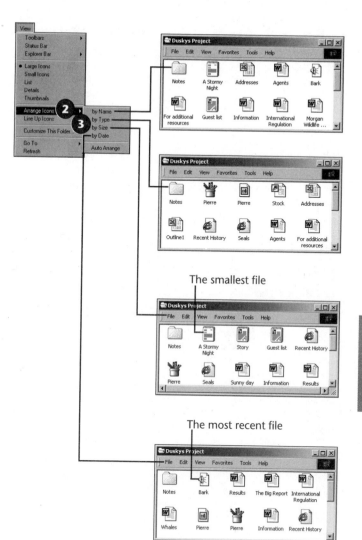

The smallest file

The most recent file

Organizing Your Folders

Windows 2000 provides the basic filing structure—drives and ready-made folders such as My Documents and Program Files. You can customize the filing system by adding your own folders or placing folders inside other folders (subfolders).

TIP

Off limits! *There are some locations in which you can't create your own folders—the Printers and Control Panel folders, for example, or any network folder to which you don't have full access. In those cases, there won't be a New command on the shortcut menu that appears when you right-click.*

TRY THIS

Quick folder. *Open the folder to which you want to add a subfolder. Press Alt to activate the menu, F to open the File menu, W to open the New submenu, and F to create a new folder. Type a name for the folder, and press Enter.*

Create a Folder

1. Open the window of the destination folder, drive, or other location.

2. Point to a blank part of the window, and right-click.

3. Point to New on the shortcut menu.

4. Choose Folder.

5. Type a name for the new folder. (The name can be as long as 255 characters, but because a long name will often be truncated by a program, a descriptive short name is a better choice.) You can use spaces and underscores, but you can't use the characters *   :   < > | ? " \ or /.

6. Press Enter when the name is correct.

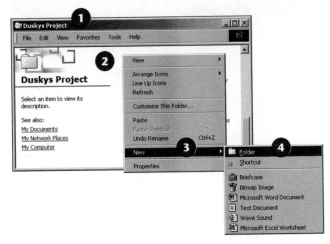

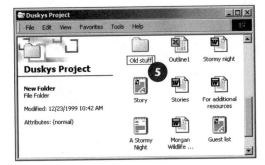

Reorganizing Your Folders

Every so often, as your needs dictate, you'll probably have to spend a little time modifying your filing system. This is a task most of us really don't look forward to! Fortunately, all it takes to reorganize your filing system in Windows 2000 is a click or two of the mouse.

TIP

Drag your folders. *You can also drag folders up or down in the Folders Explorer Bar when you need to move or copy them.*

TIP

Easy drag. *To make the dragging easier, use the vertical scroll bar in the Folders Explorer Bar to position the destination location approximately parallel to the folder you want to move or copy.*

Move or Copy a Folder into Another Folder

1 In any folder window, click the Folders button on the Standard Buttons toolbar.

2 Click the drive or folder that contains the folder you want to move or copy. If necessary, click one or more plus signs to expand the listing to locate the folder.

3 If necessary, expand the listing further by clicking plus signs until the destination folder (or drive or computer) is listed.

4 Point to the folder to be moved or copied.

5 Hold down the right mouse button and drag the folder onto the destination folder.

6 Release the mouse button and choose a command from the shortcut menu to move or copy the folder.

7 Click the Folders button on the Standard Buttons toolbar to close the Folders Explorer Bar.

The Folders Explorer Bar

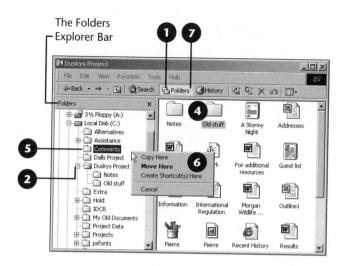

Organizing Your Files

If you have a limited number of files, you can easily keep them all in a single folder. However, if you have many files, or files dealing with different projects, you'll probably want to organize them by placing them in individual folders.

TIP

Select or deselect files.
To select a series of contiguous files, point to the first file, hold down the Shift key, and then click the last file. To deselect one of the files or to select an additional file, hold down the Ctrl key and click the file.

SEE ALSO

For information about creating a subfolder, see "Organizing Your Folders" on page 56.

Move Files into a Subfolder

1. Open the window containing the file or files you want to move.

2. Select the file or files to be moved.

3. Drag the file or files onto the subfolder.

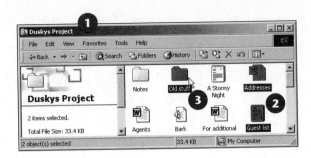

Move or Copy Files into Another Folder

1. Open the window containing the file or files you want to move or copy.

2. Click the Folders button on the Standard Buttons toolbar.

3. If necessary, expand the listing by clicking plus signs until the destination folder is displayed.

4. Select the file or files to be moved, hold down the right mouse button, and drag the file or files onto the destination folder.

5. Choose a command from the shortcut menu to move or copy the folder.

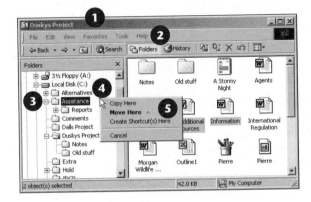

Renaming or Deleting a File or Folder

It's quick and easy to rename your files or folders, or to edit a name you've misspelled. Deleting a file or folder is even easier—in fact, it's *so* easy that Windows 2000 asks you for confirmation. However, if you delete a file or folder accidentally, you can usually retrieve it from the Recycle Bin.

SEE ALSO

For information about retrieving a deleted file or folder, see "Recovering a Deleted Item" on page 60.

TIP

It's gone! *Take the Windows 2000 confirmation check seriously. When you delete a file or folder from a floppy disk or from a network location, you won't be able to restore it from the Recycle Bin. If you do lose something, check your backup copies or consult with your network administrator.*

Rename a File or Folder

1. Right-click the file or folder.

2. Choose Rename from the shortcut menu.

3. With the name selected, type a new name, or click to position the insertion point and then edit the name.

4. Press Enter.

Delete a File or Folder

1. Open the drive or folder containing the file or folder you want to delete.

2. Select the file or folder, or hold down the Ctrl key as you point and select multiple files or folders.

3. Press the Delete key.

4. Click Yes to delete the file or folder and send it to the Recycle Bin.

5. If you're deleting a folder that contains files, click the appropriate button if Windows 2000 asks you to confirm the deletion of some types of files (program files, for example).

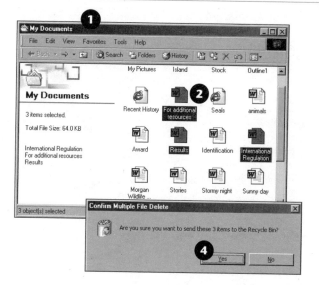

Recovering a Deleted Item

If you delete a file, folder, or shortcut by mistake, you can quickly recover it either by undoing your action immediately or by restoring the deleted item from the Recycle Bin. The Recycle Bin holds all the files you've deleted from your hard disk(s) until you empty the bin or until it gets so full that the oldest files are deleted automatically.

> **TIP**
>
> **Undo an action.** *Windows 2000 remembers as many as three of your most recent actions, so if you executed an action after you deleted something, undo the action first and then undo the deletion.*

> **TIP**
>
> **Restore a folder.** *When you've deleted a folder, you have to restore the entire folder. You can't open a deleted folder in the Recycle Bin and restore selected files.*

Undo a Deletion Immediately

1. Point to a blank part of the Windows 2000 Desktop or to a blank part of any folder window, and right-click.

2. Choose Undo Delete from the shortcut menu.

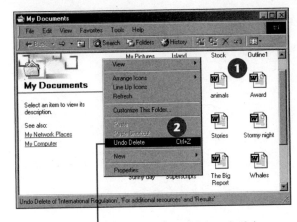

The command is available only if the deletion was your most recent action.

Restore an Item from the Recycle Bin

1. Double-click the Recycle Bin icon on the Windows 2000 Desktop.

2. Select the item or items to be recovered, and right-click.

3. Choose Restore from the shortcut menu.

4. Click the Close button to close the Recycle Bin.

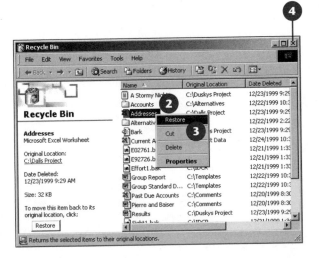

Renaming Multiple Files

If you're comfortable working with the command prompt, you can use commands with wildcard characters to change several filenames at once. The two powerful wildcard characters are the question mark (?), which can represent any single character, and the asterisk (*), which can represent any number of characters.

TIP

Filename protocol. *If the filename doesn't contain any spaces, you can type its name with or without the quotation marks.*

SEE ALSO

For information about navigating folders using the command prompt, see "Accessing Folders from the Command Prompt" on page 51.

Rename Files

1 Click the Start button, point to Programs and then Accessories, and choose Command Prompt from the submenu.

2 Go to the folder that contains the files you want to rename.

3 Type the following, enclosing all within quotation marks: *rename,* the base of the filename (that is, the characters that are common to all the files you're renaming), and any wildcards to represent the characters that are different among the filenames. Type a space, and then (again enclosing all in quotation marks) type the base of the new filename and any wildcards.

4 Press Enter.

5 Open the folder containing the files if it's not already open, and confirm that the files have been properly renamed.

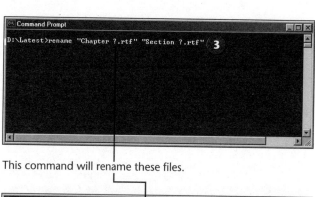

This command will rename these files.

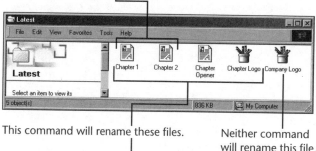

This command will rename these files.   Neither command will rename this file.

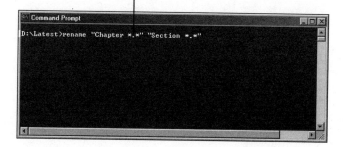

4

Copying an Item to a Special Location

A quick and easy way to copy files or folders to certain locations is to use the Send To submenu. You can then choose to copy an item to a floppy disk or to another type of removable disk; you can send a copy of a file by e-mail; or you can copy a document to your own My Documents folder for future easy access. And if there are other locations you want to use, you can add them to the Send To menu.

Copy the Item

1. Open the folder that contains the item or items you want to copy.

2. If you're copying the material onto a removable disk, verify that the disk is in place.

3. Select the item or items you want to copy. Hold down the Ctrl key while you click to select multiple files or folders.

4. Right-click one of the selected items, point to Send To on the shortcut menu, and choose the destination you want from the submenu. Wait for the files to be sent.

5. If you're sending the item or items to a mail recipient, address the mail, add any comments, and send it. The items are included as attachments.

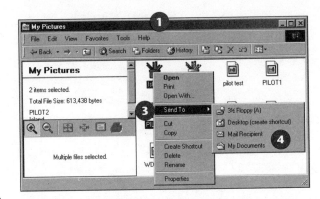

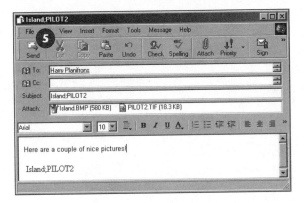

Identifying the locations.
The drive that contains your Windows 2000 files is the one that contains the WINNT folder—drive C if the computer has a single operating system installed, or possibly a different drive if multiple operating systems are installed. The folder that contains your profile uses your logon name as its name.

Remove an item. *To remove an item from the Send To menu, delete the shortcut for the item from the Send To folder.*

Start the wizard. *To start the Create Shortcut Wizard using the keyboard, press Alt, then F, then W, and then S.*

Create Your Own Special Location

1. On the drive that contains your Windows 2000 files, open the Documents And Settings folder, and open the folder for your profile.

2. If you don't see a Send To folder, choose Folder Options from the Tools menu, click the View tab, turn on the Show Hidden Files And Folders option, and click OK.

3. Open the Send To folder.

4. On the File menu, point to New, and choose Shortcut from the submenu.

5. Click the Browse button, select a location, and click OK.

6. Click Next.

7. Type the name you want on the Send To menu.

8. Click Finish.

9. Open a folder, right-click a file or folder, and confirm that the new location appears on the Send To menu.

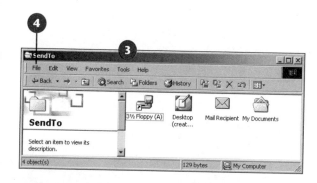

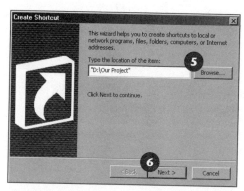

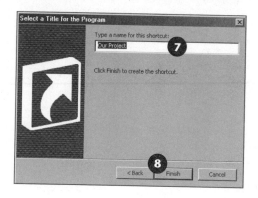

Adding Documents and Folders to the Desktop

The Windows 2000 Desktop is more than just a place for pictures and icons. You can use the Desktop to store frequently used documents and folders for quick access, or to store parts of documents for later use.

SEE ALSO

For information about accessing documents from a toolbar, see "Navigating with Toolbars" on page 40.

TIP

Where is it? *Items that you've placed on the Desktop are usually stored under your name in the Documents And Settings folder. If you can't locate this folder, right-click the item on the Desktop, choose Properties from the shortcut menu, and note the location on the General tab.*

Add a Document

1. Open the folder window that contains the document you want.

2. Hold down the right mouse button and drag the document onto the Desktop.

3. From the shortcut menu that appears, choose either to copy or move the document onto the Desktop, or to create a shortcut to the document.

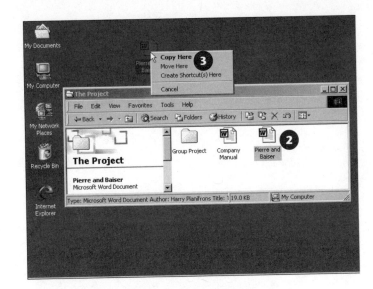

Add a Folder

1. Right-click in a blank part of the Desktop.

2. Point to New on the shortcut menu, and choose Folder from the submenu.

3. Type a name for the new folder, and press Enter.

Quick navigation. *In many programs, the Save As dialog box has a button in the left column that takes you directly to the Desktop.*

Save your scraps. *If the program you're using doesn't support dragging and dropping, and you want to save a section of text as a scrap on the Desktop, copy the selected text, right-click in a blank part of the Desktop, and choose Paste from the shortcut menu.*

Organize your scraps. *Scraps can also be stored in folders, so you can organize them just as you can any other files.*

WordPad scrap. *Start WordPad and type some text. Select the text and drag it onto the Desktop. Start a new Word 6 document in WordPad, type some text, and then drag the WordPad scrap from the Desktop into the WordPad document.*

Save a Document to the Desktop

1. Create a document in your program.

2. Choose Save from the File menu to display the Save As dialog box.

3. Select Desktop in the Save In drop-down list.

4. If you want to save the document in a folder on the Desktop, double-click the folder to open it.

5. Type a name for the document.

6. Click the Save button.

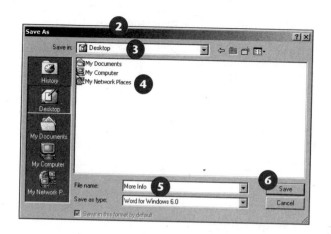

Save Part of a Document to the Desktop

1. Select the part of the document you want to save.

2. Drag the selection onto the Desktop. (You'll notice that Windows 2000 puts a "scrap" icon on the Desktop.)

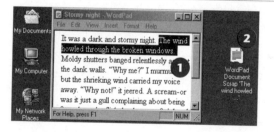

4

Arranging Windows on the Desktop

When you have several windows open, your Desktop can become littered with overlapping windows. You can arrange the open windows for easy access, or you can minimize and store some or all of them on the taskbar to keep your Desktop neat and uncluttered.

TIP

Desktop access. *If you want to access only one Desktop icon, use the Desktop toolbar. If you want full access to the Desktop, use the Desktop button on the Quick Launch toolbar to minimize all your windows.*

SEE ALSO

For information about displaying the Quick Launch and the Desktop toolbars, see "Navigating with Toolbars" on page 40.

Arrange Your Open Windows

1. Minimize any open windows other than the ones you want displayed.

2. Point to a blank spot on the Windows 2000 taskbar, and right-click.

3. Choose Cascade Windows, Tile Windows Horizontally, or Tile Windows Vertically to arrange all the open windows.

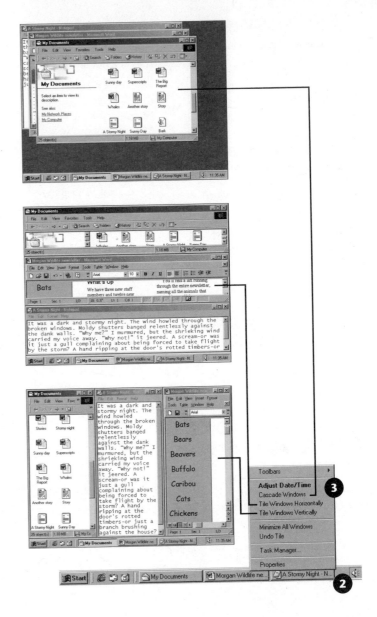

Tidying Up the Desktop

If your Windows 2000 Desktop becomes so cluttered with unused shortcuts, old scraps of text, or overlapping icons that you can't find what you want at a glance, take a minute or two to do a little housekeeping.

TIP

Auto Arrange. *The Auto Arrange command must be turned off before you can create your own arrangement of icons.*

SEE ALSO

For information about hiding the Desktop icons, see "Hiding the Desktop Icons" on page 223.

Arrange the Icons

1. Right-click in a blank part of the Desktop.

2. Point to Arrange Icons on the shortcut menu, and choose the type of arrangement you want.

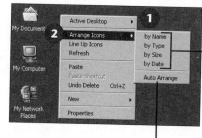

Choose the way you want the icons to be arranged.

Turn on to have Windows 2000 automatically arrange the icons after you've created, moved, or deleted them.

Create Your Own Arrangement

1. Drag the icons to the area of the Desktop where you want them.

2. Right-click in a blank part of the Desktop.

3. Choose Line Up Icons.

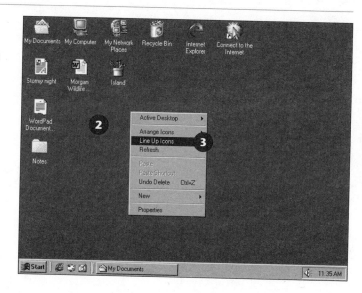

4

Organizing the Start Menu

The Windows 2000 Start menu is a wonderful resource for organizing and starting your programs and associated documents. You can organize the Start menu by adding and deleting programs, and by moving programs around to create an arrangement that's logical and convenient for the way you work.

TIP

Start menu shortcuts.
The programs listed on the Start menu are not the programs themselves but shortcuts to the programs. When you add, move, or delete an item whose name appears on the Start menu, you're affecting only the shortcut to the program, not the program itself.

Add an Item

1. Use My Computer to locate the item you want to add.

2. Drag the item to the Start button, and do either of the following:

   ◆ Place the item on the Start button to have the item appear at the top of the Start menu.

   ◆ Hold the item on the Start button without releasing the mouse button until the Start menu opens. Point to Programs, and either drag the item onto the Programs submenu, or continue dragging and pointing to submenus until you reach the desired location, and then place the item.

3. If you want to rename the item, right-click it, choose Rename from the shortcut menu, type a new name, and click OK.

The item appears at the top of the Start menu when you place it on the Start button...

...or you can place it on a submenu.

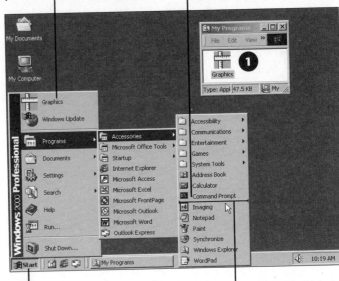

The bar shows the location at which the program will appear on the submenu.

SEE ALSO

For information about adding your own submenus, see "Reorganizing the Start Menu" on page 70.

For information about adding items to the Startup folder, see "Starting a Program When Windows 2000 Starts" on page 95.

For information about modifying the way a program starts from a shortcut menu, see "Changing the Way a Program Starts" on page 96.

TIP

Organize the menu.
If you've been adding, deleting, or moving items and the menu has become a bit disorganized, right-click any item on the menu, and then choose Sort By Name from the shortcut menu to list the items alphabetically.

Move an Item

1. Open the Start menu, and the submenus if necessary, until you locate the item you want to move.

2. Drag the item into a new location.

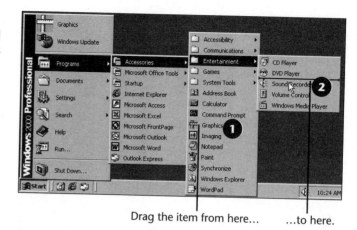

Drag the item from here...   ...to here.

Delete an Item

1. Open the Start menu, and the submenus if necessary, until you locate the item you want to delete.

2. Right-click the item, and choose Delete from the shortcut menu.

3. Confirm that you want to delete the item.

4

Reorganizing the Start Menu

The beauty of Windows 2000 is the flexibility it gives you to change things around. For example, if you'd like to reorganize the Start menu so that it works more logically for you, you can restructure it by creating or deleting submenus. Windows 2000 uses folders to organize the Start menu, so you have to create a subfolder to be able to create a submenu. You can also specify which items are displayed and how they appear.

Add a Submenu

1. Right-click the Start button, and choose Explore from the shortcut menu.

2. In the window that appears, select the folder (and thereby the Start-menu submenu) in which you want to create a submenu.

3. Right-click a blank spot in the right pane, point to New, and choose Folder from the shortcut menu.

4. Name the folder, using the name you want to appear on the submenu.

5. Close the window.

6. Open the Start menu, and drag your program or document into the new submenu.

7. After you've added all the items you want, right-click in the submenu, and choose Sort By Name from the shortcut menu.

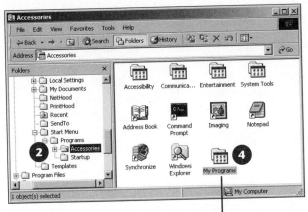

By creating this new folder...

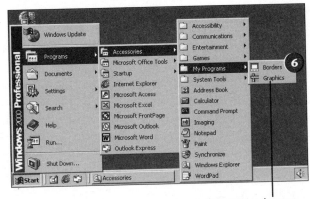

...you create this new submenu.

SEE ALSO

For information about adding items to, and moving items on, the Start menu, see "Organizing the Start Menu" on page 68.

For information about hiding or displaying the taskbar, see "Hiding the Taskbar or a Toolbar" on page 218.

TRY THIS

Fast logoff. *Display the Taskbar And Start Menu Properties dialog box, turn on the Display Logoff check box on the Advanced tab, and click OK. The next time you want to log off, choose the Log Off command instead of the Shut Down command from the Start menu.*

TIP

Use the keyboard. *To display the Taskbar And Start Menu Properties dialog box using the keyboard, press Ctrl+Esc to open the Start menu, press S, and then press T.*

Change What's Displayed

1. Right-click a blank spot on the taskbar, and choose Properties from the shortcut menu.

2. On the General tab of the Taskbar And Start Menu Properties dialog box, turn on the Use Personalized Menus check box to initially display only the menu items you use, or turn off the check box to always display the full menus.

3. On the Advanced tab, under Start Menu Settings, turn on the check boxes for features you want, and turn off the check boxes for features you don't want:

   ◆ Display... to display the specified item on the Start menu

   ◆ Expand... to display a submenu for the item, showing its contents

   ◆ Scroll The Programs Menu to add scroll bars to the Programs listing if you have too many programs to fit on the screen in a single column

4. Click OK.

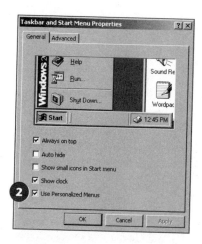

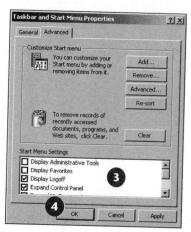

Organizing Your Favorite Items

A handy way to remember or to return to a folder or a web page is to add it to your Favorites menu. When your list of favorites becomes so long that you can't easily find an item, it's time to organize the list into categories. When you place items in a folder, the folder is displayed on the menu, and the items appear on its submenu.

SEE ALSO

For information about adding items to the Favorites menu, see "Returning to Your Favorite Sites" on page 48.

Organize the Menu

1. In any folder window, choose Organize Favorites from the Favorites menu.

2. Click Create Folder.

3. Give the new folder a descriptive name that you want to appear on the Favorites menu.

4. Create and name any other folders you want.

5. Select an item you want to place in the new folder.

6. Click Move To Folder.

7. Select the folder.

8. Click OK.

9. Repeat steps 5 through 8 to arrange other items. Click Close when you've finished.

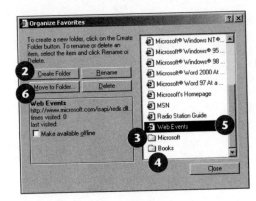

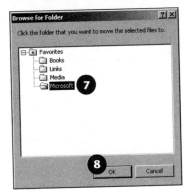

TRY THIS

Favorite project. *Create a new folder to contain all the related items for a project. Drag any items related to the project that are located on the Favorites menu into the new folder. Whenever you create or access a document, web page, or folder that is related to the project, add it to this folder on the Favorites menu. Soon you'll have easy access to all the resources for the project from any folder window.*

SEE ALSO

For information about displaying the Favorites list on the Start menu, see "Change What's Displayed" on page 71.

Rearrange the Menu

1. Open the Favorites menu.

2. Drag an item into a new location. To move an item onto a submenu, drag the item into the folder, and then, after the submenu opens, place the item on the submenu.

3. After you've added as many items as you want to the submenu, right-click in the submenu and choose Sort By Name from the shortcut menu to arrange the items alphabetically.

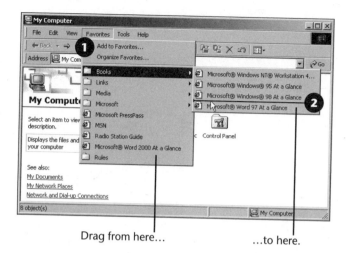

Drag from here...   ...to here.

Delete a Menu Item

1. Right-click the item you no longer want.

2. Choose Delete from the shortcut menu.

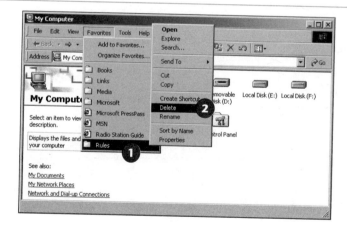

Cleaning Up Your Lists of Activities

While you work, Windows 2000 Professional keeps lists—lists of the documents you used, addresses of the web sites you visited, and even the commands you used from the Run command. Windows 2000 also keeps a chronological record—called the History—of all the documents you've used. To start fresh, or just to protect your privacy, you can delete the contents of these lists.

TIP

Delete the shortcuts.
Removing documents from the Documents menu deletes only the shortcuts to the documents, not the documents themselves.

TIP

Delete a single item.
To remove a single item from the Documents menu, right-click the item, and choose Delete from the shortcut menu.

Reset the Lists

1. Right-click a blank spot on the taskbar, and choose Properties from the shortcut menu.

2. On the Advanced tab, click the Clear button.

3. Click OK. The contents of the Documents menu on the Start menu, the addresses in the Address toolbar on the taskbar and in the Address Bar in Internet Explorer, and the commands used from the Run command on the Start menu, are all cleared.

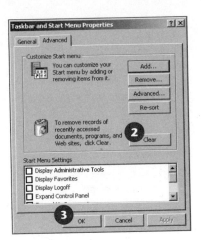

Clear the History

1. Start Internet Explorer if it's not already running.

2. Choose Internet Options from the Tools menu.

3. On the General tab, click Clear History.

4. Click OK.

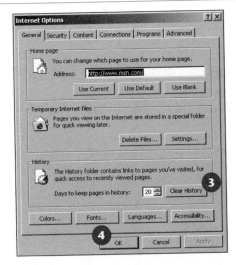

Displaying File and Folder Locations and Types

If you're a computer traditionalist who loves to know exactly where you are in the computer's directory tree, or if you'd rather see a file's full name, including its extension, than the type of file or the program with which the file is associated, Windows 2000 is ready to accommodate your preferences.

TIP

Advanced Settings list.
To obtain a description of each item in the Advanced Settings list, click the Help button in the upper right corner of the Folder Options dialog box, and then click the item in the list.

Display the File Information

1. Open the folder you want to modify.

2. Choose Folder Options from the Tools menu.

3. Click the View tab.

4. Turn on the options you want.

5. If you want all your folders to use these settings, click Like Current Folder.

6. Click OK.

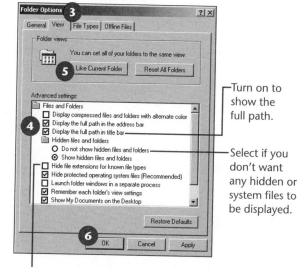

Turn on to show the full path.

Select if you don't want any hidden or system files to be displayed.

Turn off to display the filename with its extension.

The path in the title bar

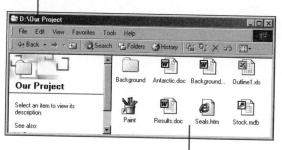

Files with their extensions shown

IN THIS SECTION

Sharing Your Computer

Groups, Permissions, and Security

Sharing Documents and Folders

Limiting Access to a Shared Folder

Monitoring Who's Connected

Making Shared Documents Always Available

Sharing Programs On Line

Sharing a Printer

5

Sharing

Today's computers, operating systems, and networks have given us the unprecedented and often dizzying ability to share or gather information locally or globally. This interconnectivity, however, comes with a cost: the need for greater security to protect your computer and its contents from harm.

You want the convenience and efficiency of being able to share the documents and files on your computer with your colleagues or coworkers, but you also want protection against lost information, hackers, prying eyes, and other evils. Microsoft Windows 2000 Professional was designed to meet those specific requirements—maintaining security while enabling sharing. One of Windows 2000's primary security measures is the ability it gives you to classify users into groups, with each group having a specific level of permission to access or change items. You can share your files and folders but can limit or deny access to shared documents. You can monitor who's connected to your computer and what they can have access to. You can set up your computer so that you can share your printer with your coworkers, but you can also limit their access to the printer if necessary. You and your colleagues can collaborate on programs in an online NetMeeting session and can keep a text version of the online meeting for future reference.

Sharing Your Computer

Windows 2000 initially sets up your computer to be shared by others. If your computer is part of a client-server network—and even if you never want to share any documents—for administrative purposes your computer needs to be set up for sharing. If sharing has been disabled or removed, you can re-enable it or install it to enhance your connection to the network.

Enable Sharing

1. Right-click My Network Places, and choose Properties from the shortcut menu.

2. In the Network And Dial-Up Connections window, right-click your network connection, and choose Properties from the shortcut menu.

3. If the File And Printer Sharing For Microsoft Networks check box is shown but isn't turned on, click it to turn it on, and then click OK.

4. If the File And Printer Sharing For Microsoft Networks check box is not present, click Install.

5. Double-click Service.

6. Select File And Printer Sharing For Microsoft Networks.

7. Click OK.

8. Click Close to close the Select Network Component Type dialog box.

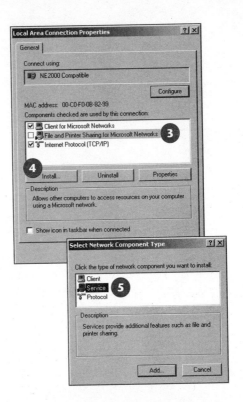

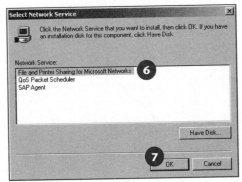

Groups, Permissions, and Security

One of the primary goals of Windows 2000 is to protect your computer from those who have no business reading your documents or modifying files *and* from your own desire to reconfigure the computer. One of the primary security measures is to classify users into different groups, described in the table at the right, with each group given a different level of authority, or permission, to access and change items. Some of these groups might look different on your computer, because someone with the proper permission—a member of the Administrators group—can create new groups and modify permissions for existing groups.

When you specify who can access a shared folder, you'll see more groups and a list of users, giving you even more options. In most cases, you can ignore the majority of the groups and either give permission to everyone or limit permission to a custom group or to certain individuals. Use the groups cautiously—you don't want to be responsible for allowing sensitive information to fall into the wrong hands.

Permissions, of course, go well beyond allowing access to shared folders. When you log on, you're logging on as a specific type of user. Even if your computer isn't part of a large network and you don't care whether others can read your documents, you should still be concerned about security. For example, if you're always logged on as an Administrator rather than a User or a Power User, all the computers to which you're connected are as vulnerable as your own to viruses, hackers, and other evil forces that copy or delete documents, change system files, or reformat hard disks. For more information about setting up groups and assigning users to groups, see "Adding New Users" on page 284 and "Defining Access Rights" on page 287.

WINDOWS 2000 USER GROUPS AND PERMISSIONS	
Group	**Permission**
Administrators	Unlimited. Have automatic share access to all computers, including access to everyone's documents.
Power Users	Can add and remove programs; can modify their computers, including Control Panel settings; can access their own documents and documents in common and shared folders; cannot access other users' documents (NTFS file system only).
Users	Can make personal settings for their computer setups, but no system changes; can access their own documents and documents in common and shared folders; cannot access other users' documents (NTFS file system only).
Guests	Can open and save common and shared documents.
Replicator And Backup Operators	Can replicate or back up data only.

5

Sharing Documents and Folders

To permit other people on different computers to access some of your documents, you share the folder that contains the documents. By specifying which groups have access and the type of permission each can have, you can limit access to the documents.

Group Project

TIP

Slow computer. *The greater the number of people who are connected to your computer and are using its resources, the more slowly your computer will run. If its sluggishness becomes unbearable when several people are connected, you'll want to consider reducing the number of people who can connect at one time.*

Share a Folder

1 Locate the folder you want to share.

2 Right-click the folder, and choose Sharing from the shortcut menu.

3 On the Sharing tab, turn on the Share This Folder option.

4 Either accept the proposed name or type a new name for the folder.

5 Type a comment if you want one.

6 Specify how many users may connect at one time:

◆ Maximum Allowed to permit as many as 10 users to be connected to your computer at the same time

◆ Allow Users, and select a number to permit the specified number (but not more than 10) to connect to your computer at the same time

The Security tab is displayed only when the folder resides on an NTFS-formatted drive. You'll also see a Web Sharing tab if your computer is set up to host a web site.

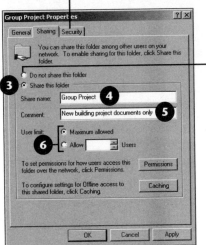

Turn on to disable sharing of a previously shared folder.

TRY THIS

Prevent accidental changes. *You can prevent accidental changes to some of your shared documents while allowing full control over other documents in the same folder. To do this, right-click the document, choose Properties from the shortcut menu, turn on the Read-Only attribute, and click OK. Note that turning on a document's Read-Only attribute will prevent a user from accidentally saving changes, but he or she can still make changes intentionally by turning off the Read-Only option.*

TIP

No sharing. *If the Sharing command doesn't appear on the shortcut menu, either you don't have the authority to modify folder sharing or sharing hasn't been set up on your computer.*

SEE ALSO

For information about specifying individual access to shared folders, see "Limiting Access to a Shared Folder" on page 82.

Set the Access

1. Click the Permissions button on the Sharing tab.

2. Specify the type of access:

   ◆ Full Control to permit users to open, save, create, move, and delete files and folders

   ◆ Change to permit users to open files and save changes

   ◆ Read to permit users to open files from the folder but not to modify the contents of the folder

3. Click OK.

4. Click OK on the Sharing tab.

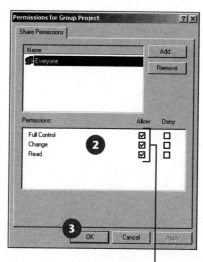

Turn on to permit access; turn off to limit access.

5

Limiting Access to a Shared Folder

A shared folder, by default, is open to anyone who has access to your computer. You can limit that access, however, by specifying which groups, individuals, or users of specific computers can access the shared folder, and you can specify the type of access each is allowed.

TIP

Specify users. *If the list of users in the domain is very long, you can type the names you want in the Names box—separating them with semicolons—instead of searching through the list to find the names. Click the Add button, and then click the Check Names button to have Windows 2000 verify the list of individuals.*

Change the Access

1. Right-click the folder, and choose Sharing from the shortcut menu. Turn on the Sharing option if it's not already selected.

2. Click the Permissions button on the Sharing tab.

3. With the Everyone group selected, click the Remove button.

4. Click the Add button.

5. Select the computer, workgroup, domain, or directory that contains the groups or individuals you want to add.

6. Select a group, an individual, or a computer.

7. Click the Add button.

8. Repeat steps 5 through 7 to add more groups, individuals, or computers.

9. Click OK.

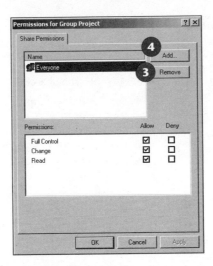

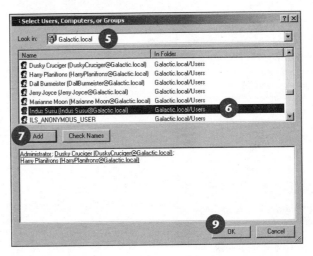

TIP

New Share button. *Once you've shared a folder, the New Share button appears on the Sharing tab of the Properties dialog box. Click the New Share button to share the folder using a different name and a different set of permissions.*

TIP

The NTFS file system. *If you're using the NTFS file system, you can use the Security tab of the folder's Properties dialog box to assign more specific access rights to folders, including shared folders. You can also specify whether a subfolder in a shared folder may also be shared. The Security tab isn't available for folders that use the FAT or FAT32 file system.*

SEE ALSO

For information about additional ways to customize shared access, see "Protecting Individual Files and Folders" on page 282, "Defining Custom Access" on page 286, and "Defining Access Rights" on page 287.

Individualize the Access

1. Select a group or an individual.

2. For each type of permission, specify the type of access:

    ◆ Turn on the Allow check box to permit access.

    ◆ Turn on the Deny check box to prohibit access, even if access was granted through a higher-level group (for example, to deny access to an individual even if his or her group has been allowed access).

3. Repeat steps 1 and 2 until you've specified the access for all groups and individuals.

4. Click OK.

5. Click OK to close the Properties dialog box for the folder.

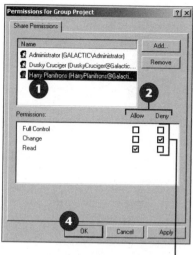

Turn on to explicitly deny access to individuals who might have been granted access permission through their membership in a group.

Monitoring Who's Connected

When you've set up your computer to share folders with your coworkers, you can see who's connected to your computer. You can, for any legitimate reason (no, bad moods and power trips are *not* legitimate reasons), "pull the plug" and disconnect someone from your computer.

Computer
Management

Control Who's Connected

1. Click the Start button, point to Settings, and choose Control Panel from the submenu.

2. Double-click the Administrative Tools icon.

3. Double-click the Computer Management icon.

4. Expand the System Tools item if it's not already expanded.

5. Expand the Shared Folders folder if it's not already expanded.

6. Click the Sessions folder.

7. Examine who's connected.

8. To disconnect an individual, right-click his or her connection, and choose Close Session from the shortcut menu. When prompted, confirm that you want to close the session.

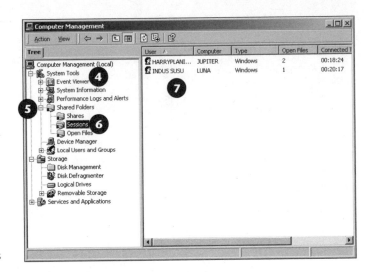

Quick display. *You can quickly display the Computer Management console by right-clicking the My Computer icon and choosing Manage from the shortcut menu.*

Don't remove sharing. *Some items on your hard disk, such as C$ and ADMIN$, are shared for administrative purposes, and, as a general rule, you shouldn't remove sharing from these items. If you do remove sharing, it will be reestablished when you restart the computer or when the Server service is restarted.*

No System Tools? *If you don't see the System Tools item, use the View window to display the Console Tree.*

Update information. *If you leave the Computer Management console open to monitor shares, press the F5 key to update the information.*

Control What's Being Shared

1. Click the Open Files folder.

2. Examine which files are being used.

3. To close a file, right-click it, and choose Close Open File from the shortcut menu.

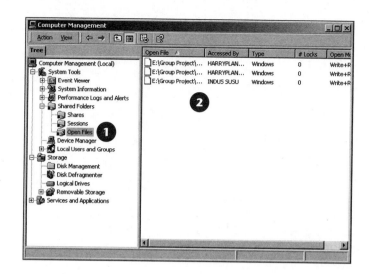

Control What's Accessible

1. Click the Shares folder.

2. Right-click a share, and choose the appropriate command from the shortcut menu:

   ◆ Stop Sharing to end sharing

   ◆ Properties to see more information about the share or to change the share permissions

3. Close the Computer Management window when you've finished.

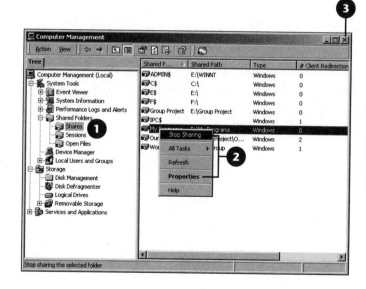

5

Making Shared Documents Always Available

Connections between computers are not always the best—networks go down, phone lines become disconnected, and so on. To prevent the problems that a broken connection can cause, you can set the shared folder to automatically *cache,* or store, documents on the computer that's visiting the shared folder. When the connection has been reestablished, you can use the locally stored (cached) documents to update the documents in the shared folder.

Set Up Automatic Caching

1. Right-click the shared folder, and choose Sharing from the shortcut menu.

2. On the Sharing tab of the Properties dialog box, click Caching.

3. Verify that the check box to allow caching is turned on.

4. Select the type of caching you want:

   ◆ Automatic Caching For Documents to specify that any documents being used on the network be cached on the local computer

   ◆ Automatic Caching For Programs to specify that any programs and read-only files being used on the network be cached on the local computer

5. Click OK.

6. Click OK to close the Properties dialog box.

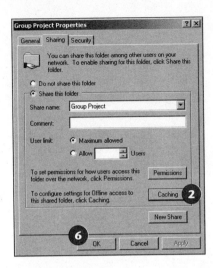

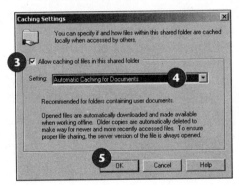

SEE ALSO

For information about manually selecting which documents or folders are cached for offline use and for information about setting up automatic synchronizing, see "Taking Along Network Files" on page 192.

Use the Files

1. Use the files on the share.

2. If the network connection is broken, note the information from the Offline Files icon in the status area of the taskbar.

3. Continue working with your documents, saving them periodically.

4. Note when the connection has been reestablished. When you've completed your work, close any documents that are still open.

5. Click the Offline Files icon in the status area of the taskbar.

6. Click OK, confirm that the offline files are closed, and wait for the files to be synchronized.

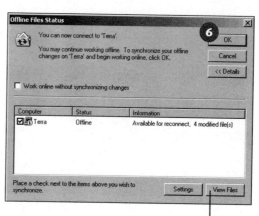

Click to view a list of all the cached offline files.

5

Sharing Programs On Line

When you're participating in an online NetMeeting, you can display programs you're working on to the other participants and can even let them use the programs themselves. That way, all your coworkers can use the programs even if they're not installed on every computer. You can also use the Whiteboard to display additional information.

SEE ALSO

For information about connecting with NetMeeting, see "Conferring on the Net" on page 184.

For information about using NetMeeting to control your computer remotely, see "Controlling Your Computer Remotely" on page 202.

Share a Program

1. With NetMeeting running and connected to the other meeting participants, start the programs you're going to share.

2. Click the Share Program button.

3. Select a program to be shared.

4. Click the Share button.

5. Repeat steps 3 and 4 to share additional programs.

6. Click Allow Control to allow meeting participants to use a program, and then click Close.

7. Have meeting participants use the Request Control command on the Control menu to take control of a program.

8. To regain control of a program, click your mouse.

9. Click the Share Program button. Click Prevent Control to deny editing access, or select a program and click Unshare to stop sharing the program.

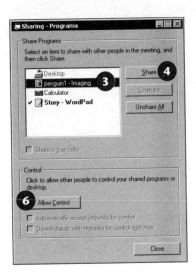

Shared programs appear in a single window on a computer that is part of the meeting.

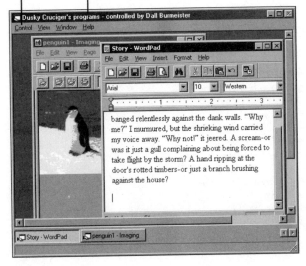

Security breach! *When you allow other people to collaborate on a shared program, they can use the program's menus to access and even delete your files. Never leave your computer unattended when a program is being shared.*

Save the information. *To pass on information in text format, use the Chat feature of NetMeeting. You can save the contents of the Chat and Whiteboard windows for later review by choosing Save from the File menu.*

Be prepared. *Before you connect to a NetMeeting, add a page to the Whiteboard, move to that page, and add the elements you want to present at the meeting. When you connect, that Whiteboard page will be available for your presentation.*

Share on the Whiteboard

1 In NetMeeting, click the Whiteboard button.

2 Use any of the following to convey information:

◆ The Pen, Line, or any of the shape tools to draw on the Whiteboard

◆ The Text tool to type text

◆ The Eraser tool to select and remove an element

◆ The Remote Pointer or the Highlighter to emphasize an area

◆ The Selection tool to select and drag elements into new locations

3 Use any of the following methods to insert additional information:

◆ The Select Area or Select Window tool to select and paste part of the screen or a whole window

◆ The Paste command to copy material from the Clipboard

Paste a graph from the Clipboard.

Show or hide the Whiteboard contents on the other computers.

Use the Select Window tool to add a program window.

Highlight text for emphasis.

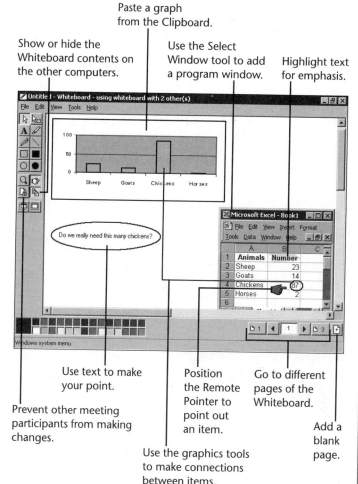

Use text to make your point.

Prevent other meeting participants from making changes.

Position the Remote Pointer to point out an item.

Go to different pages of the Whiteboard.

Use the graphics tools to make connections between items.

Add a blank page.

5

Sharing a Printer

You can set up your computer so that you can share your printer with other people on your network. However, you'll want to carefully control who has permission to print from your printer and who can remotely manage the printer. Otherwise, there's a good possibility your computer could become a dedicated print server that's so busy printing you won't be able to get any work done!

SEE ALSO

For information about enabling File And Printer sharing on your computer, see "Sharing Your Computer" on page 78.

For information about setting up, managing, and customizing your printer, or sharing someone else's printer, see the "Printing" section starting on page 121.

Share Your Printer

1. Click the Start button, point to Settings, and choose Printers from the submenu.

2. Right-click the printer you want to share, and choose Sharing from the shortcut menu.

3. On the Sharing tab, click the Shared As option.

4. Type a name for the printer.

5. Turn on or off the option to have the printer listed in the Active Directory.

6. Click the Additional Drivers button.

7. Select the appropriate drivers to support printing from computers with different operating systems.

8. Click OK. You might need to insert the Windows 2000 Professional CD or specify a network path to install the proper printer drivers.

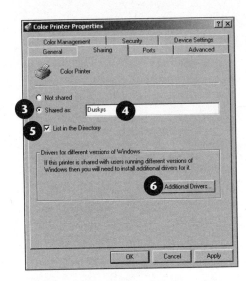

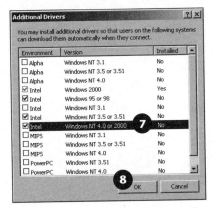

SEE ALSO

For information about adding and removing groups or individuals from the list of permissions, see "Change the Access" on page 82.

TIP

Where *is* that shared printer? *It's a good idea to include the location of the shared printer and instructions on its use in the Location and Comment sections of the General tab. The information appears in the Print dialog box, and goes a long way toward reducing the pile of unclaimed documents in your printer tray and the number of coworkers wandering the halls seeking their printouts.*

TRY THIS

Painless sharing. *On the Advanced tab, set the printer to be available during the hours you don't normally use your computer—from 6:00 PM to 6:00 AM, for example. That way, when your coworkers send documents to the printer, the print jobs will be stored and will be printed only when your computer is idle.*

Limit Access to the Printer

1. Click the Security tab.

2. Add groups or individuals to or remove them from the list.

3. Click to select a group or an individual.

4. Set the permissions for the selected group or individual.

5. Repeat steps 3 and 4 for each of the groups or individuals in the list.

6. Click the Advanced tab.

7. Set the times during which the printer will be available.

8. Click OK.

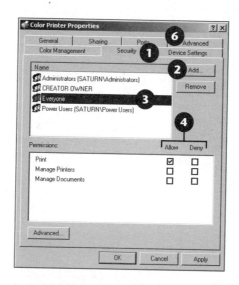

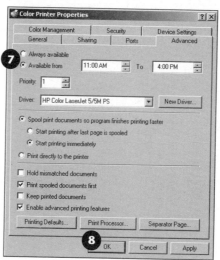

Publishing Your Own Web Pages

Need to have your presence known in the company? Why not publish web pages on your own web site on the company's intranet? With Internet Information Services (IIS) installed, hosting is an simple as posting your web pages in the proper locations.

SEE ALSO

For information about installing IIS and administering your own web site, see "Adding or Removing Windows 2000 Components" on page 276 and "Hosting a Web Site" on page 288.

Publish Your Pages

1 Create a new folder to hold your web pages.

2 Use a web-authoring tool, such as Microsoft Word or Microsoft FrontPage, to create the web pages you want to publish. Save the HTML documents and any associated files in the folder you created.

3 Create your home page, and save it in the new folder under the filename *Default.htm*. Include hyperlinks to any of the other web pages in the folder that you want listed.

4 Use the My Computer folder to copy all the files and any subfolders you created to the *wwwroot* folder, which is inside the *Inetpub* folder.

5 From the Address toolbar on the taskbar or in Internet Explorer, type the name of your computer or its IP (Internet Protocol) address, and press Enter.

6 Confirm that your web page is displayed correctly and that the hyperlinks work properly.

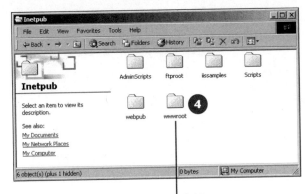

All the web pages in the *wwwroot* folder are available on the intranet.

Your home page on the intranet

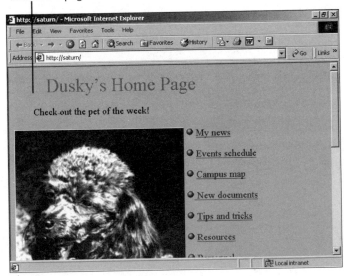

6

Running Programs

IN THIS SECTION

Starting Programs

Managing Multiple Programs

Linking to Information That Changes

Editing Inserted Material

Editing a Document in WordPad

Inserting Special Characters

Creating and Editing Pictures

Creating Your Own Font Characters

Crunching Numbers

Working at the Command Prompt

Quitting When You're Stuck

Getting to know the programs that come with Microsoft Windows 2000 Professional is a bit like moving into new living quarters. Just as your new abode has the basics—stove, refrigerator, and (dare we say it?) windows—Windows 2000 comes with many basic accessories and tools. Just as you'll add the accoutrements that transform empty rooms into a cozy home, you'll add programs to Windows 2000 to utilize its full potential.

But let's cover the basics first. There's WordPad, a handy little word processor; Paint, an easy-to-use graphics program; Calculator, for scientific calculations as well as quick basic arithmetic; and Private Character Editor for designing your own font characters. Windows 2000 provides other goodies: a web browser, mail and fax capabilities, multimedia, and many accessory programs. But right now we'll concentrate on everyday tasks: inserting characters such as © and é that don't exist on your keyboard; creating and editing text; switching between programs with a single mouse-click; copying items between documents that were created in different programs; and creating links between related documents so that updates occur automatically. We'll also discuss working at the command prompt, running MS-DOS programs, and what you can do to get out of trouble when a program isn't working properly.

Starting a Program

The real work of an operating system is to run software programs. Microsoft Windows 2000 Professional comes with a wide variety of programs, and you can install additional (and often more powerful) ones. Most programs are listed on the Start menu, but Windows 2000 gives you several ways to start your programs, so you can choose the way that's easiest for you or the one you like best.

TIP

More programs. *The programs listed in the table at the right are only some of the programs that come with Windows 2000. You'll find descriptions of others elsewhere in this book. Use the index to find details about specific programs.*

Start a Program

1 Do any of the following:

- Click the Start button, point to Programs, point to any relevant program groups to display additional submenus, and choose the program you want.

- Point to and then double-click the program icon on the Desktop.

- Open the My Computer folder, navigate to the folder that contains the program you want, and double-click the program.

- Insert the CD that contains a program that's designed to run from the CD, and wait for the program to start.

- Click the Start button, choose Run, type the full path and filename of the program, and click OK.

2 Use the program, and close it when you've finished.

FREQUENTLY USED WINDOWS 2000 PROGRAMS	
Program	**Purpose**
Address Book	Stores names, addresses, and other contact information.
Backup	Backs up your files for archiving or for restoring if a disaster occurs.
Calculator	Does arithmetic calculations and complex mathematical calculations.
CD Player	Plays music CDs and obtains additional information about CDs from the Internet.
Character Map	Inserts special characters from installed fonts.
Internet Explorer	Functions as a web browser and an HTML document viewer.
Imaging	Views, scans, annotates, and prints images.
Magnifier	Magnifies sections of the screen.
Media Player	Plays sound, music, and video.
Microsoft Fax	Sends and receives faxes.
Narrator	Describes and reads aloud the screen contents.
Notepad	Creates, edits, and views text documents.
On-Screen Keyboard	Allows keyboard input using the mouse or other pointing device.
Outlook Express	Provides e-mail, newsgroup, and directory services.
Paint	Creates and edits bitmap pictures.
Sound Recorder	Creates digital sound files.
WordPad	Creates, edits, and views text, Rich Text Format, and Word documents.

Starting a Program When Windows 2000 Starts

If you always start your workday using the same program, you can have that program start when Windows 2000 starts. And if you use the same document each day, you can have that document start automatically in the program. Windows 2000 might take a little longer to load, but your program will be ready for you right away.

TIP

No need to restart. *If you closed a program that starts automatically when Windows 2000 starts, and you now want to restart it, don't restart Windows 2000. Just open the Startup submenu and choose the program.*

Add a Program to the Startup Menu

1 Using the Start menu, locate the program you want.

2 Drag the program on top of the Startup item on the Programs submenu.

3 When the Startup submenu opens, drag the program onto the submenu.

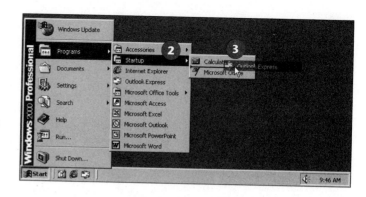

Add a Document to the Startup Menu

1 Use the My Computer window or the My Documents folder to locate the document you want.

2 Drag the document on top of the Start button, and, without releasing the mouse button, hold the document there until the Start menu opens.

3 Drag the document on top of the Startup item on the Programs submenu.

4 When the Startup submenu opens, drag the document onto the submenu.

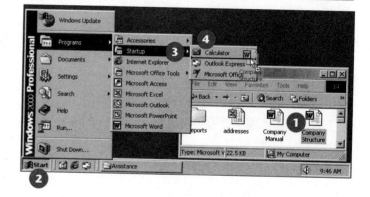

6

Changing the Way a Program Starts

Many programs have special command switches that you can use to start the program or to modify the way it starts or runs. You can add these commands to the shortcut that starts the program, as well as specify the size of the window and even a key combination that quickly switches to the program.

TRY THIS

News only. *Right-click the Outlook Express icon on the Quick Launch toolbar, and choose Properties from the shortcut menu. On the Shortcut tab, click Find Target, create a shortcut on the Desktop to the MSIMN program, and close the Properties dialog box. Right-click the shortcut, choose Properties, and, after the closing quotation marks in the Target box, add the command switch /newsonly to open Outlook Express as a news reader only.*

Modify the Shortcut

1. Locate the shortcut to the program (on the Start menu, on the Desktop, or in a folder). If there is no shortcut or if you're not permitted to modify the existing shortcut, create a new one.

2. Right-click the shortcut, and choose Properties from the shortcut menu.

3. Click the Shortcut tab.

4. Change the settings.

5. Click OK.

Add any special command switches, as specified in the program's documentation.

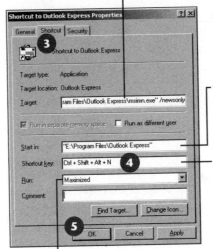

Specify the folder that contains the required related files if the program can't find them.

Press a key combination to assign a keyboard shortcut that switches to the running program.

Run the program in a normal, maximized, or minimized window.

Managing Multiple Programs

Windows 2000 lets you run several programs at the same time. You can have more than one open program window on your screen and can easily switch between programs. If you prefer, you can park your running programs neatly on the taskbar, where they'll sit snoozing quietly until you need them.

TRY THIS

Look, Ma, I'm multitasking!
Arrange your program windows by tiling them: right-click a blank spot on the taskbar and choose to tile horizontally or vertically. To make the full screen available as you work in one program, click the Maximize button. When you want to switch to another program, click the Restore button to return the first program to its tiled position.

Switch Between Program Windows

1. If you have several overlapping program windows on your Desktop, click in any visible part of an open window to bring it to the front of your screen and make it the active program—that is, the program you're working on now.

2. Click the Minimize button to remove a window from the Desktop but keep it running as a program button on the taskbar.

3. If a program window is minimized or obscured by other windows, click the program button on the taskbar. To see the full name of the program and the document, position the mouse pointer over the program button until a tooltip appears.

4. To switch between programs with the keyboard, press Alt+Tab.

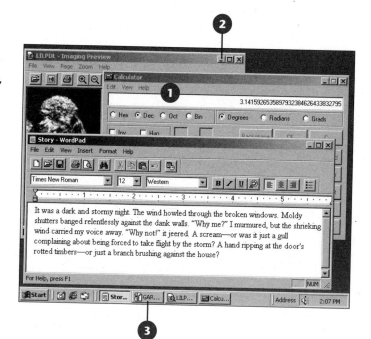

Copying Material Between Documents

It's usually very easy to copy material from a document that was created in one program into a document that was created in another program. How you insert the material depends on what it is. If the material is similar to and compatible with the receiving document—some text that's being copied into a Word document, for example—it's usually inserted as is and can be edited in the receiving document's program. If the item is dissimilar—a sound clip, say, inserted into a Word document—either it's *encapsulated,* or isolated, as an object and can be edited in the originating program only, or you simply are not able to paste that item into your document.

Copy and Insert Material

1. In the source document, select the material you want to copy.

2. Choose Copy from the Edit menu. Windows 2000 places copied items on the Clipboard. You can copy only one item at a time, so always paste the Clipboard contents into your document before you copy anything else, or you'll lose whatever was on the Clipboard. (Some programs, such as Microsoft Office 2000 programs, have their own Clipboard, which allows you to store and retrieve multiple copied items.)

3. Switch to the destination document.

4. Click where you want to insert the copied material.

5. Choose Paste from the Edit menu.

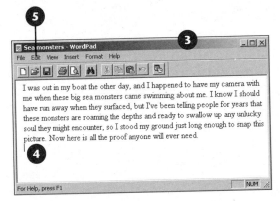

TIP

More ways to copy and paste. *Many, but not all, programs support dragging items to move them. If you can't drag a document into a program window, copy the document to the Clipboard, switch to the destination program, and paste the document. If the source document doesn't have a Copy command or if the destination document doesn't have a Paste command, try pressing Ctrl+C to copy and Ctrl+V to paste.*

TIP

Embedded or linked? *Objects can be embedded or linked. An embedded object places all its information, or data, in the document into which the object is placed. A linked object keeps most of its information in a separate file and inserts only enough information to let the program locate the linked file when necessary.*

SEE ALSO

For information about dragging, see "Mouse Maneuvers" on page 16.

For information about copying and linking, see "Linking to Information That Changes" on page 100.

Use a Different Format

1. Copy the material from the source document, and click in the destination document.

2. Choose Paste Special from the Edit menu.

3. Select the format in which you want to insert the copied material.

4. Click OK.

The source document

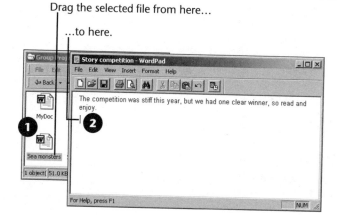

A description of the result when you use the selected format

The different formats available

Copy and Insert an Entire Document

1. Use the My Computer window or the My Documents folder to locate and select the document you want to copy.

2. Drag the document into the place in the destination document where you want it to appear.

Drag the selected file from here...

...to here.

6

Linking to Information That Changes

When you insert material from one document into another document, you can make sure the inserted material will be automatically updated whenever the content of the source document changes. You can do this by using a program that supports *linking*. But because the content resides in the source document and not in your document, the source document must be available whenever you work in your document.

TIP

Locate the source document. *If the source document has been moved or renamed and hasn't been automatically relocated, use the Links command on the Edit menu to locate and reestablish the link.*

Link to a Source Document

1. Use the My Computer window to locate the source document, and right-click it.

2. Choose Copy from the shortcut menu.

3. Switch to the destination document.

4. Click at the location where you want to insert the item.

5. Choose Paste Special from the Edit menu.

6. Select the Paste Link option.

7. Click OK.

The source document

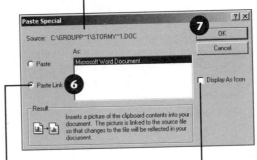

Check to display an icon instead of the content. Double-click the icon to display the content of the linked document.

Links the inserted content to an external document.

Editing Inserted Material

When material from a document that was created in a different program has been inserted into your document as an *embedded object*, you can usually edit the inserted item *in place*—that is, in your document—using the tools of the program in which the item was created.

TIP

You can't always edit in place. *Some programs won't let you edit inserted material in place. Instead, the source program opens automatically and you can make your edits there. When you've finished, choose the Update command from the source program's File menu to update the information in the embedded object before you exit the source program.*

Edit Inserted Material in Place

1 Double-click the inserted item. You can edit the content of an embedded object only when its source program is installed on your computer.

2 Use the toolbar buttons, menu commands, and whatever other tools are provided by the source program to make your editing changes.

3 Click outside the selected area to return the material into the embedded object and to restore the toolbars, menus, and other tools of your original program.

The Paint program's tools

The Paint program's menus

The WordPad window

The Paint program activated in the WordPad window

Editing a Document in WordPad

You can use WordPad to edit Microsoft Word, Microsoft Write, Rich Text Format (RTF), text (ANSI), MS-DOS text (ASCII), or Unicode text documents. When you use WordPad to edit a document that was created in Word, however, you'll lose any special formatting that WordPad doesn't support.

TIP

Open and save Word documents. *WordPad can open Word 97 and Word 2000 documents, but it can save Word documents only in the Word 6 format.*

TIP

Save both versions. *If you want to keep a copy of the original unedited document in addition to your edited version, use the Save As command on the File menu in order to save the edited document under a different filename.*

Open a Document

1. Start WordPad if it's not already running.
2. Click the Open button on the toolbar.
3. Select the type of document to be opened.
4. Find and select the document you want.
5. Click Open.

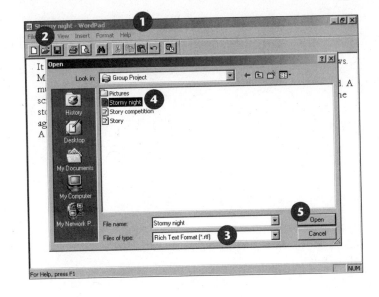

Insert and Delete Text

1. Click where you want to insert the text.
2. Type the text you want to insert.
3. Select the text you want to delete by dragging the mouse pointer over the text.
4. Press the Delete key to delete the text.

It was a dark night. The wind nearly howled through the broken windows. Moldy shutters banged relentlessly against the dank walls. "Why me?" I murmured, but the

It was a dark and stormy night. The wind nearly howled through the broken windows. Moldy shutters banged relentlessly against the dank walls. "Why me?" I murmured,

It was a dark and stormy night. The wind nearly howled through the broken windows. Moldy shutters banged relentlessly against the dank walls. "Why me?" I murmured,

It was a dark and stormy night. The wind howled through the broken windows. Moldy shutters banged relentlessly against the dank walls. "Why me?" I murmured, but the

TIP

Word association. *When Microsoft Word is installed on your computer, Word documents and RTF documents will be associated with Word and will have a Word icon, not a WordPad icon.*

TIP

Presto change-o. *To replace repetitive words or phrases throughout a document, use the Replace command on the Edit menu.*

SEE ALSO

For information about opening a document in a program other than the default program, see "Open a Document in a Different Program" on page 29.

For information about printing a document using a printer other than the default printer, see "Print a Document Using a Specific Printer" on page 124.

Replace Text

1. Select the text you want to replace by dragging the mouse pointer over the text.

2. Type the new text. The selected text is deleted.

The selected text is replaced...

It was a dark and stormy night. The wind howled through the broken windows. Moldy shutters banged relentlessly against the wet walls. "Why me?" I murmured, but the

...when you type new text.

It was a dark and stormy night. The wind howled through the broken windows. Moldy shutters banged relentlessly against the dank walls. "Why me?" I murmured, but the

Move Text

1. Select the text you want to move by dragging the mouse pointer over the text.

2. Point to the selected text.

3. Drag the text into a new location.

Drag the selected text into a new location.

It was a dark and stormy night. The wind howled through the broken windows. Moldy shutters banged relentlessly against the dank walls. "Why me?" I murmured, but the wind shrieking carried my voice away. "Why not!" it jeered. A scream—or was it just a gull complaining about

It was a dark and stormy night. The wind howled through the broken windows. Moldy shutters banged relentlessly against the dank walls. "Why me?" I murmured, but the shrieking wind carried my voice away. "Why not!" it jeered. A scream—or was it just a gull complaining about

Save and Print a Document

1. Click the Save button to save the document in the same format and with the same name.

2. Click the Print button to print the document using the default printer.

Dialog Box Decisions

You're going to be seeing a lot of *dialog boxes* as you use Windows 2000, and if you're not familiar with them now, you soon will be. Dialog boxes appear when Windows 2000 or a program (WordPad, let's say) needs you to make one or more decisions about what you want to do. Sometimes all you have to do is click a Yes, a No, or an OK button; at other times, there'll be quite a few decisions to make in one dialog box. The Print dialog box, shown below, is one you'll probably be seeing frequently, so take a look at its components and how they work.

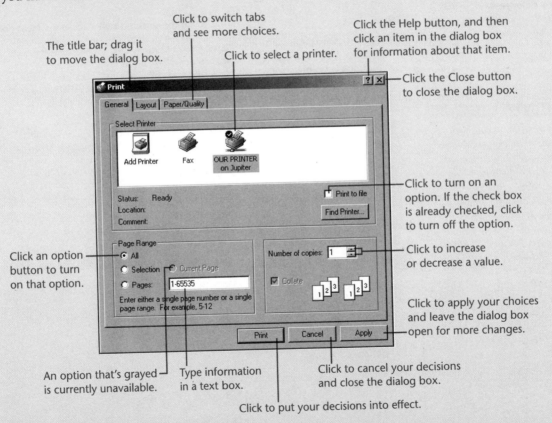

Click to switch tabs and see more choices.

The title bar; drag it to move the dialog box.

Click to select a printer.

Click the Help button, and then click an item in the dialog box for information about that item.

Click the Close button to close the dialog box.

Click to turn on an option. If the check box is already checked, click to turn off the option.

Click to increase or decrease a value.

Click an option button to turn on that option.

Click to apply your choices and leave the dialog box open for more changes.

An option that's grayed is currently unavailable.

Type information in a text box.

Click to cancel your decisions and close the dialog box.

Click to put your decisions into effect.

Inserting Special Characters

Windows 2000 provides a special accessory program called Character Map that lets you insert into your programs the characters and symbols that aren't available on your keyboard. Character Map displays all the characters that are available for each of the fonts on your computer.

TIP

The Clipboard. *The Windows 2000 Clipboard is a temporary "holding area" for items you want to copy and paste. The Clipboard can hold only one item at a time, so do your pasting right after you've done your copying.*

SEE ALSO

For information about installing Character Map if it's not already installed on your system, see "Adding or Removing Windows 2000 Components" on page 276.

Insert Special Characters

1. Click the Start button, point your way through Programs, Accessories, and System Tools, and choose Character Map from the submenu.

2. Select a font.

3. Click a character to see its enlarged view.

4. Double-click the character you want to insert.

5. Click Copy to place the character on the Clipboard.

6. Switch to your program, click where you want the character to be inserted, and press Ctrl+V (or choose Paste from the Edit menu) to paste the character from the Clipboard.

7. Close Character Map when you've copied all the characters you want.

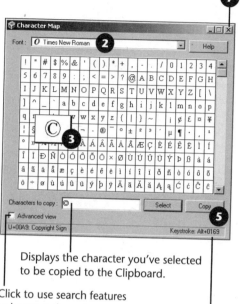

Displays the character you've selected to be copied to the Clipboard.

Click to use search features to locate a character.

Shows the keyboard shortcut for the selected character. Hold down the Alt key and use the numeric keypad to enter the numbers.

6

Creating a Picture

If you're feeling artistic, you can create a picture in Paint. The Paint program comes with Windows 2000 and was designed to create and edit bitmap (BMP) pictures. Although you can print your picture if you want to, Paint pictures are usually inserted into other documents as *embedded* or *linked objects*. You can also create a Paint picture and use it as the wallpaper for your Desktop.

TIP

Bitmaps. *A bitmap is just that: a map created from small dots, or bits. It's a lot like a piece of graph paper with some squares filled in and others left blank to create a picture.*

SEE ALSO

For information about embedding or linking, see "Copying Material Between Documents" on page 98 and "Linking to Information That Changes" on page 100.

Create a Picture

1. Click the Start button, point to Programs and then Accessories, and choose Paint from the submenu.

2. Click a drawing tool.

3. Click the color you want to use. Use the left mouse button to select the foreground color and the right mouse button to select the background color.

4. Click an option for the selected tool. (Note that options aren't available for all tools.)

5. Click to start the drawing, and drag the end or the corner of the shape to create the shape you want.

6. Keep choosing appropriate tools, colors, and options to complete your picture. Use the Undo command on the Edit menu to remove your last drawing; use the Undo command again to remove the previous drawing.

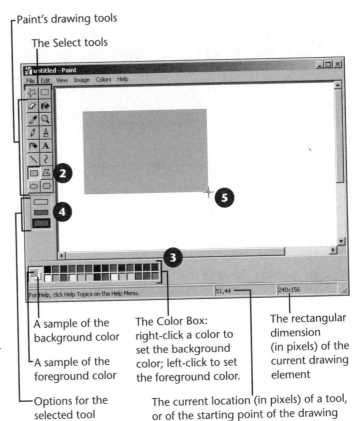

Paint's drawing tools

The Select tools

A sample of the background color

A sample of the foreground color

Options for the selected tool

The Color Box: right-click a color to set the background color; left-click to set the foreground color.

The current location (in pixels) of a tool, or of the starting point of the drawing

The rectangular dimension (in pixels) of the current drawing element

Create Desktop wallpaper.
*Start a new Paint picture.
Choose Attributes from the
Image menu, and set Width
and Height to the dimensions
of your screen in pixels (800 x
600, for example). Create and
save your picture, and then
choose Set As Wallpaper
(Centered) from the File menu.*

More formats. *If GIF or
JPEG formats are listed in the
Open or the Save dialog box,
you'll be able to work with
those formats in Paint. They'll
be listed if another graphics
program in your system has
installed the appropriate filters
for these formats.*

Text and text boxes. *To add
text to a picture, draw a text
box, and just start typing. As
long as the text box is active,
you can edit the text, change
the font, and resize the text
box. When you click outside
the text box, the text is turned
into a bitmap image that can
be edited just like any other
picture element.*

Use the Tools

1 Hold down a mouse
button and drag the
shapes you want:

♦ Hold down the left
mouse button to draw
with the foreground
color.

♦ Hold down the right
mouse button to draw
with the background
color.

2 Hold down the Shift key
for the following special
effects when you're
drawing shapes:

♦ The Ellipse tool
creates a circle.

♦ The Rectangle tool
creates a square.

♦ The Rounded Rectangle
tool creates a square
with rounded corners.

♦ The Line tool draws
a horizontal, vertical,
or diagonal line.

3 Keep choosing appropriate tools, colors, and
options to complete your
picture.

4 Save the picture
periodically.

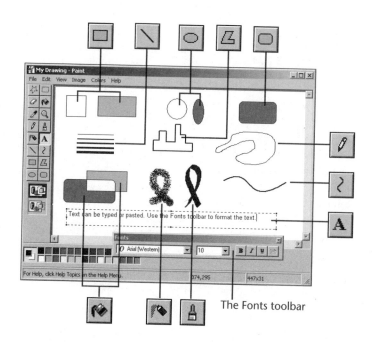

The Fonts toolbar

6

Editing a Picture

It's easy and fun to modify an existing bitmap picture to customize it, or to create a new picture using only part of the original picture. By magnifying the picture, you can even edit it a single dot, or pixel, at a time.

TIP

Quick zoom. *To quickly jump to 4x magnification (400% zoom), press Ctrl+Page Down. To return to 1x magnification, press Ctrl+Page Up.*

TIP

Thumbnails. *If you don't see a thumbnail version of your picture, point to Zoom on the View menu, and then choose Show Thumbnail.*

Edit a Picture

1. Start Paint if it isn't already running.

2. Choose Open from the File menu, locate the bitmap picture you want to edit, and click Open.

3. Use the drawing tools to edit the picture.

4. Use the Magnifier tool to magnify the details, and use the drawing tools to fine-tune your edits; click the Magnifier tool again, and choose 1x magnification to restore the view to Normal Size.

5. Press Ctrl+G to turn on the grid if it's not already turned on. (The grid isn't visible in Normal Size or at 2x magnification.) Use the Pencil tool to edit individual pixels, clicking the left mouse button for the foreground color and the right mouse button for the background color.

6. Save the picture. If you want to rename the file, choose Save As from the File menu, and type a new name for the picture.

Use the Magnifier tool.

The thumbnail shows the context for the magnified area.

Select the level of magnification.

Use the grid when you need to edit individual pixels.

SEE ALSO

For information about editing a picture that's contained in another document, see "Editing Inserted Material" on page 101.

TRY THIS

Not so opaque. *Click the Select tool, select the Opaque Paste option, and paste in a picture. With the inserted picture still selected, in the Color Box right-click the color that's the main background color for the inserted picture. With the picture still selected, click the Transparent Paste button.*

TIP

Picture this. *To save only part of a picture, use one of the Select tools to select the part you want, and then choose Copy To from the Edit menu. To insert an existing picture into your picture, choose Paste From from the Edit menu. To create a picture of something on your computer screen, press the Print Screen button on your keyboard, paste the captured image into Paint, and save it.*

Modify the Shapes

1 Use one of the Select tools to select the part of the picture you want to work on. The illustration at the right shows a few examples of what you can do.

2 Use the Eraser tool to replace any color with the background color. To replace one color with another, set the foreground color to the color to be replaced and the background color to the replacement color, and then hold down the right mouse button and drag the Eraser over the area whose color you want to replace.

3 To replace a large area with the background color, use the Select tool to select the area, and then press the Delete key.

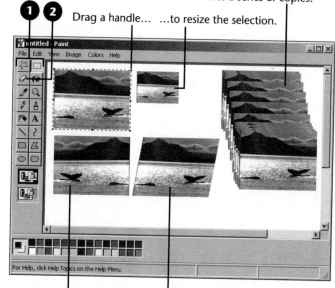

Hold down the Shift key and drag the selection to create a series of copies.

Drag a handle... ...to resize the selection.

Choose a command from the Image menu to rotate the selection...

... or to stretch and skew it. Or hold down the Ctrl key, drag the selection, and place a copy where you want it.

6

Modifying an Image

An image can be almost anything—a scanned photograph or document, a fax, or a picture from the Internet. With the Imaging program, you can view, modify, save, and print these images.

TIP

Multiple pages. *When you're creating a new document, note that only TIFF documents can have multiple pages or images.*

TIP

Thumbnails. *To see a thumbnail of a picture whenever it's selected in a folder window, make sure you have web content enabled in the Folder Options dialog box for that folder, and that there's enough room in the folder window to display the web content and the thumbnail.*

SEE ALSO

For information about viewing and annotating fax documents, see "View a Fax" on page 181.

Display and Modify an Image

1. Click the Start button, point to Programs and then Accessories, and choose Imaging from the submenu.

2. Do either of the following:
   - Click Open on the Standard toolbar, locate the image file, and click Open.
   - Choose New from the File menu, specify the file type and settings, and click OK.

3. To add an image as a new page (TIFF documents only), point to Append on the Page menu, choose Existing Page from the shortcut menu, locate the image, and click Open.

4. Use the Zoom menu to view the whole image.

5. Use the editing tools to copy, paste, or delete parts of the image, or to rotate the image; use the annotation tools to add comments or annotations.

6. Save the document. To preserve the original document, choose Save As from the File menu, and enter a new filename.

The Rotate tools

Photo by Harry Planifrons

These appear to be humpback whales!

Use the Annotation Selection tool to select an annotation that you want to move, size, or delete.

The Annotation toolbar

Annotation text can be placed directly on the image...

...or contained in a note.

Creating Your Own Font Characters

When you need a special character that doesn't exist in any of your fonts—a logo, monogram, or picture, for example—you can create your own character. Once you've created and saved it, you can insert it into any document that supports Unicode characters, and you can change its size as needed.

SEE ALSO

For information about Character Map, see "Inserting Special Characters" on page 105.

TIP

Character location. *Unless you chose a specific font to link to in the Font Links dialog box (File menu), select All Fonts (Private Characters) in the Font list of the Character Map to view your characters.*

Create a Character

1. Click the Start button, choose Run, type *eudcedit*, and click OK.

2. Click the first available blank code, and then click OK.

3. Do any of the following to create your character:

   ◆ Use the drawing tools.

   ◆ Choose Copy Character from the Edit menu, select the font and character, click OK, and then modify the inserted character.

   ◆ Create a small bitmap image in Paint, copy the image, and, in Private Character Editor, choose Paste from the Edit menu.

   ◆ Use the Flip/Rotate command on the Tools menu to rotate the image.

4. Choose Save Character from the Edit menu.

5. Press Ctrl+N to create another new character, or close Private Character Editor if you've finished.

6. Open Character Map to view and insert your new character.

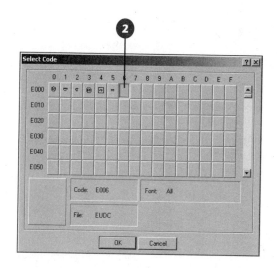

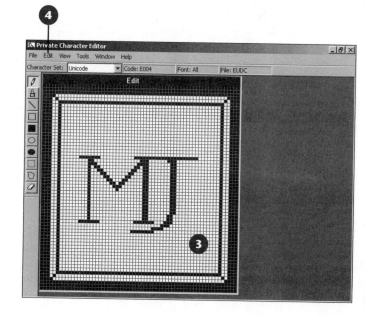

6

Crunching Numbers

Need to do a quick calculation but don't have enough fingers? Want to convert a decimal number into a hexadecimal or binary number? You can do these procedures, and even a few complex geometric and statistical calculations, with the Calculator.

Use the Calculator

1. Click the Start button, point to Programs and then Accessories, and choose Calculator.

2. Either click the number buttons or type the numerals you want. Continue until you've entered the entire number.

3. Click a function.

4. Enter the next number.

5. When you've entered all the numbers, click the equal (=) button.

6. Press Ctlr+C to copy the result if you want to paste it into your document.

Applies the function to the current value.

Clears the memory, recalls the value in memory, stores the current value in memory, or adds the current value to the value in memory.

Convert Numbers

1. Choose Scientific from the View menu.

2. Choose your numbering system.

3. Enter the number to be converted.

4. Choose the numbering system you want your number to be converted into.

What's this for? *To determine the purpose of a key and to view its keyboard shortcut, right-click the key, and choose What's This? from the shortcut menu.*

TIP

Large numbers. *When you choose Digit Grouping from the View menu, the Calculator makes large numbers easier for you to read by inserting a separator character between groups of numbers (a comma, for example, between the third and fourth digits). The separators and the decimal character are determined by your regional settings.*

SEE ALSO

For information about changing regional settings, see "Adjusting International Settings" on page 258.

Make Statistical Calculations

1. Click the Sta button. Click the title bar and move the Statistics Box so that you can see it as well as the Calculator.

2. Click the Calculator to activate it.

3. Enter a number from your data set.

4. Click the Dat button.

5. Repeat steps 3 and 4 until you've entered all the data.

6. Review your data set in the Statistics Box. If you want to delete an entry, select it and click the CD button.

7. Click the Ave, Sum, or S button to view the statistics.

8. Click the RET button to close the Statistics box, or click the CAD button to clear the data and enter a new data set.

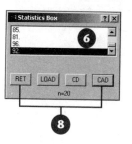

Running Commands

In Windows 2000, the command prompt is the place where you can execute command-line instructions. Most of the commands are the old standard MS-DOS commands, some are enhancements of the MS-DOS commands, and others are commands that are unique to Windows 2000. When you want or need to work from the command prompt, you can open a command prompt window and execute all your tasks there, including using the basic commands, starting a program, and even starting a program in a new window.

Run a Command

1. Click the Start button, point to Programs and then Accessories, and choose Command Prompt from the submenu.

2. At the prompt, type a command, including any switches and extra parameters, and press Enter.

3. Enter any additional commands you want to run.

The command prompt

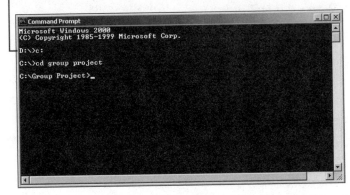

TOP 10 MS-DOS COMMANDS	
Command	**Use**
cd	Changes to the specified folder (or directory).
cls	Clears the screen.
copy	Copies the specified files or folders.
dir	Shows the contents of the current directory.
drive:	Changes to the specified drive (type the drive letter and a colon).
exit	Ends the session.
mem	Displays memory configuration.
path	Displays or sets the path the command searches.
prompt	Changes the information displayed at the prompt.
rename	Renames the specified file.

TIP

Changes. *Any changes you make to the current environment with commands such as* path *and* prompt *affect the current session only. To make the changes permanent, edit the Autoexec.nt file to include those settings.*

TRY THIS

Use command switches.
Try typing the following commands to see how the switches after each command affect the results. Use the Up arrow key to repeat previous commands, and then edit them to include the correct switches.
Type dir *and press Enter.*
Type dir /w *and press Enter.*
Type dir /? *and press Enter to see the different ways to run a command.*

SEE ALSO

For information about changing drives and moving through folders, see "Accessing Folders from the Command Prompt" on page 51.

For information about syntax and the switches that you can use with a command, see "Exploring the Command Prompt Commands" on page 116.

Repeat a Series of Commands

1 Type a command, and press Enter.

2 Type additional commands, pressing Enter after each command.

3 Use the Up and Down arrow keys to scroll through the list of previously used commands.

4 Use the Left and Right arrow keys to move the cursor within a command to edit it:

◆ Type any new text.

◆ Press the Insert key to use Overtype mode, and type over any text that you want to replace. Press the Insert key a second time to turn off Overtype mode.

◆ Use the Delete key or the Backspace key to delete text.

5 Press Enter to execute the modified command or Esc to cancel the entire command line.

6 Type *exit* to close the window when you've finished.

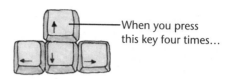

When you press this key four times...

...this command...

...is repeated on the current command line.

Exploring the Command Prompt Commands

The command prompt in Windows 2000 provides a variety of useful commands. If you're familiar with MS-DOS, you'll find that some commands in this version are new, some have been enhanced, and some have disappeared because Windows 2000 has made them obsolete.

TIP

Display the command.
To display on the command prompt line the command you just executed, press the F3 key. Press the F1 key to display the command one character at a time.

List the Commands

1. Open a command prompt window if one isn't already open.

2. Type *help* and press Enter.

3. Use the vertical scroll bar, if necessary, to review all the commands.

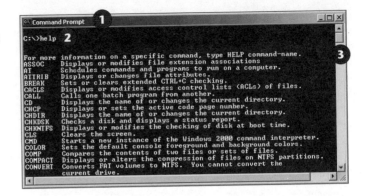

Get More Information About a Command

1. Type a command, followed by a space and /? and press Enter to get information about the command.

2. Use the vertical and horizontal scroll bars, if necessary, to review all the information about the command.

Copying Text at the Command Prompt

Among the many ways in which Windows 2000 and the command prompt work well together is the ability they give you to share text among your command output, the command line, your MS-DOS–based programs, and even your Windows-based programs.

TIP

Text problems. *If you can't select text with the mouse, or if the text isn't copied when you press Enter, right-click the title bar of the Command Prompt dialog box, and choose Properties from the shortcut menu. On the Options tab, turn on the Quick Edit Mode check box, and click OK.*

Copy Text Output

1. Run your command in a command prompt window.

2. Click to position the mouse pointer where you want to start the selection.

3. Hold down the left mouse button, drag over the area to be copied, and release the mouse button.

4. Press Enter.

5. Switch to the document into which you want to insert the text, and choose Paste from the Edit menu. For proper alignment of columnar data in a word processing program, set the text to a monospace font such as Courier New.

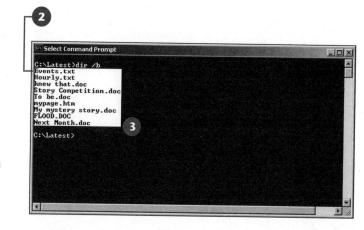

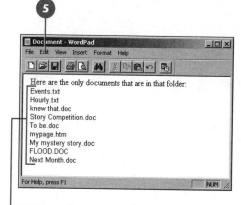

Text from the command prompt window

6

Sending Command Prompt Output to a File

Many commands and programs executed from the command prompt send a great deal of information to your screen. You can redirect the information and save it in a text file for further reference.

Redirect the Output

1. Open a command prompt window if one isn't already open.

2. Type the command, followed by a space and > *filename* (where *filename* is the name of the file you want the information sent to). If you want to store the output file in a folder other than the active folder, include the full path in the filename.

3. Press Enter.

4. Type *notepad filename* (where *filename* is the name of the file), and include the path if the file isn't in the active folder.

5. Press Enter.

6. Examine the output.

7. Close Notepad when you've finished.

Modifying the Way an MS-DOS Program Runs

To change the default settings for the way an MS-DOS program starts, or to tweak the resources used by the program, you can change the program's settings. The first time you do so, a new shortcut to the program is created to store the new settings information.

TIP

Switch to a window. *If a program starts in full-screen mode, you can switch it to a window by pressing Alt+Enter.*

TIP

Command-line switches. *Before you modify the command line in the program's Properties dialog box, use the program's documentation to determine which command-line switches can be used to modify the way the program runs.*

Change the Way a Program Runs

1. Use My Computer to locate the program you want, right-click the program, and choose Properties from the shortcut menu.

2. On the Misc tab, specify the mouse, foreground, and background options you want.

3. On the Screen tab, specify whether the program will start in a window or occupy the full screen.

4. On the Font tab, select the font type and size you want for the program window.

5. On the Memory tab, change options based on the program's documentation.

6. On the Program tab, modify the command line, the path to the working folder, any batch file that is to be run, the startup window size, whether the command prompt window closes when the program is terminated, and any different initialization files.

7. Click OK.

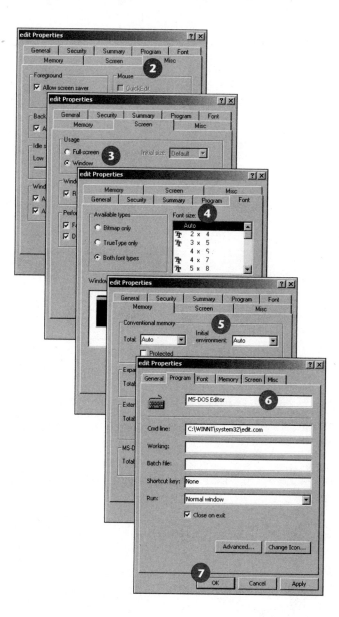

Quitting When You're Stuck

If a program isn't working properly and doesn't respond when you try to close it, Windows 2000 Professional gives you an alternative course of action that is known as "ending the task." If you can't end a specific program, you might need to shut down Windows 2000 or even turn off your computer. Whatever you do, you'll probably lose any unsaved work in the problem program.

SEE ALSO

For additional information about working with the Windows Security dialog box, see "Securing Your Computer" on page 253 and "Changing Your Password" on page 261.

For information about fixing configuration problems when you restart your computer, see "Starting Up When There's a Problem" on page 272.

End the Task or the Windows Session

1. Press Ctrl+Alt+Delete, and then click the Task Manager button.

2. On the Applications tab, select the program that's misbehaving.

3. Click the End Task button.

4. Wait for Windows 2000 to respond and to attempt to close the program. If Windows 2000 can't close the program and you're asked whether you want to end the task, click the End Now button. You'll lose any unsaved work.

5. Close Task Manager.

6. If Windows 2000 couldn't close the program, close all other running programs and choose Shut Down from the Start menu. If Windows 2000 refuses to shut down, turn off your computer.

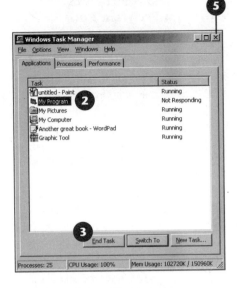

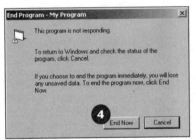

7

Printing

IN THIS SECTION

Installing a Local Printer

Printing from a Program

Printing Documents

Specifying a Default Printer

Connecting to a Network Printer

Separating Print Jobs

Controlling Your Printing

Printing a Document to a File

Printing Without a Printer

Printing from the Command Prompt to a Network Printer

Whether you're printing your documents on a printer that's attached directly to your computer or on a shared printer on a company network, you're using the print services provided by Microsoft Windows 2000 Professional. These services include sending the correct types of codes to the printer, organizing print jobs so that they print in an orderly succession, and managing output to different printers.

Whether or not your printer is a plug-and-play device, you'll see that installing it is a simple matter. If you and your computer are part of a company network, you'll learn how to connect to a network printer. If you use a shared printer, you can print separator pages to identify individual print jobs. If you take your computer on the road and can't access a printer, you'll learn how to print to a file. Then, when a printer is available, you can print your document without opening the program it's associated with. And, should you run into trouble when you try to print from an MS-DOS–based program on a network printer, you'll learn how to trick the program into thinking it's printing from a standard printer port.

If, as many people do, you feel a bit daunted by the printing process because of previous unpleasant experiences, this section of the book will guide you painlessly through the printing maze.

Installing a Local Printer

When you install a new printer for your computer, Windows 2000 needs to know about it. If you've installed a plug-and-play printer, the printer simply introduces itself and lets Windows 2000 know what drivers it needs. If your new printer isn't a plug-and-play device, you'll need to run the Add Printer Wizard.

TIP

Serial printer. *If the printer is to be connected to a serial port, turn off the computer before you install the printer.*

SEE ALSO

For information about setting up your printer so that others can share it, see "Sharing a Printer" on page 90.

For information about setting or changing the default printer, see "Specifying a Default Printer" on page 125.

Add a Printer

1. Install the printer. If Windows 2000 detects the printer, do either of the following, and ignore the remaining steps:

   ◆ Wait for the correct drivers to be installed automatically. A printer icon will appear in the status area of the taskbar when the process is complete.

   ◆ Step through the Found New Hardware Wizard that appears.

2. If Windows 2000 doesn't detect the printer, click the Start button, point to Settings, and choose Printers from the submenu.

3. Double-click the Add Printer icon, and step through the Add Printer Wizard. Make sure you select the local printer and, if your printer is not a plug-and-play printer, turn off the check box to automatically detect the printer.

4. When you've made all your settings, check the summary, and click Finish to start using the printer.

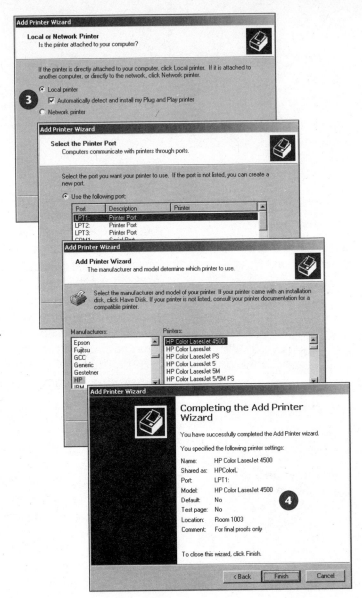

Printing from a Program

You usually print from a program in either of two ways: printing immediately to the default printer, or displaying the Print dialog box and selecting a printer and various print options.

TIP

No Print dialog box. *If the Print command isn't followed by an ellipsis (…), the document will be printed to the default printer. If the ellipsis is present, the Print dialog box will be displayed.*

TIP

Printer differences. *Because different printers have different features, the tabs in the Print dialog box might vary from one printer to another. Some programs use their own Print dialog box, so the available features might be different.*

Print

1. Create and save your document. Choose Print from the File menu.

2. In the Print dialog box, select a printer.

3. If you don't see the network printer you want to use, click Find Printer, locate and select the printer, and click OK.

4. Specify the pages you want to print.

5. Specify how many copies of each page you want.

6. Turn on the Collate check box if you're printing multiple copies and you want each set printed in order; turn off the Collate check box for faster printing and to have all the copies of one page printed before the next page is printed.

7. Use any of the other tabs in the dialog box to make additional settings.

8. Click Print.

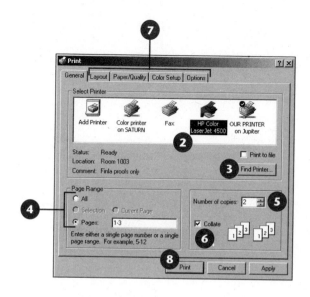

Printing Documents

When you want to print a document or a group of documents, you can print directly from Windows 2000, provided the programs associated with the documents are installed on your computer. This way, you can quickly send several documents to a printer and then walk away while Windows 2000 does all the work.

TIP

Default printer. *Some programs require the use of the system default printer. For documents associated with such programs, you'll have to either print using the default printer or have Windows 2000 switch the default-printer designation to the printer you want to use.*

SEE ALSO

For information about designating a printer as the default printer, see "Specifying a Default Printer" on the facing page.

Print a Document Using the Default Printer

1 Select the document or documents you want to print.

2 Right-click a selected document, and choose Print from the shortcut menu.

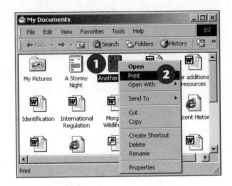

Print a Document Using a Specific Printer

1 Click the Start button, point to Settings, and choose Printers from the submenu to open the Printers folder.

2 Select the document or documents you want to print.

3 Drag the selected document or documents into the Printers folder and onto the printer you want to use.

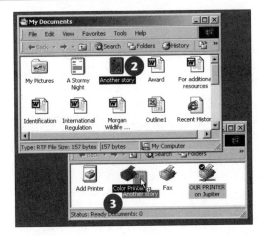

Specifying a Default Printer

Some programs are set up to print only to the system default printer; other programs are set up to print to the default printer, but you can "target," or change to, a different printer. If there are several printers available, you can designate any one of them as your default printer.

TIP

Preset default. *If there's a check mark next to the printer icon, the printer you've chosen has already been set as the default printer.*

SEE ALSO

For information about printing to different printers, see "Printing from a Program" on page 123 and "Printing Documents" on the facing page.

Change the Default

1. Click the Start button, point to Settings, and choose Printers from the submenu.

2. Right-click the printer you want to use as the default printer.

3. Choose Set As Default Printer from the shortcut menu.

4. Close the Printers folder when you've finished.

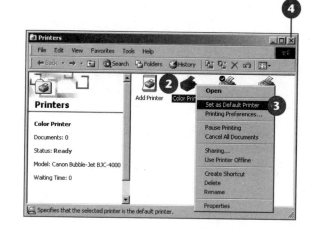

Connecting to a Network Printer

When a printer is set up to be shared, you can easily connect to it, whether it's on a print server or on someone else's workstation, and you can configure your system for that printer. If your network uses Active Directory, you can also locate a printer that meets your printing requirements anywhere on the network.

TIP

Unlisted printer. *Not all shared printers will be listed in the Active Directory. You can still connect to an unlisted printer by using My Network Places and adding the unlisted printer to your Printers folder.*

TIP

Find and print. *To search for and connect to a printer from the Print dialog box, click the Find Printer button.*

Get the Printer

1. Click the Start button, point to Settings, and choose Printers from the submenu.

2. Use the My Network Places folder to locate the computer that has the printer you want, and click that computer.

3. Drag the printer you want to use into the Printers folder.

Find a Printer Based on Its Features

1. Click the Start button, point to Search, and choose For Printers from the submenu.

2. On the Features tab, specify the features you want. Specify any other parameters you want to use on the Printers and Advanced tabs.

3. Click Find Now.

4. Right-click the printer you want, and choose Connect from the shortcut menu. The printer is added to your Printers folder.

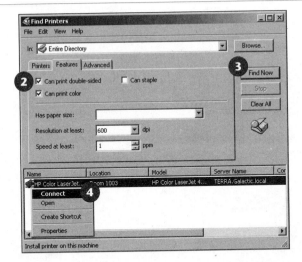

Separating Print Jobs

If your PCL or PostScript printer is shared by several people, you can specify a separator page to control which type of printing (PCL or PostScript) is being used and to print a separator page that identifies the beginning of each individual print job. Windows 2000 provides ready-made separator pages that you select depending on the type of printer you're using. The table at the right identifies the various types of separator pages and their functions.

TRY THIS

Personal message. *To personalize the message on the separator page, open the separator file in Notepad, modify the text that is printed (but nothing else), and save the file under a different name, using the .sep extension. Then choose this file as the separator page.*

Select a Separator Page

1. Click the Start button, point to Settings, and choose Printers from the submenu.

2. Right-click the printer you're using, and choose Properties from the shortcut menu.

3. On the Advanced tab, click the Separator Page button.

4. Click the Browse button.

5. Double-click the separator page you want to use.

6. Click OK.

7. Click OK in the Properties dialog box.

8. Print a document to verify that the separator page is included and that it prints correctly.

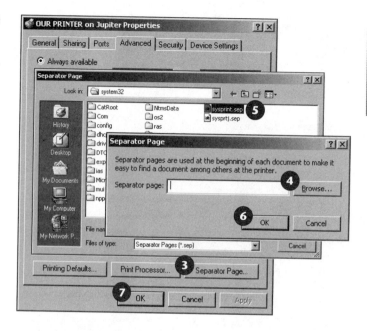

SEPARATOR PAGES	
Separator page filename	Function
pcl.sep	Switches to PCL printing and inserts a separator page.
pscript.sep	Switches to PostScript printing but doesn't insert a separator page.
sysprint.sep	Switches to PostScript printing and inserts a separator page.
sysprtj.sep	Similar to sysprint.sep but uses a different font and supports Japanese characters.

Controlling Your Printing

When you send your documents to be printed, each print job is *queued* in the order in which it's received by the print server. However, some documents might be assigned a higher printing priority than others, so your documents might not be printed in the same order in which they're received. You can see the progress of your print job in the queue, and you can temporarily suspend the printing of your document or even remove it from the queue if you want.

View the Queue

① Click the Start button, point to Settings, and choose Printers from the submenu.

② Double-click the printer you're using.

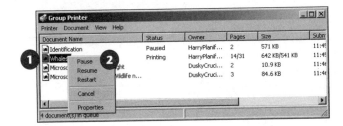

Documents in the print queue

Stop the Presses

① Right-click your document.

② Choose the action you want from the shortcut menu:

◆ Pause to temporarily stop your document from printing

◆ Resume to resume printing after the document printing was paused

◆ Restart to restart printing the document from the beginning after the document printing was paused

◆ Cancel to delete the document from the print queue

Check Your Printing Priority

1. Right-click your document.

2. Choose Properties from the shortcut menu.

3. On the General tab, take a look at the document's printing priority.

4. Click Cancel when you've finished.

5. Right-click a document that belongs to another user.

6. Choose Properties from the shortcut menu, and note that document's printing priority.

7. Complain loudly to the network administrator if a coworker repeatedly assigns his or her documents a higher priority than yours.

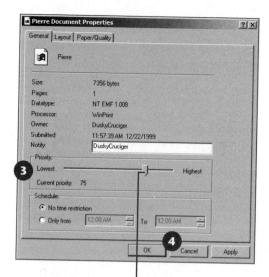

Changing the printing priority moves a document ahead of any documents that have a lower priority.

Printing a Document to a File

If you don't have immediate or direct access to a printer, you can print a document to a file. The file contains all the special printer information from the program, so you don't need to start the program again to print the document—you simply send the file to the printer when the printer is available. How convenient!

TIP

The Print To File option.
Many programs provide the option of printing to a file without requiring you to install a new printer specifically for file output. To see whether the program you're using supports this option, choose Print from the File menu, and, in the Print dialog box, check the Print To File option. If the program you're using has this option, and the printer is installed on your computer, skip the Add Printer Wizard and use the program's option.

Create a Print File

1 Use the Add Printer Wizard to install a local printer on your computer that's connected to File instead of to a printer port. Be sure to specify the same manufacturer and model specifications as those of the printer to which you'll be sending the file.

2 Use your program to print a document to the new printer.

3 Type a path and a file-name for the output file.

4 Click OK.

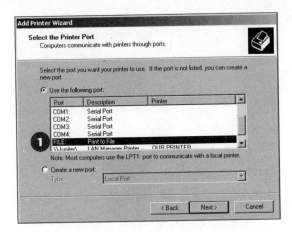

TIP

Outside printing. *Printing to a file is the best way to transfer a document to a print shop or service bureau for quality printing, because such services don't need the program you used to create the document. Before you create the file, however, find out which printer to use and what fonts the print shop or service bureau has installed.*

TIP

The printer-driver files. *If your computer doesn't have the printer or the correct printer drivers installed, you'll need access to the Windows 2000 Professional installation files (on either the server or the CD), or a disk from the printer manufacturer that contains the printer-driver files for Windows 2000 Professional.*

TRY THIS

Print from a file. *Set the printer that's connected to File as your default printer, right-click a document file (such as a bitmap image), and choose Print. Type a path and filename for the output file. Start the command prompt, and send the file to the correct printer on the print server.*

Print a Print File to a Printer

1. Click the Start button, point to Programs and then Accessories, and choose Command Prompt from the submenu.

2. At the prompt, type *print /d:printerdevice "drive:\path\filename"* (where *printerdevice* identifies the name or location of the printer, and *drive, path,* and *filename* locate and specify the print file). Note that quotation marks are optional unless the printer name or filename contains any spaces, in which case the quotation marks are essential.

3. Press Enter.

Prints the file *clrprnt.prn* using the printer connected to the LPT1 port.

Prints the file *clrprnt.prn* using the network color printer on the Neptune print server.

Printing Without a Printer

When you take your computer on the road, or if your local printer is in the repair shop, you can still print your documents. Well, not *exactly*. What you can do is create *print jobs* in the Printers folder, and then, when you reconnect to the printer, you can send all the print jobs to the printer.

TIP

Queue it up. *The lineup of documents that you see in the Printers folder is often called the print queue.*

SEE ALSO

For information about creating a print job that will be printed from a different computer, see "Printing a Document to a File" on page 130.

Queue Your Printing

1. Click the Start button, point to Settings, and choose Printers from the submenu.

2. Right-click your local printer, and choose Use Printer Offline from the shortcut menu. (You can't use a network printer off line.)

3. Print your documents as usual.

4. When you can reconnect to your printer, click the Start button, point to Settings, and choose Printers from the submenu.

5. Right-click the printer, and note that there's a check mark next to the Use Printer Offline command on the shortcut menu, indicating that the printer is off line. Click the command to set the printer to work on line.

6. Wait for your documents to print.

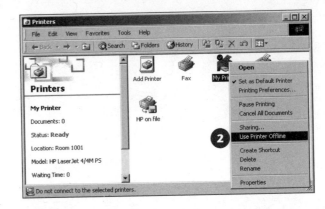

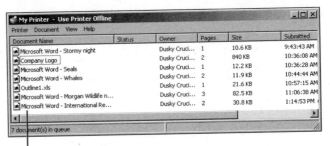

When the printer is off line, the documents are queued up until you can reconnect to the printer.

Printing from the Command Prompt to a Network Printer

Many MS-DOS–based programs are set to print to a printer that's connected to a standard printer port, such as LPT1, and these programs can't normally print to a network printer. However, you *can* print to a network printer from an MS-DOS–based program by having Windows 2000 reroute the program's output. The MS-DOS–based program is tricked into "thinking" it's printing to a standard port, but its output is really being sent over the network.

Reroute the Port

1. Click the Start button, point to Programs, and choose Command Prompt from the submenu.

2. At the prompt, type *net use lptx "\\printserver\printer" /persistent:yes* (where *lptx* is whichever parallel port you want to assign the printer to—LPT2, for example—and *printserver* and *printer* identify your network printer).

3. Press Enter.

4. Run your MS-DOS program, and print from the program to the parallel port you just assigned.

With this command, output sent to the LPT2 port goes to the Our Printer network printer on the Jupiter server.

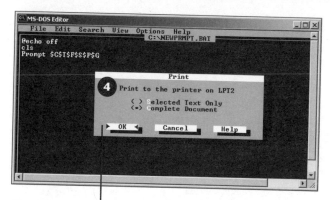

Once the program is set to print to the local port, you can print from the program to the network printer.

IN THIS SECTION

Playing an Audio File

Playing a Music CD

Listening to the Radio

Playing a Video Clip

**Playing Media
from the Net**

**Associating a Sound
with an Event**

**Multimedia Formats
and CODECs**

Creating a Sound File

Controlling the Volume

8

Working
with
Multimedia

Depending on what you use your computer for, multimedia can mean work or play—or a little or a lot of each. Microsoft Windows 2000 Professional can provide you with a vast array of audio and visual stimuli. You can play and record audio files, play music CDs while reading all the album information you'll ever want, view video clips, and listen to music or view video feeds as they're being downloaded from your network or from the Internet.

Working with multimedia can also be as simple as associating sounds with events that take place on your computer: if you'd like to hear a duck quacking every time you receive new mail, or your child's voice babbling baby language when you shut down your computer, you can make it so. And, of course, multimedia opens up a whole realm of wonderful educational and recreational tools—multimedia encyclopedias and other reference works, foreign-language courses, cooking and gardening programs, and about a zillion exciting games.

Multimedia demands a lot from your computer, however, so you'll need the proper equipment—that is, your computer must be configured for sound with a sound card or an integrated sound system, as well as speakers or a headset. For more capabilities, you'll also need a CD or DVD drive and a microphone.

Playing an Audio File

With the proper hardware installed on your computer—a sound card and speakers, for example—Windows 2000 Professional uses the multifunctional Windows Media Player to play several audio and music file formats. You can play and replay your file, control the way it plays, and even customize the player.

TIP

Media Player updates.
Windows Media Player is frequently updated to keep pace with the changing world of audio file formats. To check for an updated version, connect to the Internet, and choose Check For Player Upgrade from the Help menu.

Play an Audio File

1 Locate and double-click the file you want to play.

2 Use the controls to adjust the play:

◆ Click Play to replay the file.

◆ Click Pause to suspend the play.

◆ Click Stop to terminate the play.

◆ Drag the Seek Bar slider to resume play at a different part of the file.

◆ Click Mute to silence the play without stopping it; click Mute again to hear the file.

◆ Drag the Volume control slider to adjust the play volume.

The Seek Bar

Play

Pause

Stop

Mute

Volume control

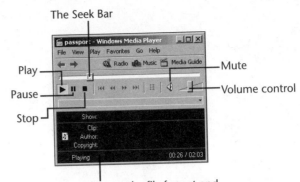

Depending on the file format and the information recorded, some files don't display any information...

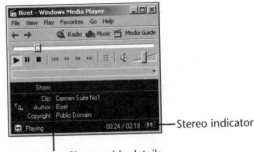

Stereo indicator

...and other files provide details.

TIP

Get more details. *To see which file formats Windows Media Player supports, choose Options from Media Player's View menu, and click the Formats tab. Click each item for more details and a list of the file extensions that are supported.*

TRY THIS

Browse for files. *Use the Open command on Media Player's File menu to browse for and then open and play another file. Click Back on the Navigation Bar to play a previously played file, and then click Forward to play the file you just opened. Click Web Events to find files to download from the Internet.*

TIP

Boss alert! *To quickly turn off the sound, press Ctrl+M.*

Change the Default Settings

1. Choose Options from the View menu.

2. Click the Playback tab, and specify the volume level, the speaker balance, and the number of times you want the file to be played.

3. Click the Player tab, and specify whether you want to open a new player for each file, which view you want the player to open in, and whether it should always appear on top of all other windows.

4. Click the Custom Views tab, and select the items you want to be displayed in the different views.

5. Click OK.

6. Close Media Player when you've finished.

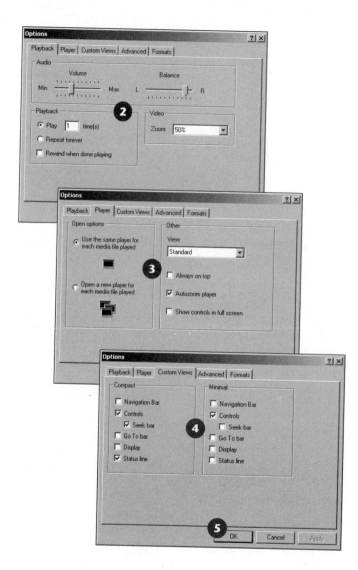

8

Playing a Music CD

You can just drop a music CD into your disc drive and play it, or you can use CD Player to download information about the album and control how the CD is played—for example, change tracks or CDs, and even rearrange the play list for each album.

TIP

Start CD Player. *If CD Player doesn't start when you insert a CD, click the Start button, point your way through Programs, Accessories, and Entertainment, and choose CD Player from the submenu. With CD Player open, click the Play button.*

TIP

Download control. *You can change any of the settings on the Album Options tab of the Preferences dialog box to control the way album information is downloaded from the Internet.*

Play a CD

1. Insert the CD into the disc drive and wait for Windows 2000 to start playing the disc.

2. If you're asked whether you want to download album information, select

   ◆ Download Information For This Album Only to be prompted to download for each new album.

   ◆ Always Download New Album Information to automatically download information each time you play a new album.

3. Click OK to download information, or click Cancel to play the album without obtaining the additional information.

4. Click any control to adjust the play, or open the Mode drop-down list to repeat tracks, to play tracks in a random order, or to preview tracks.

5. Choose Preferences from the Options drop-down list, and adjust the way CD Player is displayed. Click OK when you've finished.

Download related information from the Internet.

Pause (changes to Play when a CD isn't being played).

Stop Eject Switch tracks.

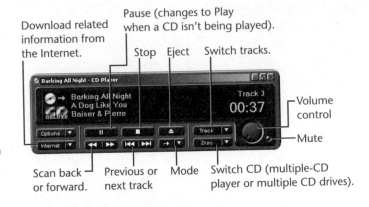

Volume control

Mute

Scan back or forward.

Previous or next track

Mode

Switch CD (multiple-CD player or multiple CD drives).

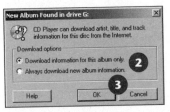

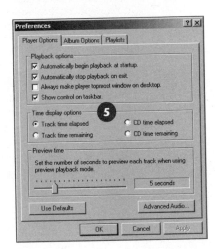

Modify the Play List

1. Choose Playlist from the Options drop-down list.

2. On the Playlists tab, select the album you want to edit, and click Edit Playlist.

3. Modify the artist's name or the album title, if desired.

4. Do any of the following:

   ◆ Drag a track into a new location to change the order in which tracks are played.

   ◆ Click a track, and click Remove to delete the track.

   ◆ Select a track from the Available Tracks list, and click Add To Playlist to add the track.

   ◆ Select a track from the Available Tracks list, type a new name for the track, and click Add To Playlist to rename and add the track.

5. Click OK when you've finished.

6. Click OK.

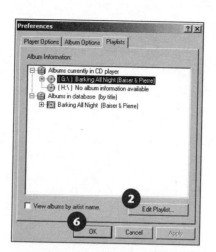

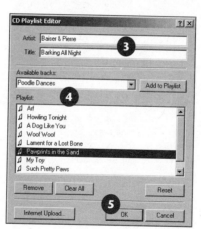

Listening to the Radio

Many radio stations broadcast their programs over the Internet. You can connect to a station by connecting to its web site and having the broadcast sent to you. Because this is digital audio, a very large quantity of data is sent to your computer, and some of the data is temporarily stored, or *buffered*, before you hear it. This means that there's usually a small time delay between the live transmission and when you hear it. Depending on your Internet connection and how busy all the servers are, the transmission might also pause while additional data is downloaded.

TIP

The Radio toolbar.
To always display the Radio toolbar, choose Internet Options from the View menu, and, on the Advanced tab, turn on the check box to display the Radio toolbar.

Find a Station

1. Start Internet Explorer if it's not already running, and connect to the Internet if you're not already connected.

2. If the Radio toolbar isn't displayed, right-click any toolbar, and choose Radio from the shortcut menu.

3. Open the Radio Stations list, and do either of the following:
   - ◆ Click a radio station that you've listened to previously.
   - ◆ Click Radio Station Guide, and locate the station you want to listen to.

4. Use the controls on the toolbar to end the broadcast, change the volume, or switch to a different radio station.

Click to jump to a preset selection.

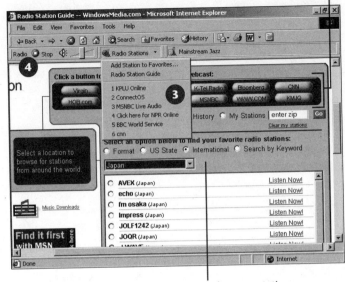

Use the search features to locate a station.

Playing a Video Clip

Most of the videos that you play on your computer are controlled by a specific program—a game or an encyclopedia, for example, or a special player such as a DVD player. Video *clips*, however, are often handled differently. These usually short video snippets are often downloaded from a web site and saved as a file, or sent as an enclosure in an e-mail message. You can control both the play of the video clip and the way it's shown on your computer.

TIP

Preview a clip. *When you select a video-clip file in a folder window, a version of Windows Media Player appears in the web content part of the window and plays the video clip. Use the play controls or right-click the player for greater control.*

Play the Video

1 Locate and double-click the file you want to play.

2 Use any of the controls to adjust the playback.

3 Do any of the following to change the appearance of the playback:

◆ Point to Zoom on the View menu and choose a different scaling factor for the video.

◆ Press Alt+Enter to use the full screen to display the video. Press Alt+Enter again to return to the standard window.

◆ Choose Compact or Minimal from the View menu to change the amount of information displayed.

◆ Choose Captions from the View menu to view closed captions if the video contains them.

4 Enjoy the video clip.

Drag to move to a different part of the video clip.

The video clip

Play

Mute

Pause

Volume control

Stop

Plays previously played video clips.

Stereo/Mono indicator

Status

Total time

Properties of the video clip, if any

Elapsed time

Playing Media from the Net

Many web sites can now provide audio or video using *streaming media,* which means that instead of waiting for a file to download and then playing it, you can listen or view while the data is downloading. This gives you the opportunity not only to play a file that's stored on a web site but also to receive live broadcasts being sent out through the web site (with a few seconds' delay for the transmission and buffering of the data). Just as you do with a multimedia file, you use Media Player to control the playback.

Start Playing

1. Locate the web site that contains the media you want to play.

2. Click the link to the media.

3. If it's available on the web site, select the best-suited speed (bandwidth) for your net connection.

4. Wait for the connection to be made, for Media Player to load, and for the first data to be transmitted and buffered.

5. Listen to and/or watch the multimedia.

6. Use Media Player's controls to monitor and modify the show.

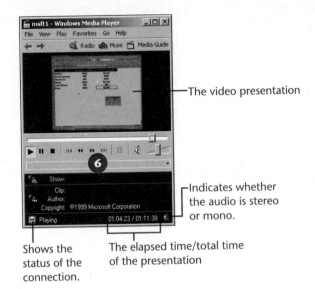

The video presentation

Indicates whether the audio is stereo or mono.

Shows the status of the connection.

The elapsed time/total time of the presentation

Improve the Playback

1 If the download pauses too often for buffering, click Stop.

2 Choose Options from Media Player's View menu.

3 On the Advanced tab, select Streaming Media.

4 Click the Change button.

5 Enter a higher number of seconds of buffered data, and click OK.

6 Close Media Player, return to the web site, and restart the downloading of the file.

7 If the download is still too slow, try downloading at a time when the servers might not be so busy.

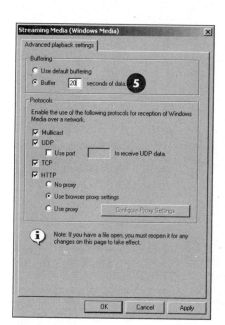

8

Associating a Sound with an Event

If you want audio cues for events in Windows 2000—the closing of a program or the arrival of new mail, for example—you can assign wave sounds to these events.

SEE ALSO

For information about assigning sounds to different events, see "Changing Your Input" on page 236.

TIP

Store your WAV files.
Put any WAV audio files that you want to use for events into the Media folder (you'll find it in the WINNT folder), and the files will appear in the Name list.

Assign a Sound to an Event

1. Click the Start button, point to Settings, and choose Control Panel from the submenu.

2. Double-click the Sounds And Multimedia icon.

3. On the Sounds tab, select an event from the Sound Events list.

4. Select a sound from the Name list, or use the Browse button to find a sound in another folder. Choose None from the list to remove a sound from an event.

5. Repeat steps 3 and 4 to add sounds to other events.

6. Click the Apply Button.

7. Click Save As, enter a name for the sound scheme you've created, and click OK.

8. Click OK.

The icon indicates that a sound has been assigned to the event.

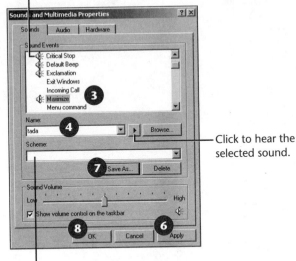

Click to hear the selected sound.

Select an existing scheme to assign a set of predefined sounds to several events.

Multimedia Formats and CODECs

Multimedia files come in a wide range of formats, because of both new and old designs and competing standards. Windows Media Player can play most audio and video files because it has a variety of *CODECs* installed. CODECs (a tech-term derived from both COder and DECoder and COmpressor and DECompressor) are programs, or *filters,* that plug into Media Player so that it can read the media files. As current formats are enhanced and new ones developed, you might find that you can't play an audio or video file from the Internet until you download a new CODEC. A well-designed web site will have the proper CODEC available for automatic download and installation. Once you've installed the CODEC, you should be able to play the audio or video file.

Of course, things are seldom this simple! If the proper CODEC isn't available or if you can't play a new multimedia format on your current player, you might be able to upgrade to a newer version of the player. This is likely enough that Media Player provides a direct link on the Help menu to the update site. Another possible complication is that the media file might be in a format that Media Player can't read. As long as the different software companies continue to squabble over which formats are best, standardization remains a distant hope.

If you want to play a file that isn't supported by Media Player, you'll need to download a different player, which you should be able to find on any major web site that uses the same format. Be aware, however, that different media players don't always interact well with each other, and that some pushy media player might seize the opportunity to become the default media player for most of your sound files. If this happens, you can always manually change the default player for each file type (see "Open a Document in a Different Program" on page 29) or simply remove the unwanted player (see "Removing a Software Program" on page 280).

8

FORMATS SUPPORTED BY MEDIA PLAYER	
Media	**Format identified by file extension**
Audio files	.aif, .aifc, .aiff, .au, .mid, .mp2, .mp3, .rmi, .snd, .wav, .wax, wma
Video files	.avi, .m1v, .mov, .mp2, .mp3, .mpa, .mpe, .mpeg, .mpg, .qt
Streaming audio and video	.asf

Creating a Sound File

With a microphone, a CD drive, or some other input device (such as a tape player) hooked up to the Line In port of your sound card or sound system, you can create your own sound files. Even without an external input device, you can create new sound files by combining and editing your existing sound files.

TIP

Beware the big wave.
A wave sound is a digital recording of a sound. Because it contains a lot of information, it's usually a fairly short recording to limit the file size.

TIP

No control. *If the device you want to use isn't listed in the Recording Control dialog box, choose Properties from the Options menu, and turn on the check box for the device.*

Set Up for Recording

1 Click the Start button, point your way through Programs, Accessories, and Entertainment, and choose Sound Recorder from the submenu.

2 Choose Audio Properties from the Edit menu.

3 Specify a recording device if your system has more than one device.

4 Click Volume.

5 Verify that the Mute check box isn't checked for the input device you want to use.

6 Set the volume for the device and, if you're recording in stereo, the balance.

7 Click the Close box.

8 If you want to modify the hardware acceleration and sampling rate for the recording, click Advanced, make your changes, and click OK.

9 Click OK.

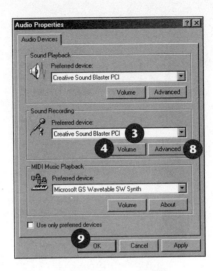

Record Sounds

1. Click the Record button.

2. Record your voice or other sounds using the microphone, or play the input device that's attached to the Line In connector.

3. Click Stop when you've finished.

4. Choose Save from the File menu.

Add Sounds and Effects

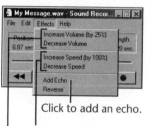

1. Move the slider to the location in the sound file where you want to add an existing sound file.

2. From the Edit menu, choose

   ◆ Insert File to add a file and record over any existing sound.

   ◆ Mix With File to merge a file with the existing sound.

3. Locate the file, and click Open.

4. Choose the type of effect you want to add from the Effects menu.

5. Save the file.

Click to add an echo.

Each click increases or decreases the speed.

Each click increases or decreases the volume.

8

Controlling the Volume

You can keep your music and other sounds muted so that you don't disturb other people, or, when you're the only person around, you can crank up the sound level and blast away! Although many programs have individual controls, you can use the Volume control to set all your sound levels.

TIP

Volume control on the taskbar. *If the Volume icon doesn't appear on the taskbar, click the Start button, point to Settings, choose Control Panel, double-click the Sounds And Multimedia icon, and, on the Sounds tab, turn on the Show Volume Control On The Taskbar check box.*

TIP

Fine-tune your sounds. *Many speakers have built-in volume controls. You can use these in conjunction with the Volume control on the taskbar to fine-tune your sound levels.*

Set the Master Volume Level

1. Click the Volume icon on the taskbar.

2. Drag the slider to adjust the volume.

3. Click outside the Volume icon to close it.

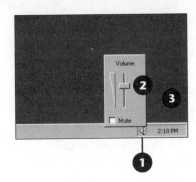

Set the Volume for Individual Devices

1. Double-click the Volume icon on the taskbar.

2. Adjust the settings for your devices.

The master control affects all devices.

Drag the slider to adjust the balance.

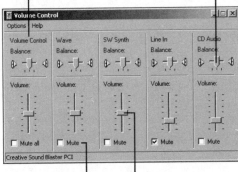

Check for no sound.

Drag the slider to change the volume.

9

Connecting

IN THIS SECTION

Adding E-Mail and News Accounts

Sending and Receiving E-Mail

Managing Messages

Subscribing to Newsgroups and Reading the News

Adding a Contact to the Contacts List

Customizing Outlook Express

Sending a Business Card

Sending and Receiving Secure Messages

Sending and Receiving Faxes

Conferring on the Net

Making a Phone Call

The ability to communicate electronically is one of a computer's most used and most valued features. In this section, we'll discuss the tools that Microsoft Windows 2000 Professional provides that let you reach out and connect with people in your immediate workgroup or on the other side of the world.

Outlook Express helps you organize and customize your e-mail and does double duty as a news reader. It can complete an address when you type only the first couple of letters and can automatically add a signature to your messages. You can enclose files, or *attachments*, with your e-mail, and you can format messages with fonts and colors. You can encrypt messages for security so that only people with the correct *digital ID* can read them. If several people use your computer, each individual can have a separate mail and news account.

Provided you have a fax modem, Windows 2000 installs Fax Service, which allows you to send and receive faxes through your computer. You can use Microsoft NetMeeting to conduct meetings or online working sessions over the Internet or your company's intranet. Meeting participants can confer using text "chats" or voice conversations. And Phone Dialer lets you make phone calls and conduct multiparty conferences or video conferences over the Internet or an intranet.

Adding E-Mail and News Accounts

You can set up Outlook Express with one or more mail accounts and one or more news servers. When you set up a service such as Hotmail, the account will probably be added automatically to Outlook Express. You can, however, add more accounts yourself.

TIP

Free Hotmail. *If you don't have an Internet e-mail account and you'd like to establish a free Hotmail account, point to New Account Signup on the Tools menu and choose Hotmail from the submenu. You do, however, still need a connection to the Internet.*

SEE ALSO

For information about the different mail protocols, see "Mail Messages, Formats, and Servers" on page 164.

Specify Your Mail Service

1. Double-click the Outlook Express icon on the Desktop, or click the Launch Outlook Express button on the Quick Launch toolbar.

2. Choose Accounts from the Tools menu to display the Internet Accounts dialog box.

3. On the Mail tab of the Internet Accounts dialog box, check to see whether the account you want has already been set up.

4. If the account you want isn't listed, click the Add button, and choose Mail from the menu that appears.

5. Complete the steps of the Internet Connection Wizard to specify your mail account.

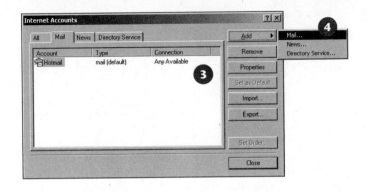

WHAT YOU NEED TO SPECIFY A MAIL ACCOUNT	
Information	**Example**
An Internet e-mail address	IndusS@InternetServiceProvider.com
Some type of incoming mail server	POP3
An incoming mail-server name	mail.InternetServiceProvider.com
An outgoing mail-server name	SMTP.InternetServiceProvider.com
Your Internet mail logon name	IndusS
Your Internet mail password	MailPassword

Specify Your News Server

1 On the News tab of the Internet Accounts dialog box, check to see whether the account you want has already been set up.

2 If the account you want isn't listed, click the Add button, and choose News from the menu that appears.

3 Complete the steps of the Internet Connection Wizard to specify your news account.

4 Click Close when you've finished.

5 When prompted, click Yes to download newsgroups from the news server.

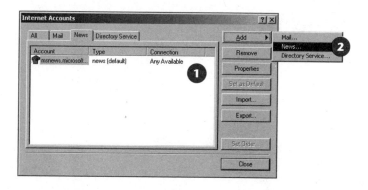

| WHAT YOU NEED TO SPECIFY A NEWS ACCOUNT ||
Information	Example
An Internet e-mail address	IndusS@InternetServiceProvider.com
An Internet news-server name	MSNews.microsoft.com
A news-server logon name (if required)	IndusS
A news-server password (if required)	NewsPassword

9

Sending E-Mail

You don't have to address an envelope or trek to the mailbox on a cold, rainy day. All you do is select a name, create a message, and click a Send button. Outlook Express and your mail server do the rest. What a great idea!

> **TIP**
>
> **Different fields.** *A From field is displayed if you have more than one e-mail account. If the BCC field isn't displayed, choose All Headers from the View menu.*

> **TIP**
>
> **A draft copy.** *When you're composing a long message, it's a good idea to frequently choose Save from the File menu to save a copy of the message in the Drafts folder.*

Address a Message

1. Double-click a message recipient's name in the Contacts list. (If the Contacts list isn't displayed, use the Layout command on the View menu to display it.)

2. To add more names, type a semicolon, and then start typing another recipient's name. Press Enter when Outlook Express completes the name, or continue typing if the proposed name is incorrect.

3. Press the Tab key to move to the CC or BCC field, and type the names of the people who are to receive a copy of the message. (The names in the CC field are included in all copies of the message; the names in the BCC—blind copy—field are not included in the messages sent to the people listed in the To and CC fields.)

4. Press the Tab key to move to the Subject line, type a subject, and press Tab again to move into the message area.

Click any of the address icons to find e-mail names in your Contacts list if you can't remember them.

Outlook Express completes the name automatically, based on the names in your Contacts list.

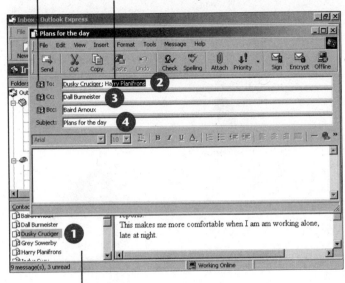

The Contacts list

TIP

Compose off line. *To econo-mize on connection and phone costs, click the Offline button, and compose your messages off line. Each time you click Send, the message will be stored in your Outbox until you go on line and choose to send and receive messages.*

TIP

Plain text. *Use Plain Text formatting if you're not sure whether the recipient has a mail reader that supports HTML formatting. Messages using Plain Text formatting are also smaller and will download faster than messages using Rich Text formatting.*

SEE ALSO

For information about adding your signature to outgoing mes-sages, see "Adding a Signature to a Message" on page 165.

For information about digitally signing and encrypting your messages, see "Sending and Receiving Secure Messages" on page 172.

Compose a Message

1. From the Format menu, choose Rich Text (HTML) or Plain Text.

2. If you're sending your messages in Rich Text Format, you can use the Format menu to add a background color, picture, or sound to your message, as well as predefined stationery to apply a background design and font style.

3. Type your message, using any of the formatting tools on the Formatting Bar. (Note that the For-matting Bar isn't available for Plain Text messages.)

4. Click any of the following on the Standard Buttons toolbar:

   ◆ The Priority button to mark the message with a high- or low-priority tag

   ◆ The Sign button to include digital identification

   ◆ The Encrypt button to scramble the mes-sage for security

5. Click the Send button to send the document.

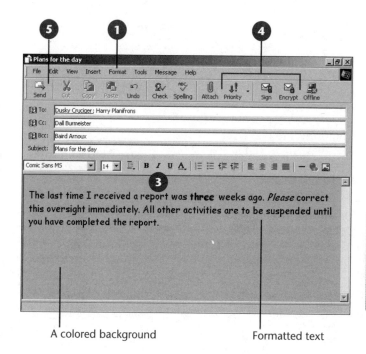

A colored background   Formatted text

9

Reading E-Mail

Outlook Express lets you specify how frequently you want it to check for incoming mail, and it notifies you when you receive new mail. You can check your Inbox and see at a glance which messages have and haven't been read, or you can set the view to list unread messages only.

TIP

I need it now! *To receive mail immediately when you don't want to wait for the system to check your mailbox for you, click the Send And Receive button.*

TRY THIS

A better view. *On the Read tab, click the Fonts button. Select a new font in the Proportional Font list and a new font size in the Font Size list, and click OK. Close the Options dialog box, and look at the messages in the preview pane.*

Set the Options

1. In Outlook Express, choose Options from the Tools menu to display the Options dialog box.

2. On the General tab, turn on the check box to play a sound if you want to be alerted by an audible signal when new mail arrives.

3. Turn on the check box to check for new mail, and specify how often you want the mail to be checked.

4. Specify whether you want to be connected automatically if you're not connected when you're checking for new mail.

5. On the Read tab, select the options you want to use.

6. Click OK.

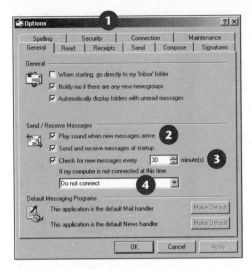

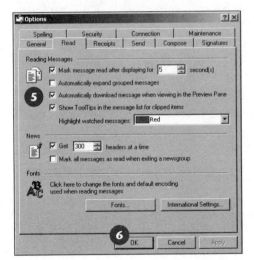

SEE ALSO

For information about saving and opening file attachments, see "Sending and Receiving Attachments" on page 156.

For information about receiving messages in a folder other than your Inbox, see "Managing Messages" on page 158.

For information about accessing and managing your messages, see "Create Automatic Rules" on page 159.

Read Your Messages

1 Switch to the Inbox for the mail service you want to view if it's not the currently active folder.

2 On the View menu, specify how you want to view your messages:

- ◆ Point to Current View, and choose the type of messages you want displayed.

- ◆ Point to Sort By, and choose the way you want the messages to be ordered.

- ◆ Choose Layout, specify whether and where you want the preview pane displayed, and click OK.

3 Do either of the following to view a message:

- ◆ Click the header, and read the message in the preview pane.

- ◆ Double-click the header to view the message in a separate window.

4 Read the message.

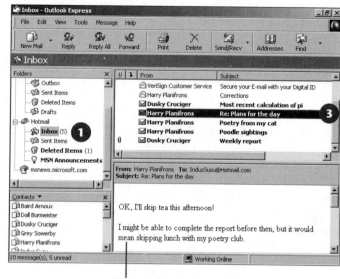

The message in the preview pane

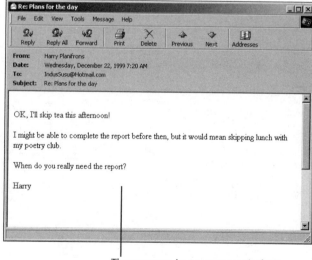

The message in a separate window

Sending and Receiving Attachments

A great way to share a file—a Word document, a picture, or even an entire program, for example—is to include it as part of an e-mail message. The file is kept as a separate part of the message—an *attachment*—that the recipient can save and open at any time.

Attach

Include an Attachment

1. Create, address, and type the message text.

2. Click the Attach button.

3. In the Insert Attachment dialog box, select the file or files to be included.

4. Click Attach.

5. Send the message just as you'd send any other message.

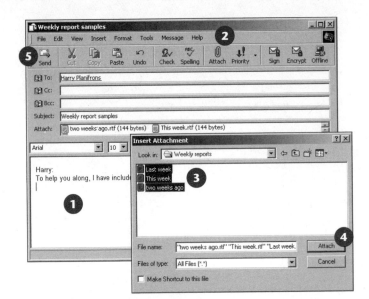

Open and Save an Attachment

1. Select the message.

2. Click the Attachment icon, and, on the menu that appears, click

   ◆ The name of the file to open the file.

   ◆ Save Attachments to save the file to disk without opening it.

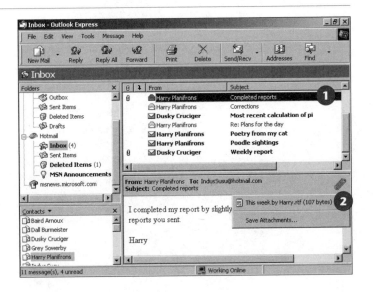

Replying to or Forwarding a Message

When you receive an e-mail message that needs a reply or that you want to forward to someone else, all it takes is a click of a button to create a new message. But be careful when you use the Reply All button! If the original message contained the names of groups, you could be replying to an entire division or the entire company instead of to one or two people.

Reply to or Forward a Message

1. Select the message.

2. Click the appropriate button:

   ◆ Reply to send your reply to the writer of the message only

   ◆ Reply All to send your reply to the writer of the message and to everyone listed in the original message's To and CC lines

   ◆ Forward to send a copy of the message to another recipient

3. Add names to or delete names from the To and CC lines.

4. Type your reply message or any note associated with the forwarded message.

5. Click the Send button.

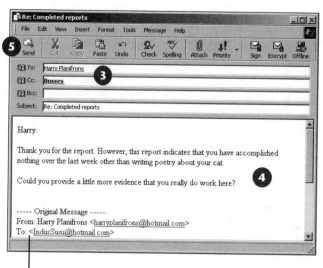

The original header information and message text are included.

Managing Messages

Tired of looking through all your messages, switching views, sorting the listings, and still having difficulty finding the message you want? You can locate your messages more easily by creating new folders and moving messages into the appropriate folders. You can even let Outlook Express do the work. All you need to do is establish a set of rules based on the different parts of the message—the From or Subject lines, for example—that automatically manage the messages for you.

TIP

Custom categories. *To customize the categories that are displayed in a new or an existing folder, choose Columns from the View menu.*

SEE ALSO

For information about POP3, IMAP, and HTTP mail formats, see "Mail Messages, Formats, and Servers" on page 164.

Create a Folder System

1. If the Folders list isn't displayed, choose Layout from the View menu, turn on the Folder List option, turn off the Outlook Bar option if you want, and click OK.

2. Right-click a folder, and choose New Folder from the shortcut menu.

3. Click the folder in which you want to create a new folder.

4. Type a name for the new folder.

5. Click OK.

6. Repeat steps 2 through 5 to create additional new folders.

7. To organize your messages, drag message headers from the message pane into the appropriate folders in the Folders list.

The Folders list

The Folder Bar

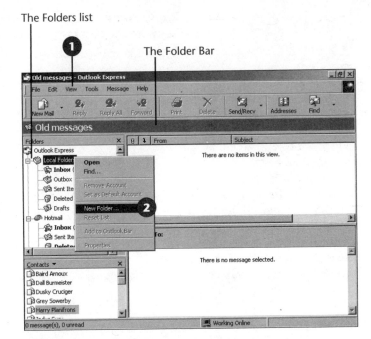

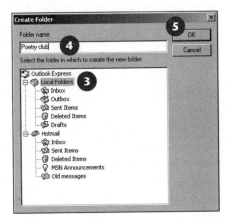

Create Automatic Rules

1. Point to Message Rules on the Tools menu, and choose Mail from the submenu.

2. Turn on the check box for each identifying condition.

3. Turn on the check box for each action to be executed when the identifying conditions are met.

4. Click a link to provide the specific information required to execute the rule.

5. Type a name for the rule.

6. Click OK.

7. Click New, and repeat steps 2 through 6 to create any additional rules.

8. Use the Move Up and Move Down buttons to change the order in which the rules are executed.

9. Click OK.

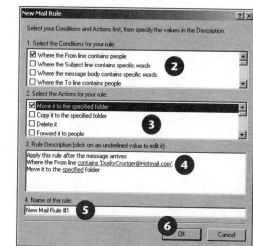

Subscribing to Newsgroups

With so many newsgroups available, you'll probably want to be selective about the ones you review. You can do so by *subscribing* to the newsgroups you like. Subscribed newsgroups appear in the message pane when you select the news server and on the Folder Bar, if it's displayed, when you expand the listing for a news server.

SEE ALSO

For information about setting up your news servers, see "Adding E-Mail and News Accounts" on page 150.

TIP

Full names. *To see the full names of the newsgroups, drag the boundary between the Newsgroup and Description labels to widen the Newsgroup area.*

Select Your Newsgroups

1. With Outlook Express connected on line and a news server selected in the Folders list, click the Newsgroups button.

2. If you have more than one news server, select the one you want to use.

3. Search for the newsgroups you want to access.

4. Double-click a newsgroup to subscribe to it.

5. Repeat steps 2 through 4 to subscribe to other newsgroups.

6. Click OK.

Limit the newsgroups to be displayed, or leave blank to view all the newsgroups.

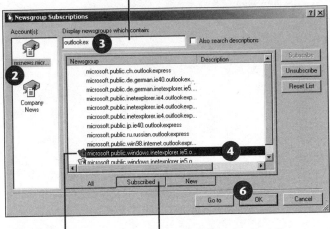

The newspaper icon shows you've subscribed to that newsgroup.

Only the newsgroups you've subscribed to are listed on the Subscribed tab.

Reading the News

Reading the news—or the gossip, tirades, and misinformation that often pass for news in Internet newsgroups—is as simple as reading your mail. All you need to do is select the newsgroup, select the message, and read it.

TIP

Threads. *A "thread" is a series of messages in which one person posts a message and other readers reply to the message and/or to the replies.*

TIP

Use a separate window. *To open the news message in a separate window, double-click the message.*

Select a Message

1 In the Folders list, expand the list under the news server if necessary, and click the newsgroup.

2 On the View menu, point to Current View, and choose the view you want:

◆ Show All Messages to see everything

◆ Hide Read Messages to display only the messages you haven't read

◆ Show Downloaded Messages to see the messages you've downloaded

◆ Hide Read Or Ignored Messages to display only the messages you haven't read or that haven't been marked to be ignored

◆ Show Replies To My Messages to see responses to your messages

3 Read the message headers.

4 Click to display a message.

5 Read the message.

The "torn page" icon shows that only the message header has been downloaded.

The "full page" icon shows that the message has been downloaded.

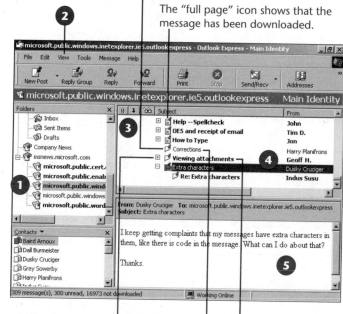

A plus sign means that there are additional messages in the thread.

The regular font shows that the message has been read.

The bold font shows that the message hasn't been read.

Downloading the News

You don't need to be connected to the Internet and a news server for the entire time you're reading the news. By downloading messages, you can work off line and read the messages at your leisure, thereby saving on connection costs.

Download the Newsgroup

1. Select a news server.

2. Select a newsgroup.

3. Select the messages you want to download. Click the Settings button if you want to change the types of messages that are downloaded.

4. Repeat steps 2 and 3 for any other newsgroups you want to download.

5. Click the Synchronize Account button.

6. If you're not connected to the news server, connect. Wait for the messages to download.

7. When you're disconnected from the news server, click a message to read it.

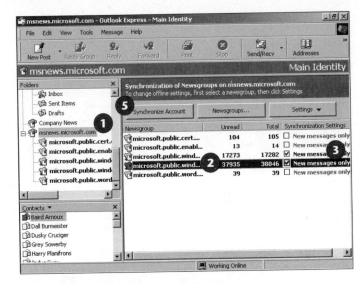

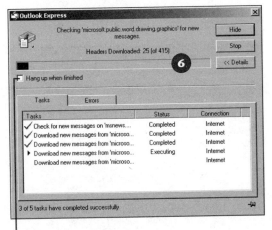

Turn on if you want to automatically hang up your dial-in connection.

Adding to the News

Most newsgroups are *interactive*—that is, you can post your own messages and reply to other people's messages. You can compose your messages on line or off line. When you're off line, the message is saved and will be posted to the newsgroup the next time you connect.

TIP

Looking for answers?
To find the replies to your messages, point to Current View on the View menu, and choose Show Replies To My Messages.

SEE ALSO

For information about using HTML format to send your messages with full formatting, see "Compose a Message" on page 153.

Create a Message

1. Open the newsgroup in which you want to post your message.

2. Select the type of message you want to post:

   ◆ Click New Post to create a new message in the newsgroup.

   ◆ Select a message, and click Reply Group to place your reply in the newsgroup as part of the original message's thread.

   ◆ Select a message, and click Reply to send an e-mail reply to the author of the message only.

3. Type a subject, and press Tab.

4. Type your message.

5. Click Send.

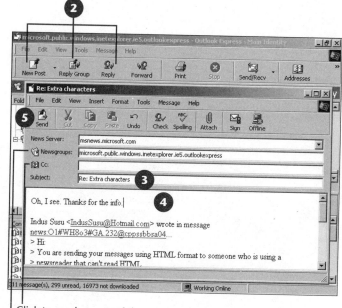

Click to send a copy of the message via e-mail.

Click to address the message to more than one newsgroup.

9

Mail Messages, Formats, and Servers

Outlook Express supports three mail formats: POP3, IMAP, and HTTP.

POP3 (Post Office Protocol 3) is the standard mail protocol used on TCP/IP networks. You connect to the mail server, your messages are transferred from the mail server to your computer, the messages are then deleted from the server, and you disconnect from the server.

With **IMAP** (Internet Message Access Protocol) and **HTTP** (Hypertext Transfer Protocol), you connect to and then interact with the server. With these two protocols, your mail messages stay on the server, and only the header, or title, of each message is copied to your computer; the body of a message is copied only when you try to access it. Any manipulation you do—creating folders or moving messages into a different folder, for example—occurs on the server.

Which protocol should you use? You must match the protocol of the mail system you're connecting to, so if you already have a mail account, you'll need to find out the protocol and the server name. But you might also have the option of choosing a different or an additional mail system. Which mail system you choose, based on its protocol, depends on how you use your mail.

If you use only one computer, the POP3 protocol works very well. All your messages are stored on your computer, and you can easily read or delete messages whether or not you're connected to the mail server.

IMAP and HTTP protocols are best if you check your mail from more than one computer. Because the messages are always on the server, you have access to everything every time you connect. These protocols also provide you with the opportunity to delete unwanted mail before you download the entire message. With an IMAP system, you can also hide and move existing folders for better organization.

Of course, all this is simply the theory behind the protocols. Outlook Express provides options that can blur some of these distinctions. You can, for example, configure your POP3 account so that your messages aren't deleted from the server when you download them and are accessible when you connect to the mail server from a different computer. With the IMAP or HTTP protocol, you can automatically download the unread messages, go off line and read the messages, move messages around in your folders, compose messages, and then connect and synchronize the contents of what you have on your computer with what's on the server.

Fortunately, you usually don't have to choose one system only. For example, you might have a mail server that provides both IMAP and POP3 services. When you're on the road, you can use a computer to read the mail using the IMAP protocol, leaving all the messages in your mailbox. When you're in the office, your computer can access the same mailbox using the POP3 account and can download all the messages.

Adding a Signature to a Message

Outlook Express can speed up your work by inserting your signature for you at the end of your messages. You can tell Outlook Express to add the information at the end of every message, or to insert it in selected messages when you click a button.

SEE ALSO

For information about sending your messages, see "Sending E-Mail" on page 152 and "Replying to or Forwarding a Message" on page 157.

TIP

HTML signature. *If your message is in HTML format, your signature file can be an HTML document too. If you enjoy experimenting with HTML, you can create anything from an attractive or ornate signature to a humorous or truly obnoxious one. The signature file, however, cannot be any larger than 4 KB.*

Define Your Signature

1. In Outlook Express, choose Options from the Tools menu.

2. On the Signatures tab, click the New button.

3. Type the signature you want to use, or specify the text or HTML document that contains the signature.

4. Repeat steps 2 and 3 to create any additional signatures you might want to use. Select the signature you'll use the most, and click the Set As Default button.

5. Specify whether you want the signature added automatically to all outgoing messages and to replies and forwarded messages.

6. Click OK.

7. Create a message. If you chose not to automatically include the signature in all messages, point to Signature on the Insert menu, and select another signature that you want to use from the submenu.

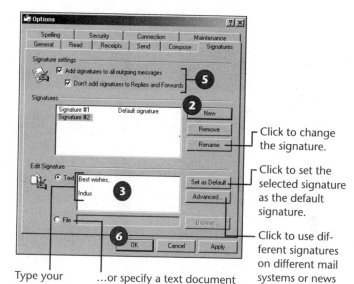

Type your signature text here...

...or specify a text document or an HTML document.

Click to change the signature.

Click to set the selected signature as the default signature.

Click to use different signatures on different mail systems or news servers.

9

Adding a Contact to the Contacts List

When you're using e-mail, you don't need to type an address every time you send a message; you can retrieve addresses from the Contacts list. All the names shown in the Contacts list are actually stored in your Address Book, a separate program that works with Outlook Express and other programs. If you frequently send one message to the same group of people, you can gather all their addresses into a *group,* and then all you need to find is that one address item. How convenient!

TIP

Add an address. *To add to your Address Book someone whose name is listed in the CC line of a message, double-click the message, and then right-click the name you want to add.*

Create a New Address

1. In Outlook Express, click Contacts at the top of the Contacts pane.

2. Click New Contact on the menu that appears.

3. On the different tabs of the Properties dialog box, enter the information you want to record.

4. Click OK.

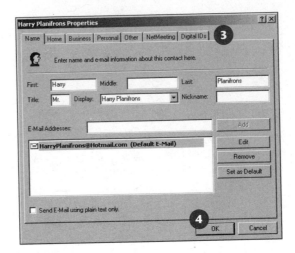

Add an Address from a Message

1. In the Inbox, right-click the message.

2. Choose Add Sender To Address Book from the shortcut menu. If the command is grayed (unavailable), click the message to download it, and then right-click it and choose the command again.

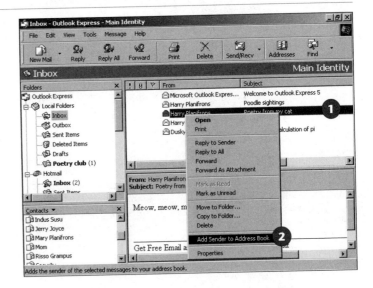

TIP

Add addresses manually.
You can collect addresses from other address books by using the Import command on the File menu, by clicking the Find button on the address book's toolbar to use a directory service, or by opening and importing an electronic business card (vCard) that someone sent you.

SEE ALSO

For information about electronic business cards and about exchanging detailed Address Book information, see "Sending a Business Card" on page 171.

TIP

Add addresses automatically. *To automatically add the addresses of all the people whose messages you reply to, choose Options from the Tools menu, and, on the Send tab, turn on the Automatically Put People I Reply To In My Address Book check box.*

Create a Group

1. Click the Addresses button on the toolbar.

2. On the Address Book toolbar, click the New button, and choose New Group from the menu.

3. Type a descriptive name, or *alias,* for the group.

4. Click the Select Members button.

5. Select from your Address Book the names of the people you want to include in the group.

6. Click the Select button.

7. When the Members list is complete, click OK.

8. Click OK.

9. Create and send a message using the group name in the To, CC, or BCC line. Everyone in the group will receive the message.

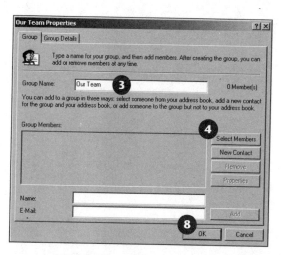

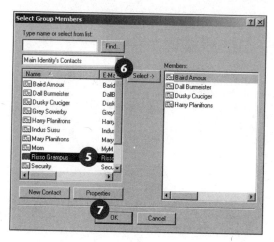

Defining Identities in Outlook Express

If more than one person uses Outlook Express on your computer, you can create individual identities so that each person has his or her own mail and news accounts, folders, and Contacts list.

TIP

Different identities.
If Outlook Express is set up to use different identities, the names in the Contacts list are the names in the Address Book for the current identity plus any names in the Shared Contacts folder of the Address Book.

TIP

Share addresses. *The Address Book stores information for individual identities in separate folders. To share addresses, open the Address Book, choose Folders And Groups from the View menu, and copy addresses into the Shared Contacts folder.*

Define an Identity

1. In Outlook Express, point to Identities on the File menu, and choose Add New Identity from the submenu.

2. Enter a name for the new identity.

3. Specify whether you want to require a password to switch to this identity, and click OK.

4. Click Yes when you're asked if you want to switch to the new identity.

5. Complete the Internet Connection Wizard to specify or set up an Internet e-mail account for the new identity.

6. Point to Identities on the File menu, and choose Manage Identities from the submenu.

7. Select the startup identity.

8. Select the default identity.

9. Click Close.

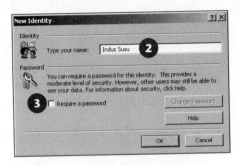

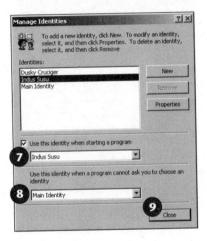

The Main Identity. *The Main Identity contains all the connections, settings, and addresses that you specified before you established the first new identity. To make all these contacts available to all the identities while you're logged on to the Main Identity in the Address Book, move all the contacts into the Shared Contacts folder.*

Switch Identities

1. Point to Identities on the File menu, and choose Switch Identities from the submenu.

2. Select an identity.

3. Type a password if one is required.

4. Click OK.

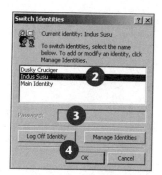

Share Contacts

1. Click the Addresses button on the Outlook Express toolbar.

2. Choose Folders And Groups from the View menu if the folders aren't already displayed.

3. Hold down the Ctrl key and click the addresses you want to share with others.

4. Drag the selected addresses into the Shared Contacts folder.

5. Close the Address Book when you've finished.

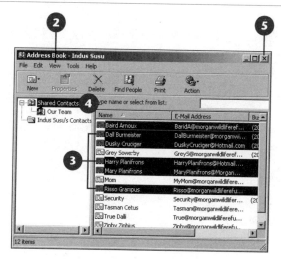

Customizing Outlook Express

Outlook Express doesn't have to look the same all the time; you can customize it to fit your individual working style. You can use the tools it provides to specify exactly how you want to navigate through your mail and news folders, and you can change the layout of the different parts of the window.

Change the Layout

1. In Outlook Express, choose Layout from the View menu to display the Window Layout Properties dialog box.

2. In the Basic section, turn on the tools you want to use.

3. Click the Customize Toolbar button if you want to add, delete, or move buttons on the toolbar. Click Close.

4. In the Preview Pane section of the Window Layout Properties dialog box, specify whether you want to use the preview pane and, if so, where you want it to be located and whether you want the message header to be shown in the preview pane.

5. Click OK.

The customized toolbar

The Outlook Bar

The Folder Bar; click to temporarily display folders.

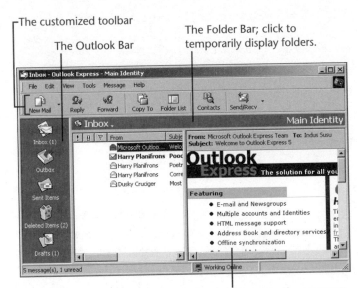

The preview pane next to the messages

The Folders list

The Views toolbar

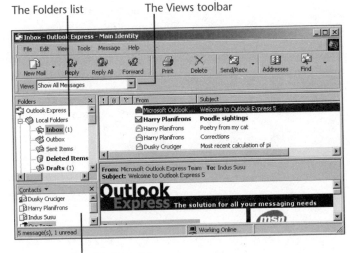

The Contacts list

Sending a Business Card

You can include an electronic business card, or *vCard,* with the e-mail and newsgroup messages you send from Outlook Express. This "virtual" card includes all the information listed in an Address Book entry, so—as well as your name, address, phone, and e-mail information—you can include your web-page address, NetMeeting connection information, digital ID, and any other information you want to provide.

SEE ALSO

For information about creating Address Book entries, see "Create a New Address" on page 166.

TIP

Delete a card. *To delete a business card from an outgoing message, choose Business Card from the Insert menu.*

Send Your Card

1. In Outlook Express, click Contacts at the top of the Contacts list, choose New Contact from the menu that appears, and create an entry for yourself, including the information you want to send to others.

2. Choose Options from the Tools menu.

3. On the Compose tab, under Business Cards, turn on the check box for Mail.

4. Select your name in the list.

5. If you want to include a business card with your newsgroup postings, turn on the check box for News, and select the same or a different card (one that contains less personal information, for example) from the list.

6. Click OK.

7. When you create a message, your business card will be included automatically.

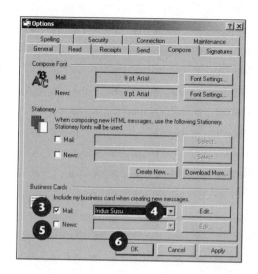

When recipients open the business card, they see all the information you've provided...

...and can easily add it to their Address Books.

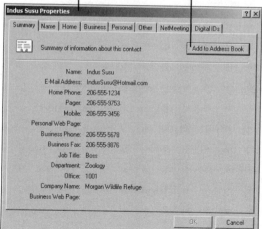

9

Sending and Receiving Secure Messages

If you're worried about prying eyes on the Internet, you can protect your mail messages by encrypting them so that only people with the correct *digital ID* can read them. You can also digitally sign your messages to authenticate their origin. You obtain your digital ID from a security provider, and then you exchange digital IDs with your intended recipients. You can't send an encrypted message without knowing your recipient's digital ID.

TIP

Network IDs. *Some networks issue their own digital IDs, so check your network documentation before obtaining an outside digital ID.*

Set Up Your Security

1. In Outlook Express, choose Options from the Tools menu, and click the Security tab.

2. Specify whether you want to digitally sign and encrypt all outgoing messages.

3. Click Get Digital ID, and follow the instructions provided to install the ID. Click OK to close the Options dialog box when you've finished.

4. Choose Accounts from the Tools menu.

5. On the Mail tab, select your mail service, and click Properties.

6. On the Security tab, under Signing Certificate, click Select, select the certificate for signing, and click OK.

7. Under Encrypting Preferences, click Select, select the same or a different certificate for encryption, and click OK.

8. Click OK to close the Properties dialog box, and click Close to close the Accounts dialog box.

Click to see detailed information about obtaining and using a digital ID.

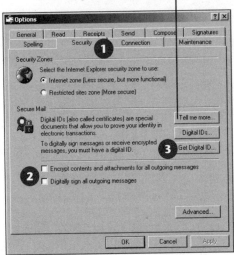

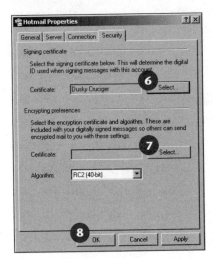

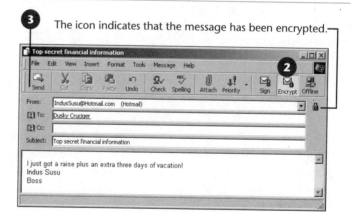

TIP

The key. *The digital ID you send out is your "public key." A private key is stored in your computer and is used along with the public key to decrypt messages. The private key exists only on your computer, so you can read encrypted messages only on that computer.*

TIP

Another way. *You can also exchange digital IDs using electronic business cards or an e-mail locator service.*

SEE ALSO

For information about sending an electronic business card, see "Sending a Business Card" on page 171.

TRY THIS

Find the key. *Click the down arrow next to the Find button on the Outlook Express toolbar, and select People. Select a directory service, type the e-mail address of the person you want to send an encrypted message to, and click Find Now. Select the person in the list, and click Add To Address Book. You should now have the public key to that person's digital ID.*

Exchange Digital IDs

1. Create a message, click the Sign button, and send the message. Have someone send you a digitally signed message.

2. In a digitally signed message you've received, click the Digital Signature button.

3. On the Security tab, click View Certificates.

4. In the View Certificates dialog box, click Add To Address Book, and click OK. Click OK again to close the message's Properties dialog box.

From: Dusky Cruciger To: Indus Susu
Subject: Here's my ID

Encryption

Encrypted contents and attachments: No
Encrypted using: n/a

View Certificates... Tell Me More...

OK Cancel

Click Add To Address Book to save the sender's encryption preferences to your address book.

Add to Address Book

OK Cancel

Send an Encrypted Message

1. Address a message to someone whose digital ID is listed in your Address Book.

2. Click the Encrypt button if you chose not to automatically encrypt all messages.

3. Send the message.

The icon indicates that the message has been encrypted.

Setting Up to Send Faxes

If your computer has a fax modem, Windows 2000 installs Fax Service, which allows you to send faxes through your computer. Before you use Fax Service, you need to provide some personal information that can be used on the fax cover page, enter the identification number for your fax, and set options for the way you want the fax to be sent.

Set the Send Options

1. Click the Start button, point your way through Programs, Accessories, Communications, and Fax, and choose Fax Service Management from the submenu.

2. In the Fax Service Management console, right-click Fax Service On Local Computer, and choose Properties from the shortcut menu.

3. Specify the options you want, and click OK.

4. Click Devices.

5. Double-click your device to display the modem's Properties dialog box.

6. Turn on the Enable Send check box.

7. Enter your fax number in the TSID box.

8. Click OK, and close the Fax Service Management window when you've finished.

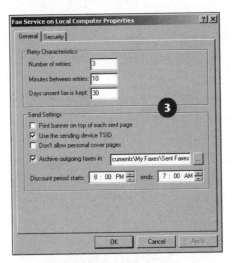

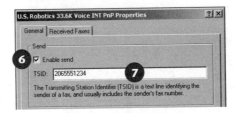

SEE ALSO

For information about creating your own cover pages, see "Creating a Fax Cover Page" on page 183.

TIP

Fax cover pages. *The Cover Pages tab is used to set up personal fax cover pages only. However, network administrators frequently set a system policy that prohibits personal fax cover pages. Check your network documentation before trying to specify a personal cover page.*

TIP

More options. *To change the paper size, image quality (resolution), or page orientation; to specify an e-mail address for notification that a fax has been sent; or to always record a billing code, right-click the Fax printer in the Printers folder, and choose Printing Preferences from the shortcut menu.*

Enter Your Information

1. Click the Start button, point to Settings, choose Control Panel from the submenu, and double-click the Fax icon.

2. On the User Information tab, enter your personal information.

3. On the Cover Pages tab, click a button to modify the available personal cover pages:

   ◆ Open to edit the selected cover page

   ◆ New to create a cover page

   ◆ Add to include an existing personal cover page

   ◆ Delete to remove the selected cover page from the list

4. Click OK.

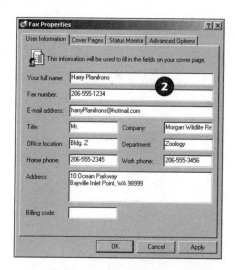

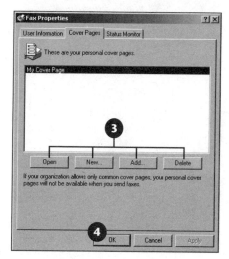

Setting Up to Receive Faxes

With a fax modem installed on your computer, you can set up your computer to receive faxes automatically or—if your have a single phone line that's used for both fax and voice—you can specify which calls you want to receive as faxes and which you want to answer yourself.

Fax

> **TIP**
>
> **The CSID.** *The CSID is the Called Subscriber Identifier. This identification is sent back to the sending fax device to confirm your identity, and it's also used in a log that records received faxes.*

Set the Receive Options

1 Click the Start button, point your way through Programs, Accessories, Communications, and Fax, and choose Fax Service Management.

2 In the Fax Service Management console, click Devices.

3 Double-click your device to display the modem's Properties dialog box.

4 Turn on the Enable Receive check box.

5 Enter your fax number in the CSID box.

6 Enter the number of times you want the modem to ring before Fax Service answers.

7 On the Received Faxes tab, specify whether you want received faxes printed, stored in a specific folder, or both.

8 Click OK.

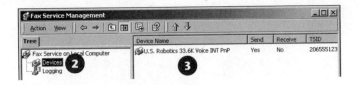

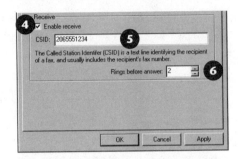

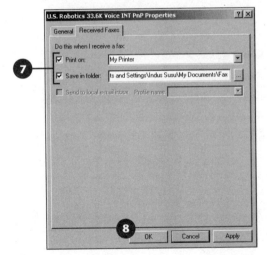

TIP

E-mail faxes. *To forward faxes to an e-mail Inbox, the computer must have a MAPI-enabled mail client, such as Microsoft Outlook, and the service must be run by someone with Administrator privileges.*

SEE ALSO

For information about receiving faxes automatically when you've set up your computer for manual reception, see "Receiving a Fax" on page 180.

Set the Receive Mode

1 Click the Start button, point to Settings, choose Control Panel from the submenu, and double-click the Fax icon.

2 On the Status Monitor tab, verify that the Display The Status Monitor check box is turned on.

3 Verify that the Display Icon On Taskbar check box is turned on.

4 Turn on the Enable Manual Answer For The First Device check box to use manual answering, or turn off the check box to have all incoming calls answered by Fax Service.

5 Click OK.

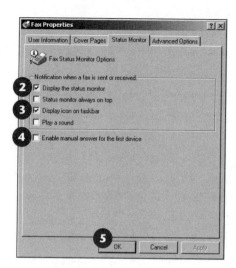

Sending a Fax

With Fax Service installed, you can send a single page with notes or a multipage document. To send some quick notes, simply enter them on a cover page. If you're sending a multipage document, you can decide whether or not to include a cover page.

TIP

About those wizards. *Some programs, such as Microsoft Word, have their own fax commands that step you through a wizard to create a cover page for a fax. After you've completed that wizard, you'll see the standard Send Fax Wizard, where you can choose not to include a cover page from Fax Service.*

TIP

Add the area code. *Turn on the Use Dialing Rules check box before you type the fax number if you want to specify the number's area code.*

Fax a Single Page

1. Click the Start button, point your way through Programs, Accessories, Communications, and Fax, and choose Send Cover Page Fax from the submenu.

2. In the Send Fax Wizard, create a list of recipients either by typing the name and fax number of a recipient or using the Address Book button to specify recipients. If you typed the information, click the Add button, and then repeat to add other recipients.

3. Specify whether you want to use dialing rules, and click Next.

4. Select a cover page.

5. Enter a subject line.

6. Type your note, and click Next.

7. Specify when you want the fax to be sent, and click Next.

8. Click Finish to send the fax to the fax queue.

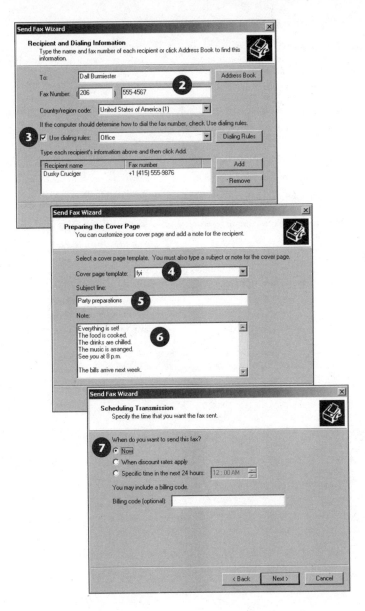

TIP

No Print dialog box? *If the program you're using doesn't display a Print dialog box, designate the Fax printer as the default printer before choosing the Print command.*

SEE ALSO

For information about setting a default printer, see "Specifying a Default Printer" on page 125.

For information about setting up Fax Service on your computer, see "Setting Up to Send Faxes" on page 174.

TIP

Identify sender and recipient. *If you're not going to include a cover page with your fax, make sure that the first page of the document contains the name of the person to whom you're sending the fax, as well as your name, fax number, and telephone number for callback in case there are any problems when you're sending the fax.*

Fax a Document

1. Open or create the document in its program.

2. Choose Print from the File menu.

3. Select the Fax printer as your printer.

4. Click Print.

5. Step through the Send Fax Wizard.

6. Click Finish to send the fax.

7. Repeat steps 1 through 6 to send any additional faxes.

8. Click the Start button, point your way through Programs, Accessories, Communications, and Fax, and choose Fax Queue from the submenu to review the status of your faxes. Close the Fax Queue window when you've finished.

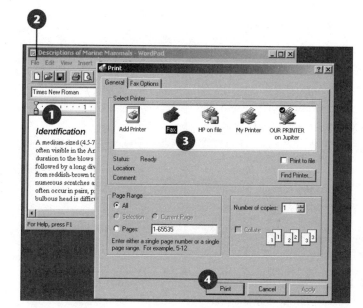

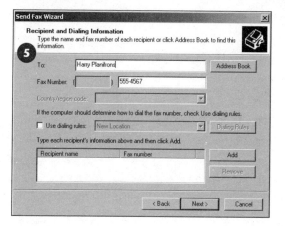

Receiving a Fax

How you receive a fax and what you do with it depends on your settings. If your computer is set up to receive and print faxes automatically, there's not much for you to do. If your computer is set up for manual fax reception, however, you'll need to tell the computer whether you want Fax Service to answer the call. Or, if you save the fax as a document without printing it, you can view it on your screen.

SEE ALSO

For information about setting your computer to receive faxes either manually or automatically, see "Set the Receive Mode" on page 177.

Receive a Fax Manually

1 When you receive the call and the Incoming Call dialog box appears, click Yes when you hear a fax tone to have Fax Service answer, or click No to use a phone to answer the call.

2 If you want to receive the next call (or a series of calls) as a fax, turn on the Answer Next Call As Fax check box in the Fax Monitor window. Turn off the check box if you want to be prompted as to whether you want Fax Service to answer incoming calls.

Displays a log listing all events since Fax Service was started.

TIP

Editing a fax. *When you open a fax for editing, you can choose to automatically open any future faxes using the Imaging program instead of the Imaging Preview program. If the fax opens in a program other than Imaging or Imaging Preview, the .tif file type association has been changed.*

SEE ALSO

For information about changing the type of program in which a file opens, see "Open a Document in a Different Program" on page 29.

For information about specifying where your received faxes are stored and whether they are to be automatically printed when received, see "Set the Receive Options" on page 176.

For information about annotating a fax, see "Annotating a Fax" on page 182.

View a Fax

1. Right-click the Fax icon on the taskbar, and choose My Faxes from the shortcut menu to open the folder containing your received faxes.

2. Double-click the fax you want to read.

3. Do any of the following:

   ◆ Choose Print from the File menu, choose a non-fax printer, and click Print.

   ◆ Use a Zoom control to view the fax.

   ◆ Use a Rotate button if the fax is oriented sideways or is upside down.

   ◆ Use the Page Control to view different pages of the fax.

   ◆ Click the Open Image For Editing button to annotate the fax.

4. Close the Imaging Preview window when you've finished.

The Open Image For Editing button   The Rotate buttons

The Zoom controls

The Page Control buttons

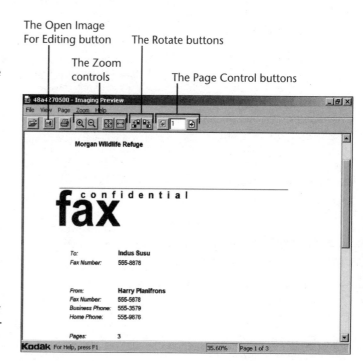

9

Annotating a Fax

When you receive a fax as a document, you can open it and annotate it—stamp it with the date on which it was received, for example, or place notes on it for others to review.

TRY THIS

The Date stamp. *Click the Rubber Stamp tool, and choose Received from the menu. Click in a blank spot near the top of the first page. Then click the Annotation Selection tool, click the received-date stamp, and drag it to a different location if you want.*

Annotate the Fax

1. Open the folder containing your received faxes, and double-click the fax you want to annotate.

2. If the fax appears in the Imaging Preview program, click the Open Image For Editing button.

3. Choose Page And Thumbnails from the View menu.

4. Click the page you want to annotate.

5. Click an Annotation tool. If the Annotation toolbar isn't displayed, choose Toolbars from the View menu, turn on the Annotation check box, and click OK.

6. Use the tool to annotate the fax.

7. Use the Annotation Selection tool to select any annotation and to move, delete, or resize the annotation.

8. Click the Save button.

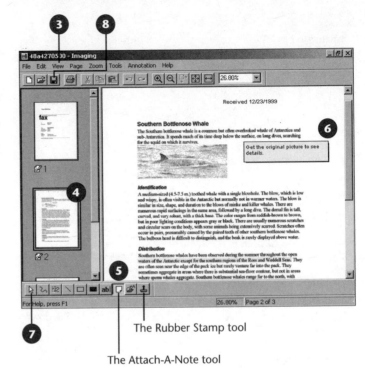

The Rubber Stamp tool

The Attach-A-Note tool

Creating a Fax Cover Page

Whenever you send a fax, it's good practice to include a cover page that contains information about the recipient and the sender, as well as the number of pages being sent. Fax Service comes with some standard cover pages, but you can create your own cover pages that contain the information you want in the design of your choice.

TIP

No personal cover pages.
Some corporate system policies prevent you from using personal cover pages. Check your network documentation to see whether such restrictions exist.

Create a Cover Page

1. Click the Start button, point to Settings, choose Control Panel from the submenu, and double-click the Fax icon.

2. On the Cover Pages tab, click New.

3. To base the page on an existing cover page, choose Open from the File menu, locate the page you want, and click Open.

4. Add elements to the cover page:

   ◆ Use the Text tool to insert a text box and add formatted text.

   ◆ Use the Insert menu to add data fields that insert information about the recipient, the sender, or the message.

   ◆ Use the Alignment tools to arrange the elements.

5. Save the cover page, using a different filename if you modified an existing cover page. Close the Fax Cover Page Editor when you've finished, and then close the Fax Properties dialog box.

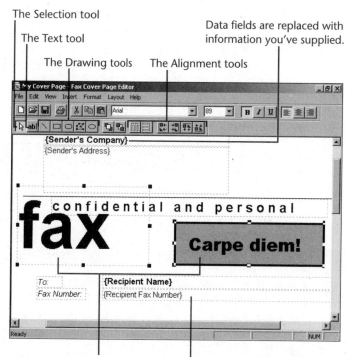

The Selection tool

The Text tool

The Drawing tools   The Alignment tools

Data fields are replaced with information you've supplied.

Select several elements by dragging the Selection tool over them, and then position them using the Alignment tools.

Drag an existing data field into a new position, or delete it. Add a new data field using the Insert menu.

Conferring on the Net

Microsoft NetMeeting provides services that let you hold a private meeting over the Internet or your company's intranet. NetMeeting lets you locate other participants, connect, and then confer using text "chats" or voice conversations; you can also deliver video from one location. The first time you run NetMeeting, a wizard walks you through the setup and asks you to provide the necessary information. After that, you can use a directory service to connect, or you can call colleagues on your network.

TIP

NetMeeting requirements. *NetMeeting must be running on a meeting participant's computer before he or she can receive a call. To receive a call using a directory service, a participant must already be logged on to the same directory you're using.*

Connect Using a Directory

1. Click the Start button, point your way through Programs, Accessories, and Communications, and choose NetMeeting from the submenu. If you haven't completed the NetMeeting Wizard, do so now.

2. From the Call menu, use the Log On command to log on to the directory if you're not already logged on. Connect to the Internet if necessary.

3. Click the Place Call button.

4. Type the e-mail address of the person you want to call.

5. Select Directory from the Using list.

6. Click Call.

7. If you don't know the person's e-mail address, click the Find Someone button, and search the directory or your Address Book to locate and call the person.

8. Repeat steps 3 through 7 to make additional connections.

Click to end a call.

A list of the meeting's participants

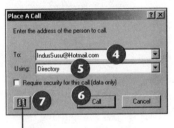

Click here to search for someone who's logged on to the directory.

Wide search. *In the Find Someone dialog box, you can choose to search the Microsoft Internet Directory, your company directory, your Address Book, or your history of previously placed calls.*

NetMeeting or Phone Dialer? *NetMeeting is best for conducting an online working session in which you're exchanging notes, sharing programs, and transferring files, or for holding a conference when you don't have access to a videoconferencing server. For simple phone calls, Internet and network voice calls, or full voice and video-conferencing when you do have access to a conferencing server, use Phone Dialer.*

For information about conducting online meetings, see "Sharing Programs On Line" on page 88.

For information about sharing your contact information, including your NetMeeting contact address, see "Sending a Business Card" on page 171.

Connect over a Network

1 Click the Place Call button.

2 Type the computer name or IP address.

3 Select Network from the Using list.

4 Click Call, and wait for the person you're calling to accept the call.

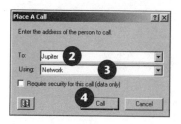

Receive a Call

Do either of the following:

◆ Choose Automatically Accept Calls from the File menu to answer incoming calls automatically.

◆ Click the Accept or the Ignore button to answer incoming calls manually.

If you don't want to accept all calls automatically, you can choose which ones to answer.

9

Making a Phone Call

If you frequently make phone calls from your computer, Phone Dialer can make your connections easy. Depending on the directory services you have—Active Directory, ILS (Internet Listing Service) directories, or conferencing servers, for example—you can also make calls over the Internet or an intranet, and conduct multiparty conferences or full videoconferencing.

TRY THIS

Phone log. *Make a series of calls using Phone Dialer. Then choose Show Log from the Tools menu. Voilà—details of all your completed calls!*

Call Someone in Your Address Book

1. Click the Start button, point to Programs and then Accessories, and choose Address Book from the submenu.

2. Right-click the name of the person you want to call, point to Action on the shortcut menu, and choose Dial from the submenu.

3. In the New Call dialog box, select the number to call if there's more than one number listed.

4. Click the Call button.

5. After you've dialed the number, pick up the phone.

6. When you've finished, hang up the phone and click Disconnect.

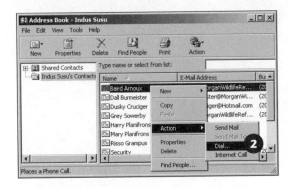

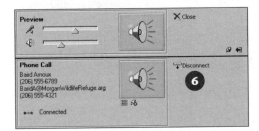

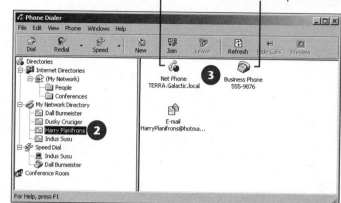

TIP

Receive a call. *To receive an Internet call or a network call on your computer, you must have Phone Dialer or NetMeeting running.*

TIP

No one there. *If your network is running Active Directory but no one is listed in the My Network Directory, choose Add User from the Edit menu to add users from the Active Directory to your local directory.*

TIP

Conferencing server. *Phone Dialer provides support for voice and video conferences only when you're connected to a conferencing server. To join an existing conference, click the Conferences folder, select the conference, and click Join.*

Call Someone in the Directory

1. If Phone Dialer isn't running, click the Start button, point your way through Programs, Accessories, and Communications, and choose Phone Dialer from the submenu.

2. Select the name of the person you want to call.

3. Double-click the type of call you want to make.

4. Wait for the call to be answered.

5. Use your computer's microphone and speakers (or headset) to talk to the recipient of a Net Phone call, or use your telephone to talk to the recipient of a standard phone call.

6. Click Disconnect when you've finished.

Double-click to make an Internet or intranet call.

Double-click to make a standard telephone call.

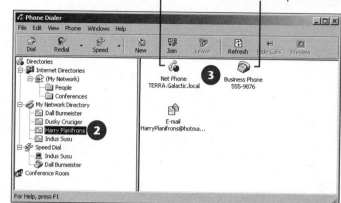

9

10

Traveling

IN THIS SECTION

Tracking Copied Files

**Taking Along
Network Files**

**Securing Files
with Encryption**

**Connecting from
Different Locations**

**Logging On
to a Network from
a Remote Location**

**Connecting to a
Computer or a Network
over the Internet**

**Connecting
with a Terminal**

**Connecting Two
Computers with a Cable**

**Storing Information
on a Removable Disk**

**Downloading Files
over the Internet**

If your work involves traveling, read this section before you take off! If you use different computers in different locations, or if your computer is connected only sporadically to a network, this section of the book will help you avoid the pesky problems that can occur when you're working long distance. We'll show you how to store network files and folders on your traveling computer so that you can access any of the files when you're not connected to the network. To easily transfer and keep track of the files you use on different computers, you can pack the files into your Microsoft Windows 2000 Briefcase and then update them back at the office.

You can connect to your network or to a specific computer from a remote location over a telephone line or with a secure connection over the Internet. You can even set up a connection that lets you control your office computer from a remote computer! If you're worried about security, you can encrypt your files to prevent unauthorized use. You can download files over the Internet using FTP (File Transfer Protocol), and you can connect directly to bulletin boards or other types of terminal services with HyperTerminal. Even without access to a network or the Internet, you can transfer files between computers via modem or by using a cable to create a temporary network connection between two computers.

Tracking Copied Files

When your work travels with you, whether it's from your office to your home or to the other side of the world, you often need to take copies of files from your main desktop computer and use them on a different computer. If you've done this a lot, and you're aware of how difficult it can be to keep track of the most recently changed version of a file, you're going to like the Windows 2000 Briefcase. Okay, so it's not made of fine Corinthian leather. You won't care when you see how easily you can synchronize the changes you make in your traveling files with the originals on your main computer.

SEE ALSO

For information about using network files on a computer that is only sometimes connected to the network, see "Taking Along Network Files" on page 192.

Use the Briefcase

1. Right-click a blank spot on the Desktop or in a folder window, point to New, and choose Briefcase from the shortcut menu. Give the new Briefcase a descriptive name.

2. Open a folder window, and drag files or folders onto the new Briefcase icon.

3. If a welcome screen appears the first time you use the Briefcase, click the Finish button.

4. Open the My Computer window, and drag the Briefcase onto the removable disk.

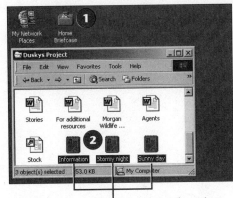

Dragging these files onto the Briefcase icon copies the files into the Briefcase.

SEE ALSO

For information about adding the Briefcase to the Send To menu, see "Create Your Own Special Location" on page 63.

TIP

Disk capacity. *Be aware of the capacity of the removable disk you'll be using to hold the Briefcase, and be careful not to add so many files to the Briefcase that it won't fit on the disk.*

TIP

Orphaned files. *Once you've copied a file into the Briefcase, don't move or make changes to the original file. If you do, the file in the Briefcase will become an "orphan," and you won't be able to update the original file from the file in the Briefcase. If you have orphaned a Briefcase file, you'll need to save it using a different filename.*

Use the Files

1. Insert the removable disk into your other computer, drag the Briefcase from the disk onto the Desktop or into a folder window, and double-click the Briefcase icon.

2. Double-click a file to use it, and save the file to the Briefcase. When you've finished, drag the Briefcase from the Desktop to the removable disk.

Update the Files

1. Insert the disk into your main computer. Open the My Computer window, open a window for the disk, and drag the Brief-case onto the Desktop.

2. Double-click the Briefcase icon.

3. To update

   ◆ A single file, select the file, and choose Update Selection from the toolbar.

   ◆ All files, choose Update All.

4. Click Update to confirm the updating.

The Briefcase records the location of the original files...   ...and tracks which files have been changed.

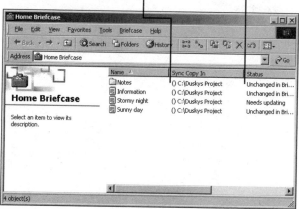

The Update All button   The Update Selection button

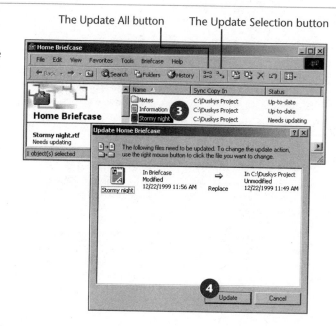

10

Taking Along Network Files

If your computer isn't always connected to your network, you can set up your system so that specific network files and folders are stored locally on your computer, using the identical folder structure as that of the network. Then, when you're traveling—or if you simply want to work off line—you can work as if you were still connected to the network. When you reconnect to the network, you can synchronize the contents of the files and folders on your computer with those on the network.

TIP

Offline documents. *For quick access to offline documents, leave a folder window open to a folder that's set to be used off line when you disconnect from the network.*

Make Files Available Off Line

1. Open the My Computer window, and choose Folder Options from the Tools menu.

2. On the Offline Files tab, turn on the Enable Offline Files check box.

3. Click OK.

4. Locate and select the files or folders on the network that you want to be available to you off line, right-click one of the selected items, and choose Make Available Offline from the shortcut menu.

5. Step through the Offline Files Wizard, specifying whether you want the offline files automatically synchronized when you log on and log off.

6. If you selected any folders that contain subfolders, specify whether you want the subfolders to be available off line.

7. Wait for the files to be synchronized. Repeat step 4 for any additional files or folders that you want to use off line.

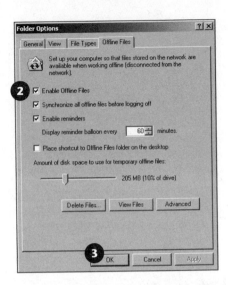

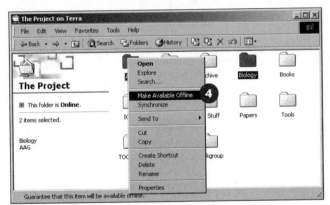

SEE ALSO

For information about making your files automatically available to others when they work off line, see "Making Shared Documents Always Available" on page 86.

TIP

Manual synchronization.

If you chose not to have the files synchronized automatically when you log on and log off, select the folders you want to use off line before you disconnect from the network, and choose Synchronize from the File menu. After you've reconnected to the network, choose Synchronize again.

TIP

Forced synchronization.

If—despite having been set up for automatic synchronization—your files aren't synchronized after your computer has reconnected to the network, right-click the Offline Files icon, and choose Synchronize from the shortcut menu.

Use the Files

1 Disconnect from the network.

2 Work with the files off line just as you would if you were on line.

3 If you can't find a particular offline file, right-click the Offline Files icon in the status area of the taskbar, and choose View Files from the shortcut menu.

4 When you reconnect to the network, wait for the files to be synchronized.

5 If changes have been made to both your local version of a file and the original network file, specify how you want to resolve the conflict in the Resolve File Conflicts dialog box that appears.

Folders and files marked as being off line are available to you when you've disconnected from the network.

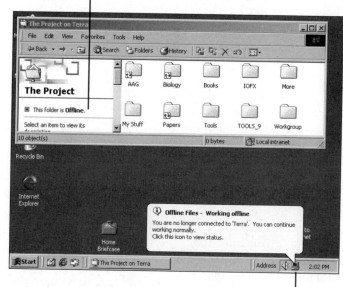

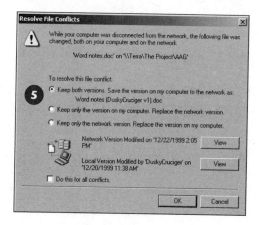

The Offline Files icon

Securing Files with Encryption

When you're traveling, your computer and your files are at risk. Windows 2000 can't prevent your computer from being stolen, but if your hard disk is set up with NTFS (the NT file system), you can encrypt your sensitive files and thereby prevent anyone from hacking into the computer and reading them. Encrypting also prevents those who do have permission to access your computer from viewing any sensitive files. Only when you log on are those files available.

SEE ALSO

For information about setting up your hard disk with NTFS, see "Changing Your Disk Format" on page 299.

Encrypt the Files

1. Right-click the folder containing the files you want to encrypt, and choose Properties from the shortcut menu.

2. On the General tab of the folder's Properties dialog box, click the Advanced button.

3. Turn on the Encrypt Contents To Secure Data check box.

4. Click OK.

5. Click OK.

6. In the Confirm Attribute Changes dialog box that appears, click the Apply Changes To This Folder, Subfolders And Files option.

7. Click OK.

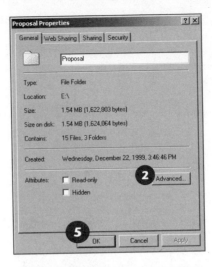

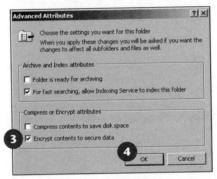

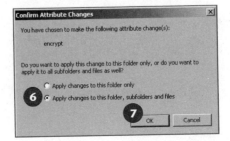

Connecting from Different Locations

If you travel around a lot—breakfast in New York, lunch in Chicago, and dinner in Seattle, perhaps—and you dial in to your corporate network or your online service, or you use other telephone features from your computer from each location, you need to tell Windows 2000 where you're calling from so that it can use the correct dialing properties for that location.

Phone and
Modem
Options

TIP

Easy dialing. *Once a dialing location has been set up, you can select it from the Dialing From list.*

Create a New Location

1 Click the Start button, point to Settings, and choose Control Panel from the submenu.

2 Double-click the Phone And Modem Options icon.

3 Click the New button.

4 On the General tab, type a name for the location, and enter the dialing information.

5 On the Area Code Rules tab, click New. In the New Area Code Rule dialog box, enter an area code, and specify the prefixes you want to include. Under Rules, specify whether to include the area code and/or an access number when dialing. Click OK when you've finished.

6 If you want to use a calling card, provide your calling card information on the Calling Card tab.

7 Click OK.

8 Specify the location from which you'll be calling.

9 Click OK.

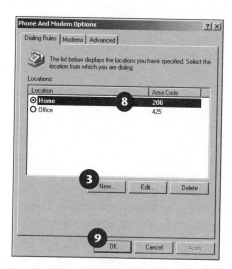

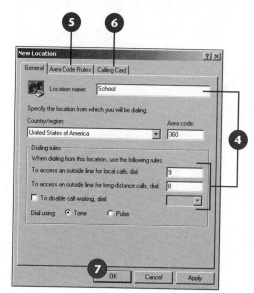

Calling to Your Computer

If you want to connect to your computer by telephone from another computer or give access to others to facilitate file transfer between computers, you can set your computer to automatically accept incoming phone calls. By specifying the users who are authorized to connect, you control who can gain access to your computer. Once connected, the connecting computer can access shared folders on the host computer.

SEE ALSO

For information about sharing folders, see "Sharing Your Computer" on page 78.

For information about controlling your computer remotely, see "Controlling Your Computer Remotely" on page 202.

Create a Host Computer

1. On the computer to which you want to gain access, right-click the My Network Places icon on the Desktop, and choose Properties from the shortcut menu.

2. Double-click the Make New Connection icon.

3. In the Network Connection Wizard, click the Accept Incoming Connections option.

4. Select the modem to be used, and specify that you don't want to permit a virtual private connection.

5. Specify the users who are authorized to connect.

6. Complete the wizard by specifying the networking protocols and supplying a name for the connection. Click the Finish button.

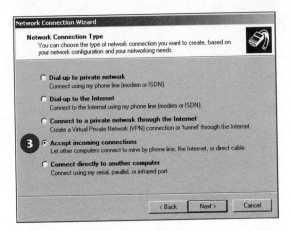

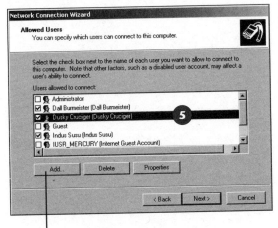

Click to add a user who's not already registered on this computer.

TIP

Adding users. *The users who are listed in the wizard are those who have been authorized to log on locally to the computer. When you add users to the dial-in connection, you're also adding them to the list of users who can log on locally to the computer.*

SEE ALSO

For information about connecting to a server on the network and gaining full access to network resources, see "Logging On to a Network from a Remote Location" on page 199.

For information about adding new users to a computer, see "Adding New Users" on page 284.

TIP

Reconnecting. *To reconnect to the host computer, either double-click the shortcut the Network Connection Wizard created on your Desktop (if you selected that option) or double-click the connection in the Network And Dial-Up Connections window.*

Connect to the Host Computer

1. On the computer from which you want to connect to the host computer, right-click the My Network Places icon on the Desktop, and choose Properties from the shortcut menu.

2. Double-click the Make New Connection icon.

3. In the Network Connection Wizard, click the Dial-Up To Private Network option.

4. Enter the phone number of the host computer, and turn on the Use Dialing Rules option if the number is outside your own area code.

5. Complete the wizard, enter a name for the connection, and click the Finish button.

6. Enter your user name and password.

7. Click Dial, and wait to be authorized.

8. Click the Dial-Up icon in the status area of the taskbar to disconnect from the host computer when you've finished.

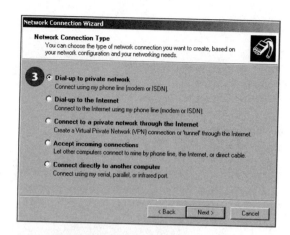

10

Connecting to a Network by Modem

If you have permission to dial in to a network that has dial-up network services, you can connect to the network using your modem. Once you're connected, your access to network resources depends on the permission you've been granted by the network administrator. You need to set up the connection only once; you can reuse it by double-clicking it in the Network And Dial-Up Connections window.

> **TIP**
>
> **Who goes there?** *If your name and password are validated by the dial-up server but your computer or domain name isn't recognized, you might be asked for your user name and password each time you open a folder or use a network resource.*

Connect

1 Get your connection specifications from the network administrator.

2 Right-click the My Network Places icon on the Desktop, and choose Properties from the shortcut menu.

3 Double-click the Make New Connection icon.

4 In the Network Connection Wizard, click the Dial-Up To Private Network option, and step through the wizard. When you've completed the wizard, click the Finish button.

5 In the dialog box that appears, enter the user name and password you've been assigned.

6 Click the Properties button.

7 Use the connection specifications you received to set the options on the Options, Security, and Networking tabs, and click OK.

8 Click Dial. If prompted, enter your user name, password, and domain name for network access.

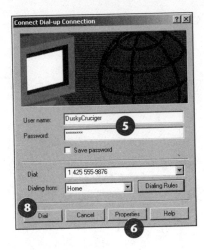

Your options settings must match your connection specifications; otherwise, the connection will fail.

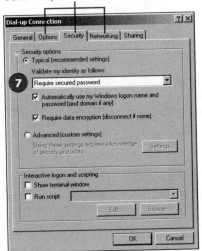

Logging On to a Network from a Remote Location

When you log on to a network from a remote location, you can access the network just as if you were in the office, although everything might work a bit more slowly. In order for you to log on remotely, your computer must be configured exactly as if it were connected directly to the network. If possible, set your computer up before you go traveling.

SEE ALSO

For information about creating a dial-up connection, see "Connecting to a Network by Modem" on the facing page.

For information about creating a VPN connection, see "Connecting to a Computer or a Network over the Internet" on page 200.

Log On to the Network

1. Create a dial-up or a VPN (Virtual Private Network) connection to the network if one doesn't already exist.

2. If your computer is already running, log off. When you log on, enter your network user name and password, and, if necessary, your domain name.

3. Turn on the Log On Using Dial-Up Connection check box, and click OK.

4. In the Network And Dial-Up Connections dialog box, select the dial-up connection you created, and click Dial.

5. In the Connect Dial-Up Connection dialog box, verify the user name, password, and number to dial, and click Dial.

6. Work on the network as usual. When you've finished, log off.

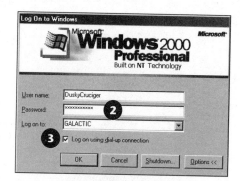

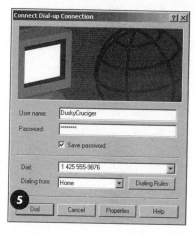

10

Connecting to a Computer or a Network over the Internet

Remote telephone connections to a network can be expensive and troublesome, especially if you're connecting from a long distance. With a VPN (Virtual Private Network) connection, you need only be connected to the Internet, and the VPN connection creates a secure, private connection to the network.

Create a VPN Connection

1. Get the connection specifications from the computer administrator or the network administrator.

2. Right-click the My Network Places icon on the Desktop, and choose Properties from the shortcut menu.

3. Double-click the Make New Connection icon.

4. In the Network Connection Wizard, click the Connect To A Private Network Through The Internet option, and click Next.

5. Specify
   - Whether you'll need to dial in to connect to the Internet, and, if so, the connection.
   - The host computer name or IP address.

6. Complete the wizard. In the Connect dialog box, click Properties, and use the connection specifications you received to set the options on the Security, Networking, and Options tabs. Click OK. Then click Dial to connect or Cancel to use the connection at a later time.

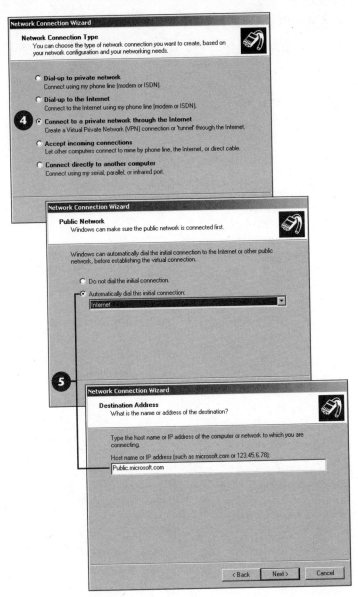

TIP

Connect. *The first time you create the connection, the connection process starts automatically. For subsequent connections, either double-click the shortcut the wizard created on the Desktop (if you selected that option) or double-click the connection in the Network And Dial-Up Connections window.*

TIP

More about VPNs. *A VPN connection is not exclusive to the Internet; it can be used on a company's private network to provide extra security for sensitive information.*

SEE ALSO

For information about logging directly onto the network using a remote connection, see "Log On to the Network" on page 199.

Connect to the Network

1. Double-click the connection if the connection process hasn't started automatically.

2. If you're not connected to the Internet, click Dial in the Connect dialog box that appears for your Internet connection.

3. In the Connect dialog box for the VPN connection, enter your user name and password, and click Connect.

4. If you're prompted for additional information, provide your user name, password, and domain name for the computer, and click OK.

5. Once you're logged on, work on the network as usual. When you've finished, log off from the network if you're prompted to do so.

6. Click the VPN Dial-Up Networking icon on the taskbar.

7. Click the Disconnect button.

First connect to the Internet...

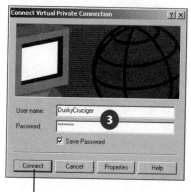

...and then create the VPN connection to the network.

10

Controlling Your Computer Remotely

Do you need access from your home computer to the computer at your workplace? Or do you need to access your workplace computer from another office or from somewhere on the network? No problem! You can use Microsoft NetMeeting to allow one computer to be controlled remotely by another computer.

SEE ALSO

For information about starting NetMeeting, see "Conferring on the Net" on page 184.

For information about using a password-protected screen saver, see "Using a Screen Saver" on page 230.

Share the Desktop

1 Log on as a user with Administrator rights to the computer you want to access from other locations, and start NetMeeting if it's not already running.

2 From the Tools menu, choose Remote Desktop Sharing.

3 Step through the Remote Desktop Sharing Wizard. Be sure to set up a password-protected screen saver when you're prompted to do so.

4 Close NetMeeting when you've finished.

5 Right-click the NetMeeting Remote Desktop Sharing icon in the status area of the taskbar, and choose Activate Remote Desktop Sharing from the short-cut menu.

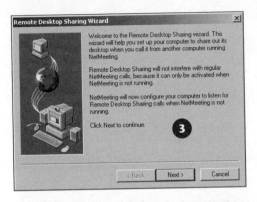

The NetMeeting Remote Desktop Sharing icon

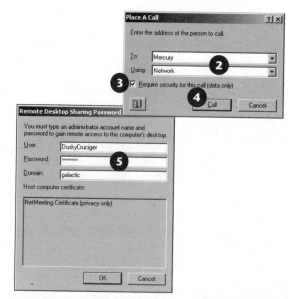

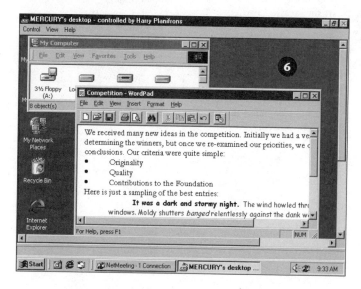

TIP

Hands off! *Using a password-protected screen saver prevents other people from using your computer while it's unattended.*

TIP

Deactivate Remote Desktop Sharing. *To deactivate Remote Desktop Sharing on your computer, right-click the NetMeeting Remote Desktop Sharing icon on the taskbar, and choose Turn Off Remote Sharing from the shortcut menu to temporarily deactivate the feature. To permanently remove the Remote Desktop Sharing feature, start NetMeeting, choose Remote Desktop Sharing from the Tools menu, and turn off the Enable Remote Desktop Sharing On This Computer check box.*

Connect to the Computer

1 On the computer that you'll use to remotely control your office computer, connect to your company's network if necessary, start NetMeeting if it's not already running, and click Place Call.

2 Enter the name of the computer you're calling.

3 Turn on the check box to require security.

4 Click the Call button.

5 Enter your user name, password, and domain, and click OK. (You must have administrative rights for the computer you're connecting to.)

6 Work from the Desktop of the computer you're controlling remotely.

7 Click the End Call button in the NetMeeting program when you've finished.

Connecting with a Terminal

When you need to connect by modem with a terminal—a bulletin board, for example—you can do so using HyperTerminal. HyperTerminal is a program provided by Windows 2000 that lets your computer function as a terminal. And if you have problems connecting or communicating, you can modify the settings to improve the connection.

TIP

Telnet. *To connect to a server as a Telnet terminal, click the Start button, choose Run from the menu, type* telnet *in the Open box, and click Enter.*

Set Up Your Terminal

1. Click the Start button, point your way through Programs, Accessories, and Communications, and choose HyperTerminal from the submenu.

2. Type an identifying name for the connection, select an icon, and click OK.

3. Enter your phone information and your connection method, and click OK.

4. Select the location you're dialing from, and click the Dial button.

5. Use the sign-on information you've been assigned, and verify that the information is being displayed correctly.

6. Sign off, and click the Disconnect button.

Scroll up to see text that has scrolled off the window. Text from previous sessions is also shown.

Click to disconnect.

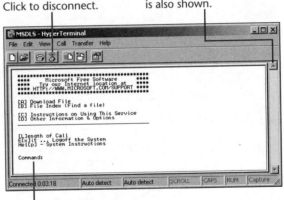

Follow the directions of the host terminal.

Cable connection. *Your connection to another computer doesn't have to be a modem connection. To connect two computers with a cable, choose the correct COM port from the Connect Using list in the Connect To dialog box that appears when you're setting up HyperTerminal.*

Window size. *To change the size of the terminal window, choose Font from the View menu, and select a different font and/or font size. Then choose Snap from the View menu to have the entire HyperTerminal window snap to the size of the terminal window.*

Terminal Services. *Don't confuse HyperTerminal with Terminal Services. Terminal Services is a Windows 2000 Server feature that allows a client computer (not necessarily one that's running Windows 2000) to run programs directly on the server.*

Modify the Connection

1 Click the Properties button on the HyperTerminal toolbar.

2 On the Settings tab, click the ASCII Setup button.

3 Modify the settings as shown in the table, below right.

4 Click OK.

5 Click OK in the Properties dialog box.

6 Choose Save from the File menu.

7 Try your connection again.

CONNECTION-SETTING TROUBLESHOOTING	
If you have this problem	**Make this setting**
The text you send is in one long line.	Turn on the Send Line Ends With Line Feeds check box.
You don't see what you send.	Turn on the Echo Typed Characters Locally check box.
Some of the text you send isn't received.	Enter *1* for Line Delay. Increase the value if necessary.
Some of the characters you send drop out.	Enter *1* for Character Delay. Increase the value if necessary.
The text you receive is in one long line.	Turn on the Append Line Feeds To Incoming Line Ends check box.
The text you receive is garbled.	Turn on the Force Incoming Data To 7-Bit ASCII check box.
The ends of lines aren't visible.	Turn on the Wrap Lines That Exceed Terminal Width check box.

10

Transferring Files by Modem

If you want to transfer files directly between computers via modem, you can transfer them the old-fashioned way—that is, from terminal to terminal. There is no limitation on file size, and you'll probably get the maximum speed from your modem. You can even use this method to transfer data between two computers of different types, including mainframes and computers that aren't running Windows 2000 Professional, provided the other computer has a modem and communications software. However, the procedure described here assumes that both computers are using HyperTerminal.

SEE ALSO

For information about setting up a HyperTerminal connection, see "Connecting with a Terminal" on page 204.

Set Up the Terminals

1. On the host computer, click the Start button, point your way through Programs, Accessories, and Communications, and choose HyperTerminal from the submenu.

2. In the Connection Description dialog box, name the connection, and click OK.

3. In the Connect To dialog box, click Cancel.

4. Click the Properties button on the toolbar, and click the ASCII Setup button on the Settings tab.

5. Turn on the Send Line Ends With Line Feeds and Echo Typed Characters Locally check boxes. Click OK, and click OK again to close the Properties dialog box.

6. On the calling computer, repeat steps 1 through 5, but in step 3, enter the phone number of the host computer in the Connect To dialog box. Click OK, and then click Cancel in the Connect dialog box.

7. On each computer, choose Save from the File menu to save the settings.

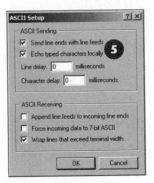

Transmission speed. *If the transmission is extremely slow, verify that the modem or the COM port is set to work at its maximum speed. If you're getting too many errors, reduce the transmission speed. To adjust the speed, choose Properties from the File menu, and click the Configure button on the Connect To tab.*

For information about transferring a file by attaching it to an e-mail message, see "Sending and Receiving Attachments" on page 156.

For information about transferring a file over the Internet using NetMeeting, see "Conferring on the Net" on page 184.

For information about making a network connection to your computer via modem, see "Calling to Your Computer" on page 196.

For information about connecting to your network via modem, see "Connecting to a Network by Modem" on page 198.

Connect the Computers

1. On the answering computer, choose Wait For A Call from the Call menu.

2. On the calling computer, click the Connect button and then the Dial button.

3. Type messages to each other to coordinate the transfer.

4. On the computer that will receive the file, click the Receive button on the HyperTerminal toolbar, specify the folder and protocol for the file, and click Close.

5. On the computer that's sending the file, click the Send button on the HyperTerminal toolbar, locate the file, and click Send.

6. Wait for the file to be sent.

7. Click the Disconnect button when you've finished.

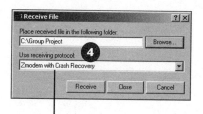

Use the same protocol on both computers.

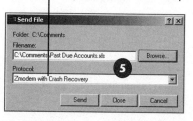

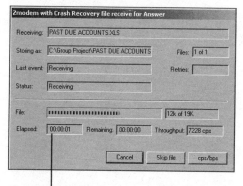

The status of the file transfer is displayed. Both computers receive the status information.

10

Connecting Two Computers with a Cable

To transfer information between two Windows 2000 computers that aren't normally connected—a notebook computer and a desktop computer, for example—you connect them with a cable that links their parallel or serial ports. The cable creates a network connection between the two computers so that you can use the network computer to access the files and folders on the portable computer.

Configure the Computers

1. Connect the cable between the two computers.

2. On the portable computer, right-click the My Network Places icon on the Desktop, and choose Properties from the shortcut menu.

3. Double-click the Make New Connection icon.

4. In the Network Connection Wizard, click the Connect Directly To Another Computer option, and click Next.

5. Step through the wizard, specifying that this computer is the host, which port the cable is connected to, and who is authorized to connect. Type a name for the connection.

6. Repeat steps 2 through 4 for the desktop computer. Then step through the wizard again, specifying that this computer is the guest and which port the cable is connected to.

Specify which computer is the host and which the guest.

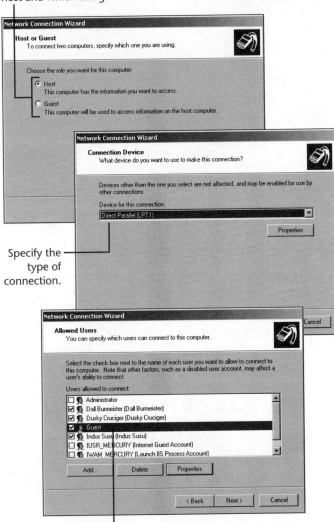

Specify the type of connection.

On the host computer, specify who is authorized to connect.

TIP

Infrared ports. *If both computers are equipped with infrared communication ports, you can use these ports instead of using a cable.*

SEE ALSO

For information about sharing folders, see "Sharing Documents and Folders" on page 80, "Limiting Access to a Shared Folder" on page 82, and "Monitoring Who's Connected" on page 84.

TIP

Cable connection. *The fastest way to transfer information between computers when you're using a cable connection is with a parallel connection. For more information, connect to the Parallel Technologies web site at http://www.lpt.com. You can make a serial connection with an RS-232 null-modem cable.*

TIP

Reverse the roles. *To use your portable computer to access the files and resources on your desktop computer, designate the portable computer as the guest and the desktop computer as the host.*

Exchange Information

1. On the guest computer, double-click the Direct Connection icon in the Network And Dial-Up Connections window.

2. Enter the assigned user name and password.

3. On the guest computer, click the Search button in any folder, and search for the computer you're connected to. In the Search Results pane, double-click that computer.

4. From the guest computer, explore the shared folders on the host computer, copying any necessary files between computers.

5. When you've finished, right-click the Direct Connection icon on the guest computer's taskbar, and choose Disconnect from the shortcut menu.

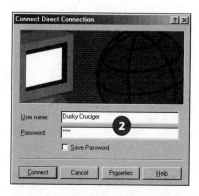

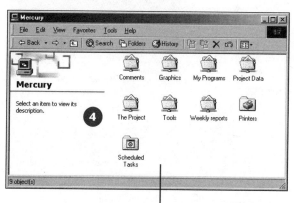

The guest computer has access to the shared files on the host computer.

10

Storing Information on a Removable Disk

If you use floppy disks or other removable disks such as ZIP disks to transport or archive information, Windows 2000 provides easy access to your disks. If you have a disk that's not correctly formatted, or if you want to quickly erase all the items on a disk, you'll need to format it before you can use (or reuse) it. For many disk types you can also select the type of file system to be used on the disk.

Format a Removable Disk

1. Place the disk in its drive, and double-click the My Computer icon on the Desktop.

2. Right-click the drive, and choose Format from the shortcut menu.

3. Select a file system.

4. Type a name for the disk if you want one (up to 11 characters long, or up to 32 for NTFS-formatted disks).

5. Turn on the Quick Format check box to create a new system directory for the disk, or turn off the check box to create a new system directory and to fully remove all remnants of files from the disk.

6. Turn on the Enable Compression check box (NTFS format only) for standard compression.

7. Click Start, and then click OK to confirm the format.

8. Click OK, and then click Close when the formatting has been completed.

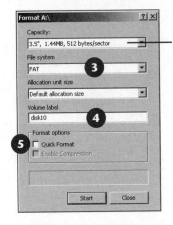

Only some removable disks support different capacities.

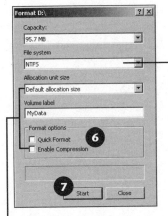

Only some removable disks support different file systems.

Only NTFS file systems support different allocation unit sizes and compression.

Copy Files or Folders to a Removable Disk

1. Place a disk in the disk drive.

2. Open the window containing the files and folders to be copied, and select the items you want to copy.

3. Right-click one of the selected items, point to Send To on the shortcut menu, and click the drive that contains the disk.

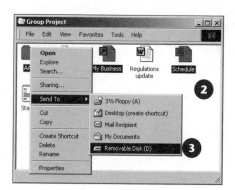

Duplicate a Floppy Disk

1. Place the disk to be duplicated in the floppy drive.

2. Open the My Computer window, right-click the drive containing the disk, and choose Copy Disk from the shortcut menu.

3. Select the drives to be used.

4. Click Start.

5. Click Close when the copying has been completed.

You can copy only between drives of the same type. If you're using a single drive, switch disks when prompted.

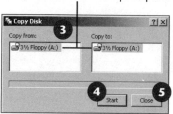

Downloading Files over the Internet

One of the quickest—but not the friendliest—ways to retrieve files over the Internet is to use FTP (File Transfer Protocol) to download the files from an FTP server. FTP is designed specifically for the Internet and TCP/IP connections. You run FTP from the command prompt, where you use a series of arcane commands to connect to, explore, and download files.

Connect to the FTP Server

1. Get your connection information from the server administrator. Connect to the Internet if you're not already connected.

2. Click the Start button, point to Programs and then Accessories, and choose Command Prompt from the submenu.

3. At the prompt, change to the folder in which you want to store the downloaded files.

4. Type *ftp://servername* (where *servername* is the name of the FTP server), and press Enter.

5. Type your assigned user name when prompted. If you weren't assigned a name, type *anonymous*. Press Enter.

6. Type your assigned password. If you weren't assigned a password, leave the box empty or follow the instructions on the screen. Press Enter.

7. Use the FTP commands to explore the site and download the files. When you've finished, type *quit*, press Enter, and close the command-prompt window.

COMMON FTP COMMANDS	
Command	**Function**
ascii	Switches to text mode to transfer non-executable files.
binary	Switches to binary mode to transfer executable files.
cd	Changes directories on the server.
dir	Lists the contents of a directory.
get	Retrieves a specified file.
help	Lists all the FTP commands.
mget	Retrieves multiple files if the wildcards * and ? are used.
prompt	Turns off the confirmation of the downloading of each file.
put	Sends a specified file from your computer to the FTP server.
quit	Ends the FTP session and disconnects from the server.

Customizing

IN THIS SECTION

**Rearranging or
Hiding the Taskbar
or the Toolbars**

**Changing the
Look of the Desktop**

Customizing Toolbars

**Customizing
Folder Windows**

Changing Your Click

**Customizing
Mouse Pointers and
Mouse Actions**

**Changing Your
Input and Output**

Enlarging the View

**Fitting More Items
on the Desktop**

Changing Screen Colors

Using Two Monitors

Whether the computer you use is yours or your employer's, you can customize it so that it looks and works exactly the way you want it to. You can keep the classic Windows look, change the look to that of a web page, or design your own look with elements from both styles. You can change the size and color of almost everything; set items to open with one click instead of two; rearrange or hide the taskbar, toolbars, Start menu, and Desktop items; and customize your Active Desktop with pictures, animated items, and links. You can use a single window in which to open all your folders, or use a separate window for each folder; and you can customize folder windows with colors, pictures, and comments. You can choose a screen saver, use the Magnifier to enlarge anything on your screen, try different mouse pointers, and change your mouse's behavior.

If you have any problems with your vision, hearing, or manual dexterity—or if you simply want to try a different way of working—you can use some innovative tools: press key combinations one key at a time instead of simultaneously, use high-contrast color schemes for better visibility, control mouse movements with the numeric keypad, specify visual cues to replace the computer's beeps, use the On-Screen Keyboard, or let Narrator describe aloud the elements and text on your screen.

Customize Your Environment

Windows 2000 Professional lets you customize your Desktop so that it functions the way you want it to. If you're a traditionalist, you can use Windows 2000 just the way it came—that is, with icons and folders that you open by double-clicking, and with the Start button, toolbars, and taskbar always visible. If you like the look and feel of the Internet, you can set your icons to launch with a single click, and you can place all sorts of jumps and HTML features right on your Desktop. If you'd prefer to use toolbars to navigate and to run programs, you can arrange predefined toolbars, or new toolbars that you create, around your screen, and then have them

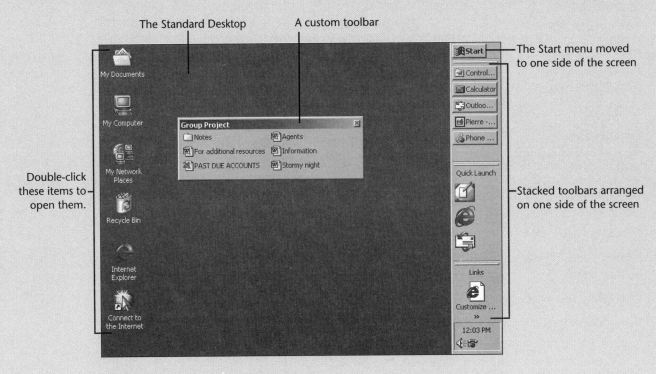

The Standard Desktop

A custom toolbar

The Start menu moved to one side of the screen

Double-click these items to open them.

Stacked toolbars arranged on one side of the screen

disappear when you don't need them. If none of these options is exactly to your liking, you can mix and match them to create your own unique environment.

And customization goes far beyond the Desktop. Whatever alterations you want to make for your own pleasure or comfort—putting pictures in your folder windows, adjusting the way your mouse moves, changing the colors on your screen or the sounds your computer makes—you'll find out how to accomplish them in this section of the book.

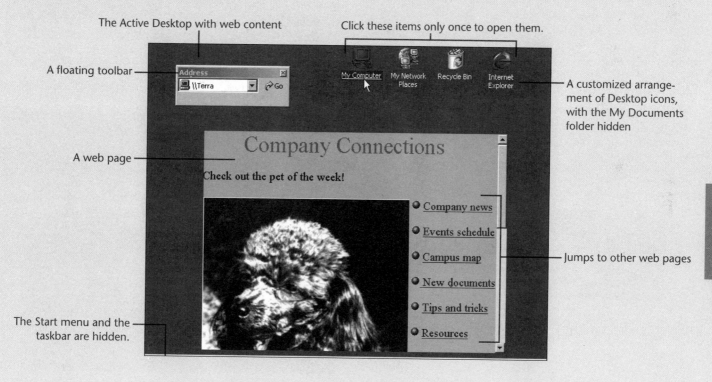

The Active Desktop with web content

Click these items only once to open them.

A floating toolbar

A customized arrangement of Desktop icons, with the My Documents folder hidden

A web page

Jumps to other web pages

The Start menu and the taskbar are hidden.

11

Rearranging the Taskbar and the Toolbars

The taskbar and the tool-bars are indispensable tools for working efficiently in Windows 2000. If you want, you can rearrange them so that they're tailored even more closely to your working style. For example, you can change the size of a toolbar or the taskbar, and you can "dock" either at any of the four sides of your screen. You can also "float" the toolbars—but not the taskbar—anywhere on your Desktop.

Move Them

1 Point to a blank spot on the taskbar or to the small "raised" bar on a toolbar.

2 Do any of the following:

- ◆ Drag the taskbar or toolbar to the top, bottom, or either side of your screen to dock it.

- ◆ Float a toolbar by dragging it into an empty spot on the Desktop.

- ◆ Drag a floating toolbar to a side of the screen or onto a docked toolbar to dock the floating toolbar.

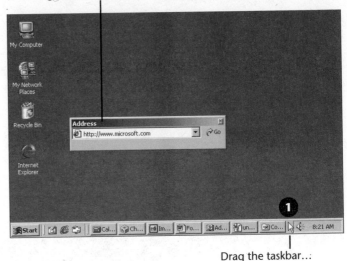

A floating toolbar created by dragging a toolbar onto the Desktop

Drag the taskbar…

…to a side of the screen.

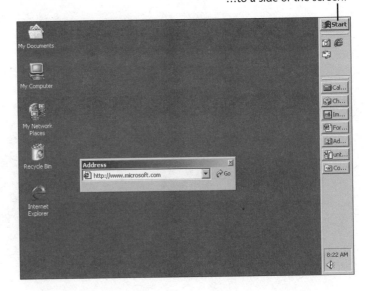

TRY THIS

Show or hide them. *Display several toolbars together with the taskbar on a single line along the bottom of the screen. Drag the top edge of the task-bar up. Observe that as you drag the taskbar up, the tool-bars stack under each other. Keep dragging up until all the toolbars and the taskbar are on separate lines. Now set the task-bar and the toolbars to Auto Hide, and click the Desktop.*

SEE ALSO

For information about the Auto Hide option, see "Hiding the Taskbar or a Toolbar" on page 218.

TIP

Customize them. *To change the size at which icons are dis-played on a toolbar, right-click a blank spot on the toolbar, point to View on the shortcut menu, and choose Large or Small. To show or hide a text label to identify each icon, right-click the toolbar, and choose Show Text from the shortcut menu. To show or hide a text label to identify a docked toolbar, right-click the toolbar, and choose Show Title from the shortcut menu.*

Resize Them

1 Move the mouse pointer over an edge of the taskbar or toolbar until the pointer turns into a two-headed arrow.

2 Drag the border until the taskbar or toolbar is the size you want.

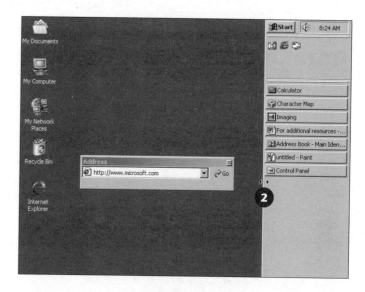

Stack Them

1 With the taskbar and the toolbars docked at the top or bottom of the screen, drag the inside edge of the taskbar.

2 Release the mouse button when the taskbar and the toolbars are stacked.

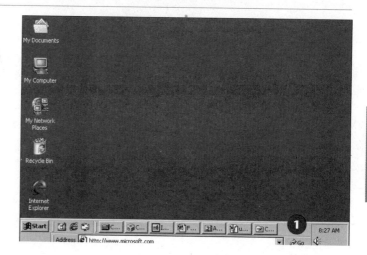

11

Hiding the Taskbar or a Toolbar

The taskbar and the toolbars are handy navigational devices, but they can sometimes get in your way. If you want to, you can hide the taskbar and any of the toolbars and have them appear only when you need them.

TIP

Find the taskbar. *If you can't find the taskbar because it's hidden or because something else is on top of it, press the Ctrl+Esc key combination. This will display the taskbar with the Start menu open.*

TIP

Toolbar behavior. *Any toolbar that's connected to the taskbar will be hidden when the taskbar is hidden and will be displayed when the taskbar is displayed.*

Hide the Taskbar

1. Right-click a blank spot on the taskbar, and choose Properties from the shortcut menu.

2. Turn on the Auto Hide check box.

3. Turn on any other options you want.

4. Click OK.

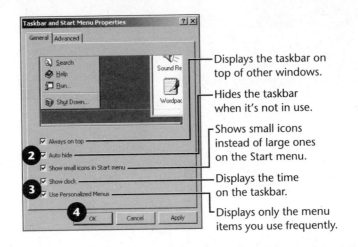

Displays the taskbar on top of other windows.

Hides the taskbar when it's not in use.

Shows small icons instead of large ones on the Start menu.

Displays the time on the taskbar.

Displays only the menu items you use frequently.

Hide a Toolbar

1. Move the toolbar to an edge of the screen that doesn't contain the taskbar.

2. Right-click a blank spot on the toolbar or on the text title of the toolbar.

3. Choose Auto-Hide from the shortcut menu.

4. Right-click a blank spot on the toolbar, and choose Always On Top from the shortcut menu if the command doesn't already have a check mark next to it.

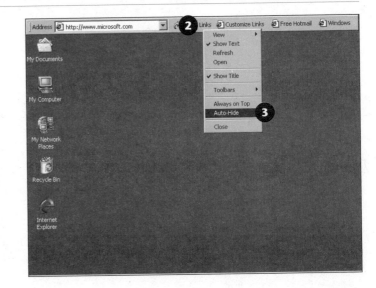

TIP

Multiple monitors. *If you're working with two (or more) monitors attached to your computer, you can move the taskbar and any of the toolbars onto the part of the Desktop that's displayed on the second monitor. You can then dock the taskbar or toolbars at the edge of that monitor's screen.*

SEE ALSO

For information about moving a toolbar, see "Rearranging the Taskbar and the Toolbars" on page 216.

For information about working with multiple monitors, see "Using Two Monitors" on page 246.

Display the Taskbar or a Toolbar

1 Move the mouse pointer to the edge of the screen where the taskbar or a toolbar is hidden. The taskbar or toolbar slides into view.

2 Use the taskbar or toolbar as you normally would: click buttons, type an address, or select an item from a drop-down list.

3 Move the mouse pointer off the taskbar or toolbar to hide the taskbar or toolbar again.

When the mouse pointer reaches the edge of the screen...

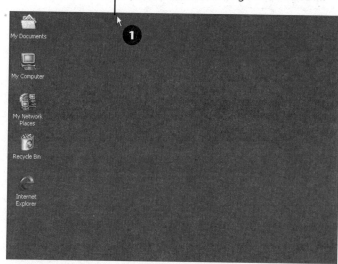

...the hidden toolbar appears.

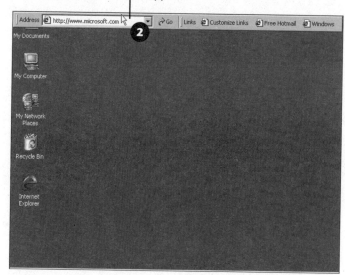

Changing the Look of the Desktop

Just as your physical desktop might be constructed from solid oak, printed plastic, or glass, your Windows 2000 Desktop can have a patterned surface. You can add a picture for more interest, and you can have it occupy the entire Desktop surface or only part of it. You can even combine a picture with a patterned background. Keep experimenting until you find the look you like.

SEE ALSO

For information about using an HTML document (a web page) as your Desktop background, see "Creating a Custom Desktop Background" on page 222.

Add a Pattern

1. Right-click a blank spot on the Desktop, and choose Properties from the shortcut menu.

2. Click the Background tab if it's not already selected.

3. Click the Pattern button.

4. Select the pattern you want to use from the Pattern list.

5. Click OK.

6. Click Apply to see the pattern on your Desktop.

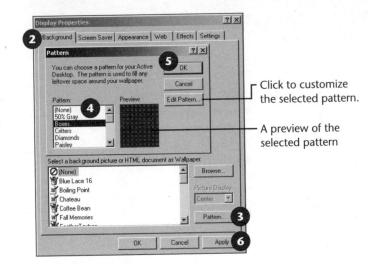

Click to customize the selected pattern.

A preview of the selected pattern

Add a Picture

1 Select the picture you want to use from the Wallpaper list. The items in the list are the bitmap files in the WINNT folder and the JPEG picture files in the Wallpaper folder (which is in the Web folder inside the WINNT folder).

2 Click the Display option you want:

◆ Center places a single copy of the picture in the center of the Desktop.

◆ Tile repeats the image to fill the Desktop.

◆ Stretch scales the image to fit the Desktop. However, the image might be distorted or its quality might have deteriorated.

3 Click OK.

A centered picture on top of the selected pattern

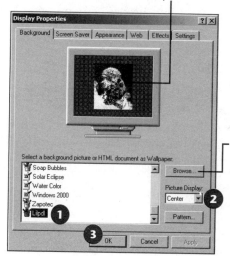

Click to find and use a picture file that isn't listed.

11

Creating a Custom Desktop Background

With the Active Desktop enabled, you can use a web page as the background for your Desktop. By using a web page, you can include multiple items—pictures, tables, animated items, and anything that's supported by HTML—and can place them exactly where you want them. If you want the page to be active, you can use a web page that's updated frequently or that contains links to other locations. And if the background is just *too* active for you, you can turn it off, or back on again, with a couple of clicks of the mouse. .

> **SEE ALSO**
>
> *For information about placing web content in a window on your Desktop, see "Adding Links to the Desktop" on page 49.*

Choose a Web Page

1. Right-click a blank spot on the Desktop, point to Active Desktop on the shortcut menu, and choose Customize My Desktop from the submenu.

2. On the Web tab, verify that the Show Web Content On My Active Desktop check box is turned on.

3. On the Background tab, click Browse, locate and select the web page you want, and click Open.

4. Click OK.

5. If the web page is one that's updated periodically, right-click a blank spot on the Desktop, and choose Refresh from the short-cut menu to update your background.

6. To hide the background, right-click a blank spot on the Desktop, point to Active Desktop on the shortcut menu, and choose Show Web Content. Choose Show Web Content again to redisplay your custom Desktop.

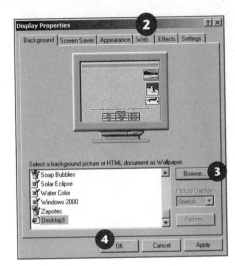

Any open windows sit on top of the custom Desktop background.

A web page as a custom background for the Desktop

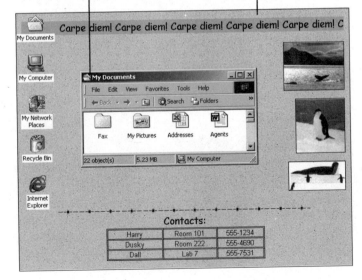

Hiding the Desktop Icons

Although the Desktop icons are useful, you might want to remove one or all of them from your Desktop. For example, if you don't usually open the My Documents folder from the Desktop, or if you're concerned that it gives other people quick access to your documents, you can hide the icon. If you're using the Active Desktop, and you don't want the icons cluttering it up, you can hide all the icons and use a different method to access the items on your computer.

TIP

You can still use hidden icons. *Even if you hide all the Desktop icons, you can still use them by displaying and using the Desktop toolbar. However, hiding only the My Documents folder removes its icon from the Desktop toolbar.*

Hide the My Documents Folder

1. Open the My Computer window from the Desktop.

2. Choose Folder Options from the Tools menu.

3. On the View tab, under Advanced Settings, turn off the Show My Documents On The Desktop check box.

4. Click OK.

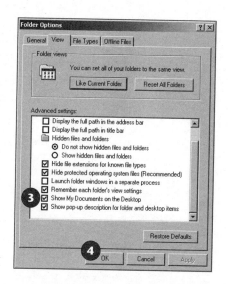

Hide All the Icons

1. If you're not using the Active Desktop, right-click a blank spot on the Desktop, point to Active Desktop on the shortcut menu, and choose Show Web Content from the submenu.

2. Right-click a blank spot on the Desktop, point to Active Desktop on the shortcut menu, and choose Show Desktop Icons from the submenu.

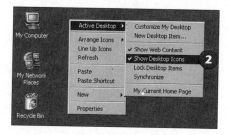

11

Customizing Toolbars

You can customize the toolbars in folder windows to include only the tools you need. When you customize a toolbar in one folder window, the toolbars will be changed in all your folder windows. You can use this same procedure to customize the toolbars in Internet Explorer and Outlook Express.

SEE ALSO

For information about creating your own toolbars, see "Creating Your Own Toolbars" on page 41.

For information about customizing the Links toolbar, see "Changing Links" on page 46.

TIP

Restore it. *To restore a toolbar to its original configuration, click the Reset button in the Customize Toolbar dialog box.*

Add, Delete, and Move Items

1. In any folder window, use the View menu to display the Standard Buttons toolbar if it's not already displayed.

2. Right-click a blank spot on the Standard Buttons toolbar, and choose Customize from the shortcut menu.

3. To add an item, select it in the list on the left, and click the Add button.

4. To remove an item, select it in the list on the right, and click the Remove button.

5. To move an item, select it in the list on the right, and use the Move Up or Move Down button to change the item's position.

6. Specify whether you want text included on the toolbar buttons.

7. Specify whether you want large or small icons.

8. Click Close when you've finished.

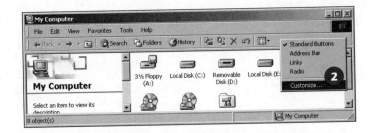

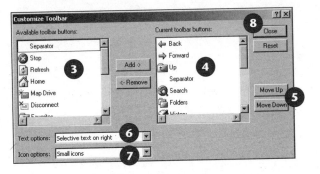

A customized toolbar with large icons

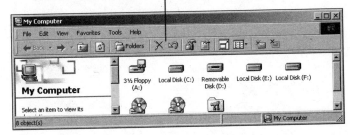

Opening a Folder in Its Own Window

When you open a folder from a within a "parent" folder window, the contents of the parent window are usually replaced by the contents of the folder you just opened. If you want each folder you open to open in a new window and want to have the other folder windows remain open, let Windows 2000 know your preference.

TIP

One window or more?
Use a single window if you keep all your documents for a project in one folder and usually work in one folder at a time. Use a separate window for each folder if you often use documents from different folders or if you frequently copy documents between folders.

Use a New Window for Each Folder

1. In any folder window, choose Folder Options from the Tools menu.

2. On the General tab, click the Open Each Folder In Its Own Window option, and then click OK.

3. Open a series of folder windows.

4. Manage the windows by using any of the following methods:

   ◆ Click the Close button to close windows you don't need.

   ◆ Hold down the Shift key and click the Close button on one of the last windows you opened to close the window and all the open parent-folder windows.

   ◆ Right-click a blank spot on the taskbar, and choose a command from the shortcut menu to arrange the windows.

   ◆ Click the Show Desktop button on the Quick Launch toolbar to minimize all the windows.

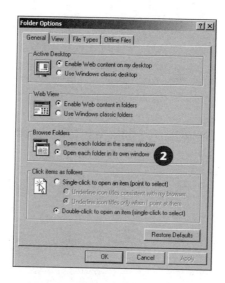

Each folder opens in its own window.

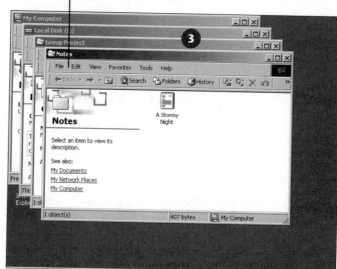

11

Adding a Comment to a Folder Window

If there's enough room, Windows 2000 Professional automatically uses part of a folder window that contains web content to display information about the folder itself or about an item that you've selected in the folder window. You can modify the web content so that it includes a comment about the folder each time it's accessed.

SEE ALSO

For information about showing or hiding web content in a folder, see "Displaying Classic Folder Windows" on page 229.

Add Your Text

1. Open the folder you want to modify.

2. From the folder's View menu, choose Customize This Folder. (If the command doesn't appear on the menu, you can't customize the folder.)

3. In the welcome window of the Customize This Folder Wizard, click Next.

4. In the Customize This Folder window, turn off both the check box for choosing or editing the template and the check box for modifying the background appearance, if either is checked.

5. Turn on the Add Folder Comment check box, and click Next.

6. Type your comment.

7. Click Next, and then click Finish.

8. If the comment doesn't appear in the folder window, close and then reopen the window.

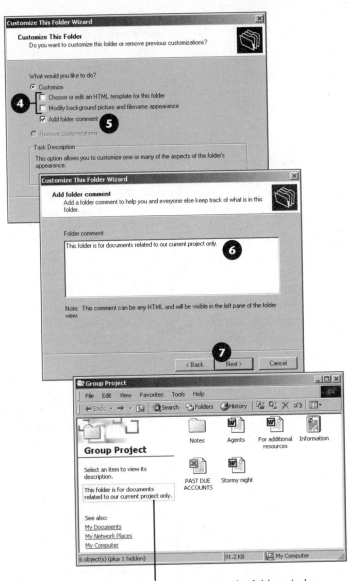

Your comment appears in the folder window.

Adding a Background Picture to a Folder Window

You can add interest to a folder window that's set to display web content by using a picture for the background of the folder. If necessary, you can also change the color of the text for the icons to make it clearly visible against the background.

TIP

No customization allowed. *If the Customize This Folder command isn't displayed on the folder's View menu, you can't customize the folder.*

TIP

Remove the picture. *To remove the picture or any other customization, rerun the Customize This Folder Wizard, and click the Remove Customizations option.*

Set the Background

1. Open the folder you want to modify, and, from its View menu, choose Customize This Folder.

2. In the welcome window of the Customize This Folder Wizard, click Next.

3. In the Customize This Folder window, turn off both the check box for choosing or editing the template and the check box for adding a folder comment, if either is checked.

4. Turn on the Modify The Background Picture And Filename Appearance check box, and click Next.

5. Select a background picture from the list, or click the Browse button to locate a picture file.

6. Click the Text button to specify the color of the icon text.

7. To place a contrasting background color behind the icon text, click the Background button, and specify the color.

8. Click Next, and then click Finish.

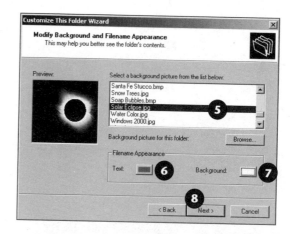

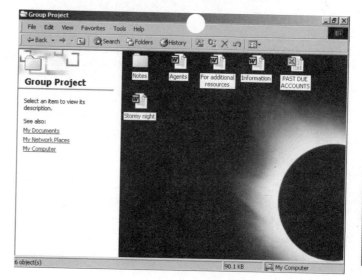

11

Customizing a Folder Window for Pictures

Windows 2000 provides a special folder—the My Pictures folder—which is designed to hold pictures. It provides a powerful preview tool in the web content area of the folder window so that you can preview a selected picture. However, if you store your pictures in folders other than the My Pictures folder and would like the same preview functionality in any folder that contains pictures, you can customize the appropriate folder windows.

Select the Template

1. Open the folder you want to modify.

2. From the folder's View menu, choose Customize This Folder. (If the command doesn't appear on the menu, you can't customize the folder.)

3. In the welcome window of the Customize This Folder Wizard, click Next.

4. In the Customize This Folder window, make sure that only the Choose Or Edit An HTML Template For This Folder check box is checked, and then click Next.

5. Select the Image Preview template.

6. Click Next, and then click Finish.

7. Select a picture.

8. Use the preview tools to view or print your picture.

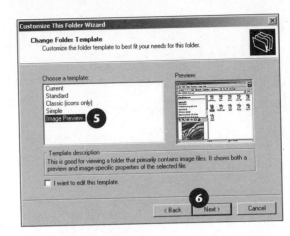

Displaying Classic Folder Windows

Windows 2000, by default, displays all your folder windows with web content. Even if you shrink a window until it's so small that the web content disappears, your computer's resources are still being used to generate the web content. If you'd rather work in folder windows without content—giving you more space to display icons and possibly speeding up your computer just a bit—you can turn off the web content features of all your folder windows.

SEE ALSO

For information about changing the size of a window, see "Managing a Program Window" on page 10.

Switch to Classic Folders

1 In any folder window, choose Folder Options from the Tools menu.

2 On the General tab, under Web View, click the Use Windows Classic Folders option.

3 Click OK.

A folder window with web content

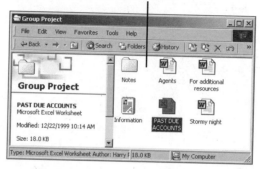

The same folder window without web content

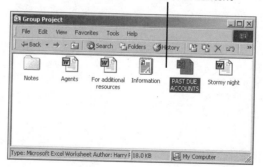

11

Using a Screen Saver

When you work at a computer, it's good for your eyes—and for your mental health—to take a break and look at something different once in a while. If you work with other people, you might not want them to be able to read your screen—albeit unintentionally—any time your computer is unattended. A screen saver can provide a nice little respite from your work as well as some privacy. To prevent anyone from using your computer—but still allowing network access to it—when you're away from your desk, you can use the password option. You'll need to enter the password to end the screen saver when you're ready to get back to work.

SEE ALSO

For information about securing your computer without using a screen saver, see "Securing Your Computer" on page 253.

Choose a Screen Saver

1. Right-click a blank spot on the Desktop, and choose Properties from the shortcut menu.

2. Click the Screen Saver tab.

3. Select a screen saver.

4. Click Settings to set options for the screen saver.

5. Turn on the Password Protected check box if you want to require your logon password to terminate the screen saver.

6. Set the length of time you want your computer to be inactive before the screen saver starts.

7. Click Preview to see the screen saver in full screen. Move your mouse to end the preview.

8. Click OK.

A preview of the selected screen saver

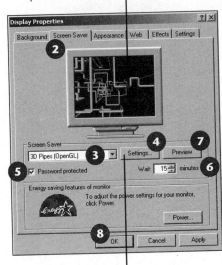

The settings are different for each screen saver.

Changing Your Click

One of the big differences between exploring your computer with Windows 2000 and exploring the Internet with Internet Explorer is the way you use a single or double mouse-click. If you prefer to use the single-click style of the web browser, just let Windows 2000 know your preference.

TIP

Links. *To specify the way Internet Explorer underlines links, choose Internet Options from the Tools menu of Internet Explorer, and change the setting on the Advanced tab. The table at the right describes the way Internet Explorer's settings for underlining links affect the way icons are underlined.*

Set the Style

1 In any folder window, choose Folder Options from the Tools menu.

2 On the General tab, click the Single-Click To Open An Item (Point To Select) option.

3 Select an option to determine when icon text is underlined:

◆ Underline Icon Titles Consistent With My Browser to use the same settings as those used by Internet Explorer or other browsers for under-lining links

◆ Underline Icon Titles Only When I Point At Them to have the icon text underlined only when the mouse pointer is pointing to the icon

4 Click OK.

5 Verify that pointing to, selecting, and clicking an icon works as you expect.

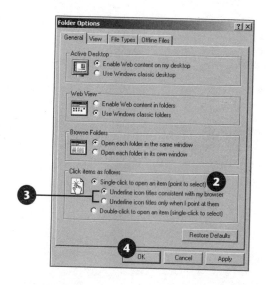

INTERNET EXPLORER'S ICON-UNDERLINING OPTIONS	
Use browser settings when browser is set to	**For this icon underlining**
Always	All the icons are underlined.
Hover	Only the icon you point to is underlined.
Never	No icons are ever underlined.

11

Changing the Mouse Pointers

Would you like something more exciting than an arrow as a mouse pointer? Do you sometimes have difficulty finding the pointer on the screen? You can make your work more interesting and even a little easier by using any of the different pointers for the standard Windows 2000 events shown on the Pointers tab of the Mouse Properties dialog box. Your choices are varied, from three-dimensional pointers to oversized black pointers that are impossible to miss.

Change the Pointer Scheme

1 Click the Start button, point to Settings, and choose Control Panel from the submenu.

2 Double-click the Mouse icon.

3 Click the Pointers tab.

4 Select a new scheme from the Scheme drop-down list.

5 Review the pointers to make sure that you like the scheme.

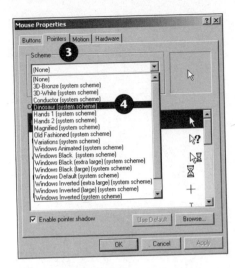

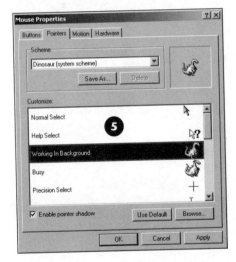

Big mouse. *Besides breaking the tedium of using standard mouse pointers, changing the pointer scheme can substantially increase the visibility of all your mouse pointers. If you have difficulty seeing the pointers on your screen, try either a larger pointer scheme or one with inverted colors.*

For information about using a wheel mouse, see "Wheeling Around with the Mouse" on page 18.

For information about customizing your mouse's performance, see "Adjusting Mouse Actions" on page 234.

Customize the Pointers

1. Select the event and the pointer you want to change.

2. Click the Browse button. If necessary, navigate to the Cursors folder (located in your WINNT folder).

3. Click the pointer you want for the selected event.

4. Click the Open button.

5. Repeat steps 1 through 4 to change other individual pointers.

6. Save the modified scheme with a new name.

7. Click OK.

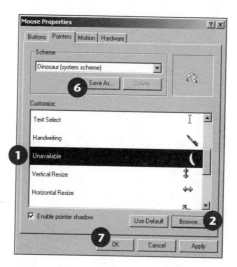

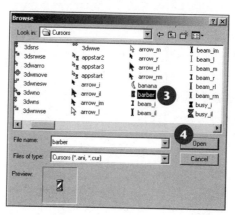

11

Adjusting Mouse Actions

Few things are more frustrating than an uncooperative mouse that doesn't do what you want it to do. A dirty—and thus unhappy—mouse is often the cause of many problems, but, if you've attended to your mouse's *toilette* and you're still having problems, you can make some simple adjustments for better mouse performance.

SEE ALSO

For information about using a wheel mouse, see "Wheeling Around with the Mouse" on page 18.

For information about specifying the way Windows 2000 responds to your mouse clicks, see "Changing Your Click" on page 231.

For information about using the keyboard to control mouse actions, see "Changing Your Input" on page 236.

Switch Buttons

1 Click the Start button, point to Settings, and choose Control Panel from the submenu.

2 Double-click the Mouse icon.

3 On the Buttons tab, select the Right-Handed or Left-Handed button configuration.

The text shows the button assignment for the configuration you selected.

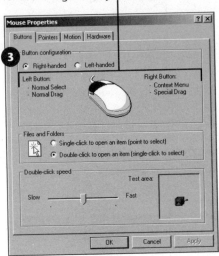

Set the Double-Click Speed

1 Drag the Double-Click Speed slider to set your double-click speed.

2 Double-click the jack-in-the-box. If it doesn't pop up (or go back into the box if it's already popped up), change the double-click speed and repeat the test.

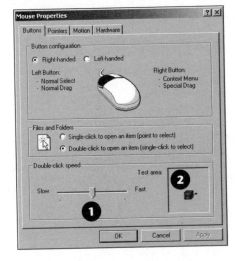

TIP

IntelliPoint software.
You have many more settings options with the Microsoft IntelliPoint software installed. Although the IntelliPoint software isn't part of Windows 2000, it's often installed when any Microsoft Mouse products are installed. With IntelliPoint software installed, the Mouse Properties dialog box contains additional tabs that let you fine-tune mouse speed, improve pointer visibility, customize the way you select items, and re-define the use of the wheel if you have a wheel mouse.

SEE ALSO

For information about using different mouse pointers, see "Changing the Mouse Pointers" on page 232.

TIP

The Snap To Default option. *To enable the mouse pointer to snap to a button in a dialog box, one button must be defined as the default button. Because some programs don't always define a default button, you won't be able to use the Snap To Default option in those programs.*

Set the Pointer Speed

1. Click the Motion tab.

2. Drag the Speed slider to set the speed at which the pointer moves. Move the mouse around, and drag the slider to adjust the speed as necessary.

3. Specify how quickly you want the pointer to accelerate when you move the mouse. Move the mouse around, and adjust its acceleration and speed as necessary.

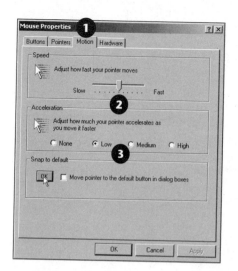

Set the Pointer Action in a Dialog Box

1. Under Snap To Default, turn on the check box to have the mouse pointer automatically move to a default button (for example, the OK or the Open button) in a dialog box.

2. Click OK.

3. Experiment to see whether you like the settings. If necessary, return to the Mouse Properties dialog box and adjust the settings.

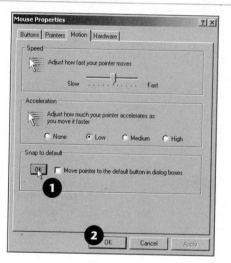

11

Changing Your Input

Windows 2000 provides several tools that let you change the way you enter information into the computer. These tools, although designed primarily for those who experience difficulty when typing or when using the mouse, can be used by anyone who wants to customize keyboard or mouse actions. For example, the keyboard can be used to execute mouse actions, or the mouse or another pointing device can be used for keyboard input. Some other tools that can help you customize keyboard input are described in the table at the right.

TIP

The Accessibility tools.
You can use the Accessibility Wizard on the Accessibility submenu of the Start menu to provide a quick way to set up several tools at one time and to help you identify which tools you might want to use.

Set the Input Options

1 Click the Start button, point to Settings, and choose Control Panel from the submenu.

2 Double-click the Accessibility Options icon.

3 On the different tabs of the Accessibility Properties dialog box, turn on the options you want to use, as described in the table.

4 Click the Settings button for the option you selected, and specify how you want the option to function. Click OK.

5 Repeat steps 3 and 4 to set all the options you want to use.

6 On the General tab, specify whether you want the features you selected to be turned off after the computer has been idle for a set period of time.

7 Click OK to close the dialog box.

ALTERNATIVE INPUT OPTIONS	
Feature	**What it does**
StickyKeys	Sets key combinations with the Alt, Ctrl, and Shift keys to be pressable one key at a time.
FilterKeys	Ignores repeated characters or too-rapid key presses.
ToggleKeys	Makes different sounds when you turn the Caps Lock, Num Lock, or Scroll Lock key on or off.
MouseKeys	Sets the numeric keypad to control mouse movements.
SerialKey devices	Provides support for alternative input devices.

SEE ALSO

For information about changing the way your computer can handle sound and text, see "Changing Your Output" on page 238.

For information about increasing the visibility of items on the screen, see "Enlarging the View" on page 240.

TIP

Regional locales. *The keyboard layout reflects the regional locale. If you change your locale, the keyboard characters will change accordingly.*

SEE ALSO

For information about changing the locale, see "Adjusting International Settings" on page 258.

Use the On-Screen Keyboard

1. Click the Start button, point your way through Programs, Accessories, and Accessibility, and choose On-Screen Keyboard from the submenu.

2. Click in a program window or dialog box where you want to enter some text.

3. Click each character to enter it.

4. To modify the keyboard:

   ◆ From the Keyboard menu, choose a keyboard type and layout style, and the number of keys to be displayed.

   ◆ From the Settings menu, choose Typing Mode, and specify whether characters will be selected by clicking them, hovering the pointer over them, pressing a keyboard key, or using a device such as a joystick.

   ◆ From the Settings menu, choose Font to specify the font in which the keyboard characters will be displayed.

When you select a key here...   ...the character appears here.

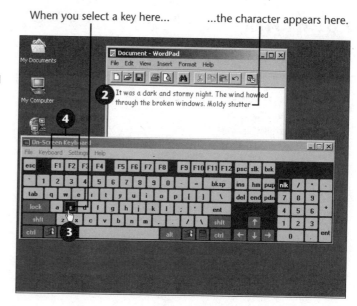

Changing Your Output

Just as you can modify the way you enter information, you can change the way you receive it. If you can't or don't want to hear sounds, you can replace the computer's warning beep with a visual indicator and, provided a program supports it, you can display text captions instead of sound. Alternatively, if you'd rather hear verbal descriptions of the current screen elements and have the text—screen text or text that you're typing—read aloud, you can have Narrator do the work.

SEE ALSO

For information about modifying the way you enter information, see "Changing Your Input" on page 236.

Set the Sound Options

1. Click the Start button, point to Settings, and choose Control Panel from the submenu.

2. Double-click the Accessibility Options icon.

3. Click the Sound tab.

4. Turn on the Use SoundSentry check box if you want a specified screen component to flash when the system beeps. Click the Settings button to specify which screen component you want to flash.

5. Turn on the Use ShowSounds check box if you want programs to display text instead of sounds. (The programs must be designed to support this feature.)

6. Click OK.

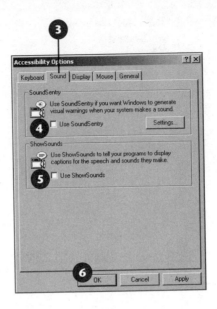

Accessibility Options

Keyboard | Sound | Display | Mouse | General

SoundSentry
Use SoundSentry if you want Windows to generate visual warnings when your system makes a sound.

☐ Use SoundSentry   Settings...

ShowSounds
Use ShowSounds to tell your programs to display captions for the speech and sounds they make.

☐ Use ShowSounds

OK | Cancel | Apply

Narrator. *Narrator is designed to be used with Windows 2000 Professional and some of its accessory programs, such as WordPad, Notepad, and Internet Explorer, but it doesn't work in all programs.*

SEE ALSO

For information about starting Narrator when Windows 2000 starts, see "Starting a Program When Windows 2000 Starts" on page 95.

Use Narrator

1 Make sure that you have a sound system installed on your computer and that the speakers are turned on.

2 Click the Start button, point your way through Programs, Accessories, and Accessibility, and choose Narrator from the submenu.

3 Turn on the check boxes for the items you want to use.

4 Click the Voice button.

5 Change the values in the Speed, Volume, and Pitch boxes to adjust the voice until it's appropriate for your use, and then click OK.

6 Work on your documents with Narrator's assistance.

7 When you no longer need Narrator, click the Exit button in the Narrator dialog box, and then click Yes to confirm your choice.

Describes aloud all the elements in the active window, items on the Desktop, and so on.

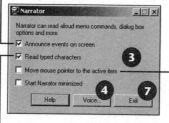

Moves the mouse pointer to the item being described.

Reads aloud any editable text in the active window.

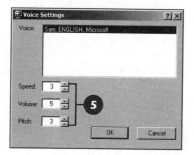

Enlarging the View

If you have difficulty seeing the items on your screen, you can increase the size of many Windows 2000 elements. You can also change the color scheme for greater contrast. But if you need to enlarge *everything*, including all the text in a program, Microsoft Magnifier is the answer. With it, you can increase the size of anything on your screen, whether it's a Windows 2000 component or a program that you've installed.

TIP

Large text, large icons.
Many programs, including Microsoft Office programs, have zoom controls that let you increase the size of text as it's being viewed on the screen. Many programs also have options that let you display large icons.

Increase the Size of Screen Elements

1 Click the Start button, point your way through Programs, Accessories, and Accessibility, and choose Accessibility Wizard from the submenu.

2 Step through the wizard, specifying whether you want to use large window titles and menus only or whether you also want to use Microsoft Magnifier.

3 Turn on the check box to set options for someone who is blind or has difficulty seeing items on the screen.

4 Continue through the wizard, specifying

◆ The size of scroll bars.

◆ The size of icons.

◆ Whether to use a high-contrast color scheme.

◆ The size and color of the cursor.

5 When you've completed the wizard, click Finish.

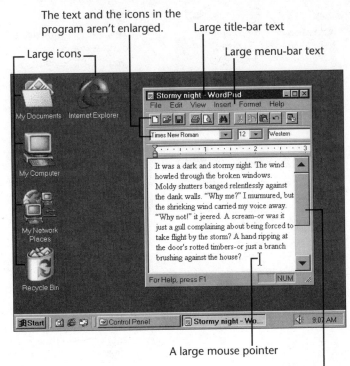

The text and the icons in the program aren't enlarged.

Large title-bar text

Large menu-bar text

Large icons

A large mouse pointer

Large scroll bars and scroll arrows

TIP

Color schemes. *The Invert Colors option affects only the Magnifier. The Use High Contrast Mode option changes the color scheme for all Windows 2000 elements.*

SEE ALSO

For information about setting other accessibility options, see "Changing Your Input" on page 236 and "Changing Your Output" on page 238.

TIP

Hide the Magnifier. *To temporarily hide the Magnifier, turn off the Show Magnifier check box.*

TIP

Quick moves. *To quickly hide the Magnifier, to restore the minimized Magnifier Settings dialog box, or to exit the Magnifier, right-click in the Magnifier, and choose the appropriate command from the shortcut menu.*

Set Up the Magnifier

1. If you didn't start the Magnifier from the Accessibility Wizard, click the Start button, point your way through Programs, Accessories, and Accessibility, and choose Magnifier from the submenu.

2. Set a magnification level.

3. Turn on check boxes to specify how the Magnifier is to follow your actions and whether you want high-visibility colors.

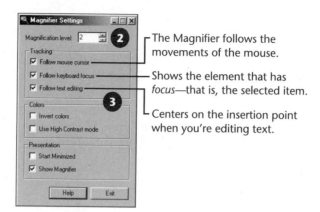

The Magnifier follows the movements of the mouse.

Shows the element that has *focus*—that is, the selected item.

Centers on the insertion point when you're editing text.

Use the Magnifier

1. Depending on the options selected, move the mouse, type text, or select an item to display your actions.

2. Observe your actions in the Magnifier.

3. When you've finished, click the Exit button in the Magnifier Settings dialog box.

What you do here... ...is shown here.

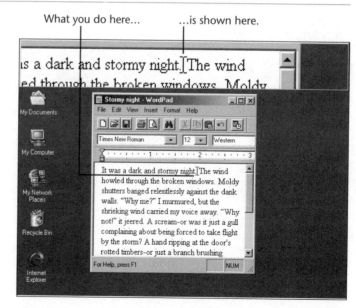

Improving the Look of Your Screen

You can turn on several enhancements to improve the look of your screen, especially if you're running at a high resolution and in High Color or True Color.

TIP

Caution. *Some enhancements use a lot of memory, so be selective. If, after you apply them, your computer runs slowly, turn off the enhancements one at a time until your computer's performance improves.*

TIP

Refresh rate. *If the screen flickers a lot, try adjusting the adapter's refresh rate. To do so, click the Advanced button on the Settings tab of the Display Properties dialog box. Verify that you've specified your monitor on the Monitor tab, and then, on the Adapter tab, select a different refresh rate. (You can't adjust the refresh rate on all systems.)*

Turn On the Enhancements

1. Right-click a blank spot on the Desktop, and choose Properties from the shortcut menu.

2. Click the Effects tab.

3. Turn on the check boxes for the options you want.

4. Click OK.

Places shading around screen fonts to reduce their jagged look on the screen, but doesn't affect printed fonts.

Animates menus, windows, and drop-down lists so that they fade in or out or scroll up and down when you open and close them.

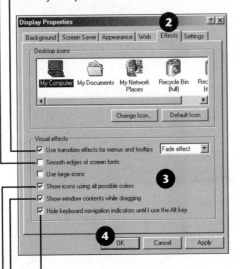

Hides the underlines under letters in menus that indicate the keys you use with the Alt key to open the menus.

Moves the window itself when it's being dragged, instead of showing a placeholder rectangle.

Removes "dithering" from icons when the system is set to High Color or True Color.

Fitting More Items onto the Desktop

If you want to squeeze more items onto your Desktop, you can change its size... sort of. You "enlarge" the available space by changing the screen resolution, and thereby the *scaling*, which lets you fit more items onto the Desktop even though its area on your screen doesn't get any larger. Your gain in "virtual" area comes at a cost, though—everything will be smaller and harder to read.

TIP

Valid settings. *If Windows 2000 has properly identified your monitor and graphics card, it will display valid settings only.*

SEE ALSO

For information about increasing the size of your Desktop by using more than one monitor, see "Using Two Monitors" on page 246.

Increase the Screen Area

1. Right-click a blank spot on the Desktop, and choose Properties from the shortcut menu.

2. Click the Settings tab.

3. Drag the slider to select a screen area.

4. Click the Advanced button.

5. Select a different font size if you want. (If you change the font size, you'll need to restart the computer when you resize the Desktop.)

6. Click OK.

7. Click OK or Close.

8. Click OK to confirm that you want to resize the Desktop.

9. After the Desktop has been resized, click Yes to accept the new settings or No to revert to the original settings. If you don't click Yes within 15 seconds, Windows 2000 restores the original settings.

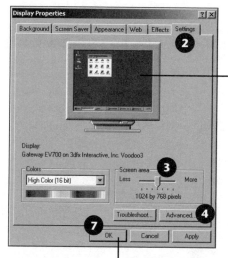

Preview the change in the Desktop area.

The OK button changes into a Close button when you change the font size.

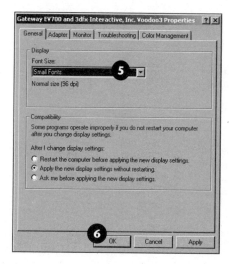

Changing Screen Colors

If you're tired of looking at the same old screen colors, you can brighten them up— or tone them down. You can select a predefined color scheme or define your own color scheme.

TIP

Disappearing act! *Change your colors with caution, and be sure to keep enough contrast between a text color and its background. If, for example, you change the menu font color to the same color as the menu itself, you won't be able to see the names of the menu items until you select them.*

TIP

Easier visibility. *The High Contrast and the Large and Extra Large schemes provide settings that make the Windows 2000 components more easily visible on your screen.*

Select and Modify a Color Scheme

1 Right-click a blank spot on the Desktop, and choose Properties from the shortcut menu.

2 On the Appearance tab, select a color scheme.

3 Preview the scheme. If you like all the colors, skip steps 4 through 8, and click OK.

4 To modify the color scheme, select an item from the Item list.

5 Select a different color for the item.

6 Select a different font, font size, and font color for an item that displays text.

7 Repeat steps 4 through 6 to make changes to any other items.

8 Click the Save As button, type a name for your color scheme, and click OK.

9 Click OK to apply the changes.

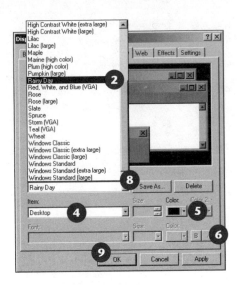

Making Everything More Colorful

Most computers can display different ranges of color, from a simple 256-color palette that's fine for displaying colors in dialog boxes to a more complex true-color palette that produces photographic-quality colors. The higher levels of color use up a lot of memory, so—depending on the capabilities of your video adapter and monitor—you might have to work with reduced screen resolution if you need to use the highest color settings.

SEE ALSO

For information about setting the screen resolution, see "Fitting More Items onto the Desktop" on page 243.

Change the Color Palette

1 Right-click a blank spot on the Desktop, and choose Properties from the shortcut menu.

2 Click the Settings tab.

3 Select a setting in the Colors drop-down list. (The colors available depend on your computer system.)

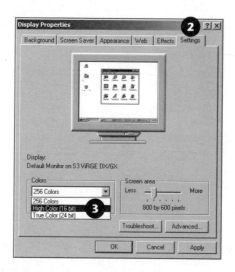

Set the Compatibility Options

1 Click the Advanced button in the Display Properties dialog box .

2 On the General tab, specify whether you want your computer to restart automatically, to ask you if it should restart, or not to restart when you change the color settings.

3 Click OK, and then click OK to close the Display Properties dialog box.

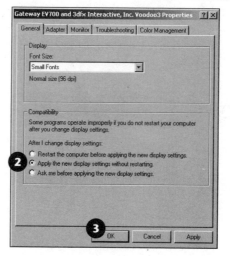

11

Using Two Monitors

Desktop not big enough for you? Well, you can literally spread it out on two—or more—monitors. You need to have a video adapter card installed for each monitor, or an adapter card that supports multiple monitors. Once the card is installed, you can set each monitor to its own color and screen-resolution settings and spread your work out over a *big* desktop.

TIP

Video adapter. *Windows 2000 has strict requirements for the type of video adapter that can be used with the second monitor. Be sure to check the latest Windows 2000 hardware compatibility list (available at* http://www.Microsoft.com/hcl/) *before you try to install a second adapter card. If—despite your having a qualifying second video card installed—Windows 2000 doesn't set up multiple monitors, try switching the slots in which the adapter cards are installed.*

Set Up the Monitors

1. Right-click a blank spot on the Desktop, and choose Properties from the shortcut menu.

2. On the Settings tab, select the primary monitor. (If you don't know which is the primary monitor, click the Identity button, and you'll see a large "1" on the screen of the primary monitor.)

3. Adjust the colors, screen area, and any advanced settings for that monitor and adapter.

4. Select the second monitor.

5. If it's not already checked, turn on the check box to extend the Desktop onto the second monitor.

6. Adjust the colors, screen area, and any advanced settings for the second monitor and adapter.

7. Drag the monitors into the arrangement you want.

8. Click OK.

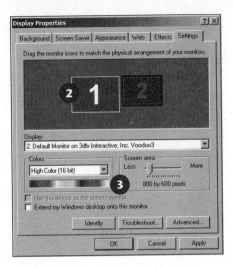

When the monitors are placed side by side, the Desktop is wider than it is tall. When one monitor is placed above the other, the Desktop is taller than it is wide.

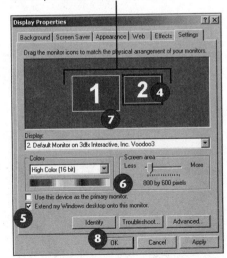

Work on the Desktop

1. Open a window or start a program on your primary monitor. (Monitor 1 is your primary monitor and is the one in which Windows 2000 starts.)

2. Drag the program to whichever edge of the primary monitor is adjacent to the other monitor, as shown in the Display Properties dialog box. Continue dragging the program until you can see and place it on the second monitor.

3. Arrange your windows, programs, and toolbars on the two monitors.

4. Use standard techniques to switch between programs—pressing Alt+Tab, using shortcut-key combinations, or clicking items on the taskbar, for example—regardless of which monitor the programs are located on.

With the monitors arranged one above the other, you see this on your secondary monitor...

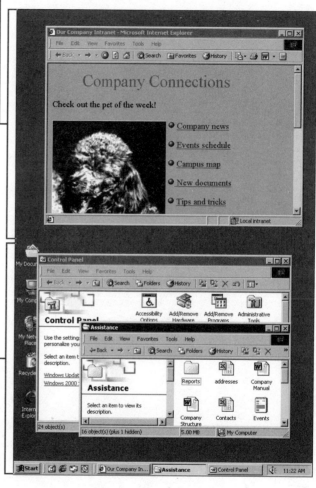

...and this on your primary monitor.

Managing Windows 2000

IN THIS SECTION

Backing Up Your Files

Securing Your Computer

Managing Your Computer's Power

Changing the Date and Time Format

Adjusting International Settings

Changing Your Password

Adding Fonts

Updating Your System

Maintaining the Drives

Diagnosing Problems

Documenting the System Configuration

Creating an Emergency Repair Disk

Starting Up When There's a Problem

Managing Microsoft Windows 2000 Professional includes diverse tasks that range from changing your password to setting an alarm that warns you when your laptop's battery is running low to repairing your system. If your files aren't automatically backed up on a network, it's imperative that you back up your work so you can restore it if a disaster occurs. You set a backup schedule, and Windows 2000 creates automatic backups for you. If security is an issue, you can lock your computer whenever it's unattended. And you can reset almost everything on your computer—the currency system, the keyboard layout, the time and date—for use in another country or time zone.

Because of rapid changes in technology, Microsoft provides the Windows Update site; just connect over the Internet and install fixes, updates, or patches. If you need to do some troubleshooting, use the disk-maintenance tools to find and re-order bits of files that have become scattered or lost, delete unused files, or test for disk errors. View the logs that Windows 2000 keeps, and find and fix errors or diagnose hardware problems. Document and print your system configuration in case you need technical support. Create an emergency repair disk so that you can reinstall missing or damaged files, and use special modes to repair Windows 2000 if it refuses to start.

Backing Up Your Files

You can back up, or dupli-cate, your files to another location for safekeeping— a tape drive or another hard drive, for example. That way, if you need a file that you've deleted or if there's been a disaster (human or mechanical), you can restore your files. You can back up selected files or all your files, or you can back up system data only.

TIP

Network backup. *If you're working on a large network, your files might be backed up automatically. Check with the network administrator before you back up your files.*

TIP

Normal backup. *The first backup you create should be a Normal backup, which backs up all your files and marks them as backed-up files. You'll also need the Normal backup to restore files you saved using the Differential or Incremental backup.*

Select What You Want to Back Up

1 Click the Start button, point your way through Programs, Accessories, and System Tools, and choose Backup from the submenu.

2 On the Welcome tab, click the Backup Wizard button, and then click Next to step through the Backup Wizard.

3 Specify what you want to back up, and click Next.

4 If you chose to back up selected items, select the items, and click Next.

5 Specify where the files are to be backed up. If you're backing up to a network share or a removable disk, click the Browse button to specify the location, and either select an existing backup file or enter a new filename to create a new backup file.

6 Click Next.

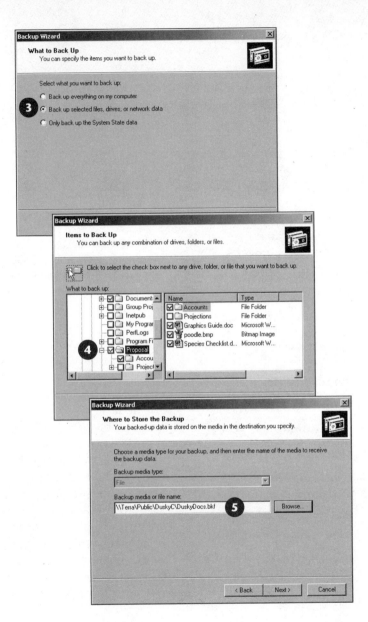

Daily backup. *Start the Backup Wizard, select the folders you want to back up every day, and specify where you want them to be stored. Click the Advanced button, select Daily as the backup type, and specify that the backup be appended to the media. Set the backup to be run later with a job title of "Daily Backup," and schedule the task to be done daily at a time when you won't be using the computer. Complete the wizard, and close the Backup program. From now on, any files that you create or change will be automatically backed up every day.*

Change the schedule.
To change your backup schedule, open the Scheduled Tasks folder from the Control Panel, and double-click the backup task. To delete the backup schedule, right-click the backup task, and choose Delete from the shortcut menu.

Set the Backup Options

1. Click the Advanced button in the Backup Wizard.

2. Specify the type of backup you want, and click Next.

3. Step through the wizard, setting your preferences for verification and compression, appending or replacing the data, and labeling the backup.

4. Specify when the backup is to be run. If you choose Later, click the Set Schedule button, and specify whether the backup is to be run once at a specific time or routinely at specified time increments.

5. Complete the wizard.

6. If the backup is set to run immediately, wait for the data to be backed up, and then close both the Backup Progress dialog box and the Backup program when the backup has been completed. If the backup is scheduled to run later, close the Backup program.

TYPES OF BACKUP	
Type	**Files copied**
Copy	All files. The files are not marked as backed up.
Daily	Files created or modified on the current day only. The files are not marked as backed up.
Differential	Any files created or modified since the last Normal or Incremental backup. The files are not marked as backed up.
Incremental	Any files created or modified since the last Normal or Incremental backup. The files are marked as backed up.
Normal	All files. The files are marked as backed up.

12

Restoring Backed-Up Files

Have you deleted or otherwise lost files that you now need? If those files were routinely backed up from your computer, you can restore them from the backup to your computer.

TIP

Catalog. *When a backup is executed, information about the items that were backed up and the storage location of the backup is saved in a "catalog" on your computer. If you're restoring a backup that wasn't created by you on your own computer, or if the original catalog was deleted or damaged, the Backup program will read the backup file you specify and will add its contents to the catalog.*

Restore the Files

1. Click the Start button, point your way through Programs, Accessories, and System Tools, and choose Backup from the submenu.

2. On the Welcome tab, click the Restore Wizard button, and then click Next to step through the wizard.

3. Select the data set and the files to be restored. Click Next.

4. Click the Advanced button.

5. Specify where you want the files to be copied to.

6. Specify whether you want the restored files to replace any existing files of the same name.

7. Complete the wizard, and wait for the files to be restored. Click Close in the Restore Progress dialog box when all the files have been copied, and then close the Backup program.

Click to use a backup file that's not cataloged on this computer.

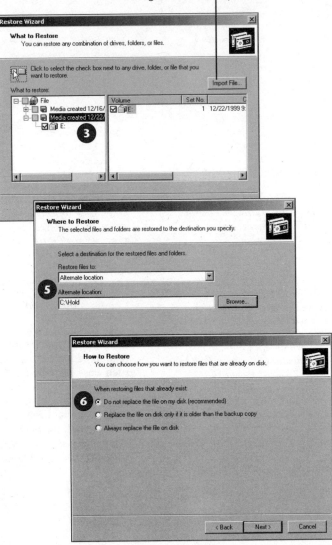

Securing Your Computer

Secure passwords and security policies will do you no good whatsoever if you leave your computer running unattended and at the mercy of anyone who wants to slip in and gain access to your files. To protect your files from such an intrusion, you can lock your computer and keep it secure until you unlock it. When a computer is locked, however, your colleagues who have permission to do so can still access its resources over a network.

SEE ALSO

For information about locking your computer automatically, see "Using a Screen Saver" on page 230 and "Managing Your Computer's Power" on page 254.

Lock It

 1 Press Ctrl+Alt+Delete.

2 Click Lock Computer.

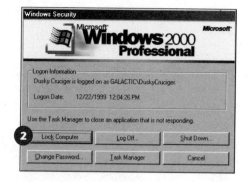

Unlock It

1 Press Ctrl+Alt+Delete. Yes, sometimes this familiar key combination is strung together with minus signs (or hyphens) instead of the usual plus signs, as in this dialog box. Do what you've always done—just press the keys simultaneously.

2 Enter your password.

3 Click OK.

12

Managing Your Computer's Power

Different computers sometimes have different power-management requirements and abilities. You might want the monitor on your main desktop computer to shut down after a few minutes of idleness, but you might also want the hard disk to "stay awake" constantly. On your laptop computer, you might want everything to shut down after a few minutes of idleness. Depending on the features and abilities of your computer, you can set these power schemes, as well as some other features.

Power Options

Use a Power Scheme

1 Click the Start button, point to Settings, and choose Control Panel from the submenu.

2 Double-click the Power Options icon.

3 Select a power scheme.

4 If the preset power schemes don't meet your specific needs, modify the settings. Click Save As, and save your settings as a new scheme.

Different tabs might be displayed, depending on the setup of your computer.

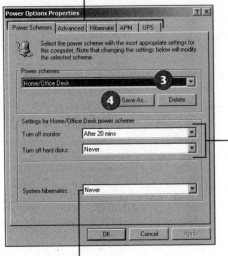

The settings are different for each power scheme.

Displayed only when the Hibernation option is turned on.

Different tabs, different items. *You won't see the Alarms tab if your computer isn't a portable computer with a battery, and you won't see the APM tab if the computer doesn't support APM or if it does support ACPI. Also note that many computers don't support hibernation. Only the items supported by your computer will appear on the different tabs.*

No ACPI? *Windows 2000 has very strict standards for supporting ACPI. If, although your computer is designed to support ACPI, Windows 2000 doesn't enable ACPI features, contact the computer manufacturer about obtaining an updated version of the BIOS that's designed to work with Windows 2000.*

Choose Your Options

1 Click the appropriate tab, and select

◆ Advanced to display the power icon on the taskbar and to require a password.

◆ Alarms to set a warning alarm when the battery is low.

◆ APM to enable the APM (Advanced Power Management) feature when the ACPI (Advanced Configuration And Power Interface) feature isn't available on the computer.

◆ Hibernate to enable hibernation.

◆ UPS to configure the settings for any Uninterruptible Power Supply attached to the computer.

2 Click OK when you've finished.

POWER-MANAGEMENT OPTIONS	
Option	Function
Alarm Action	The action that's executed when the low or critical battery alarm is activated.
Always Show Icon On The Taskbar	Shows the power source when pointed to; switches power schemes or shows the battery state when clicked.
Critical Battery Alarm	Activates the battery alarm when the battery power level is critical.
Enable Advanced Power Management Support	Enables the computer to go on standby or to hibernate. The feature is activated automatically when ACPI is installed on the computer.
Enable Hibernate Support	Enables the computer to write the information in its memory to the hard disk and then shut down. When you turn the computer back on, the information is restored to its memory.
Low Battery Alarm	Activates the battery alarm when the battery's power level is low.
Prompt For Password When Computer Goes Off Standby	Requires your logon password when the computer returns from standby or hibernation.
When I Press The Power Button On My Computer or When I Close The Lid Of My Portable Computer	Determines whether the computer shuts down, goes on standby, or hibernates when the power button (the on/off button) is pressed, or when the lid of a portable computer is closed.

12

Changing the Date and Time Format

Windows 2000 Professional uses the most commonly accepted formats to display the date and time, but you can change the display to the formats you prefer.

DATE FORMATS

1/25/00

or

01/25/2000

or

January 25, 2000

TIME FORMATS

3:05:30 P

or

03:05:30 PM

or

15:05:30

TIP

What's the date? *To see whether the date is correct, point to the time on the task-bar and hold the mouse steady until the date appears.*

Change the Date Format

1. Click the Start button, point to Settings, and choose Control Panel from the submenu.

2. Double-click the Regional Options icon.

3. Click the Date tab.

4. Select or type a different format for the short date. See the table for valid codes.

5. Click Apply, and inspect the date in the Short Date Sample box.

6. Select or type a different separator for the short date.

7. Click Apply, and inspect the date in the Short Date Sample box.

8. Select or type a different format for the long date.

9. Click Apply, and inspect the date in the Long Date Sample box.

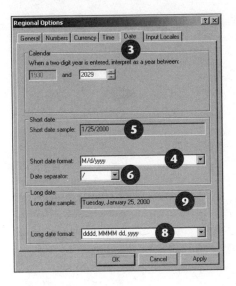

CODES FOR DATE FORMATS	
Code	**Result**
M	The month number
MM	The month number, always two digits
MMM	The three-letter month abbreviation
MMMM	The full name of the month
d	The day number
dd	The day number, always two digits
ddd	The three-letter day abbreviation
dddd	The full name of the day
yy	The year number, last two digits only
yyyy	The full number of the year

SEE ALSO

For information about changing the settings for a different region or country and an associated language, see "Adjusting International Settings" on page 258.

TIP

Different date and time formats. *Many programs format the date and time using their own codes; such programs might not utilize the settings shown in our tables. If the date and time appear in a different format in one of your programs, consult the program's Help for formatting details.*

TRY THIS

Change formats. *On the Date tab, set the long-date format to ddd, MMM, d, YY, and click Apply. Then, on the Time tab, set the time format to HH:mm:sst, and click OK. Take a look at the time on the taskbar, and then point to the time to see the date.*

Change the Time Format

1. Click the Time tab.

2. Select or type a different format for the time. See the table for valid codes.

3. Click Apply, and inspect the time in the Time Sample box.

4. Select or type a different separator for the time.

5. Click Apply, and inspect the time in the Time Sample box.

6. Select or type a different AM symbol.

7. Click Apply, and inspect the time in the Time Sample box.

8. Select or type a different PM symbol.

9. Click Apply, and inspect the time in the Time Sample box.

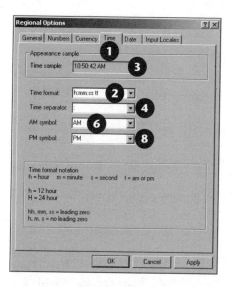

CODES FOR TIME FORMATS	
Code	**Result**
h	The hour in 12-hour format
hh	The hour in 12-hour format, always two digits
H	The hour in 24-hour format
HH	The hour in 24-hour format, always two digits
m	The minute
mm	The minute, always two digits
s	The second
ss	The second, always two digits
t	The AM or PM symbol, the first character only
tt	The AM or PM symbol, both characters

12

Adjusting International Settings

If you're working in, or producing documents for use in, a region or country other than the one for which your computer was configured, you can change the default region and have Windows 2000 adjust the numbering, currency, time, and date schemes used by your programs. If you're working with a different language, you can switch the layout of your keyboard to conform to that language.

Regional Options

SEE ALSO

For information about different ways to display the date and time, see "Changing the Date and Time Format" on page 256.

Change the Default Region

1. Click the Start button, point to Settings, and choose Control Panel from the submenu.

2. Double-click the Regional Options icon.

3. On the General tab, select a language and, if necessary, the associated country.

4. Click the Apply button.

5. Use the Numbers, Currency, Time, and Date tabs to make any other adjustments to the settings.

6. Click Apply on any tabs where you've made adjustments to put those changes into effect without having to close the dialog box.

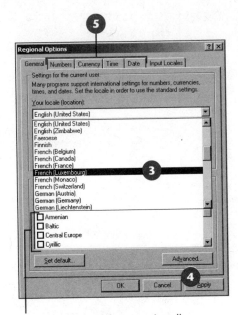

Turn on the check boxes to install additional language groups.

Change the Keyboard

1. Click the Input Locales tab.

2. Click the Add button. In the Add Input Locale dialog box, select a language, the associated country, and the keyboard layout you want, and click OK.

3. Specify how you want to turn off the Caps Lock key.

4. Specify the key combinations (hot keys) you want to use to switch quickly between locales.

5. Turn on the Enable Indicator On Taskbar check box.

6. Click OK.

Switch Layouts

1. Click the keyboard layout abbreviation on the taskbar.

2. Select the keyboard layout you want.

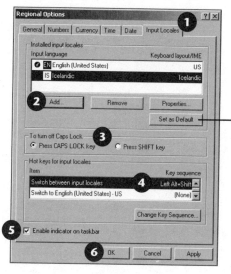

Click to always start up in the selected language.

Adjusting the Date and Time

If you take a laptop computer with you when you travel, or if your computer's battery has run down, you'll need to adjust the computer's clock to the correct time zone. If you've had your computer repaired, you'll probably need to correct the date and time.

Date/Time

TIP

Got the time? *If the time isn't shown on the taskbar, right-click a blank spot on the taskbar, choose Properties from the shortcut menu, and, on the Taskbar Options tab, turn on the Show Clock option. To adjust the date or time without displaying the clock, double-click the Date/Time icon in the Control Panel.*

Adjust the Time Zone

1. Double-click the time on the taskbar.

2. Click the Time Zone tab.

3. Select your time zone from the list.

4. Specify whether you want the clock to adjust automatically for daylight saving time changes.

Adjust the Date and Time

1. Click the Date & Time tab.

2. Select the current month from the drop-down list.

3. Select the current year.

4. Click today's date.

5. Click the hour, minute, second, and the AM or PM to be adjusted.

6. Click the arrows to adjust the time.

7. Verify the time on the clock face.

8. Click OK.

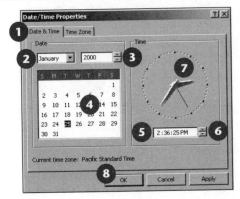

Changing Your Password

As if it's not difficult enough to remember your password, security procedures—not to mention ruthless network administrators—sometimes require you to change your password periodically. Annoying as this task might be, the few seconds it takes can keep prying eyes out of your computer and off the network.

TIP

Different tools. *Some networks require you to use different methods for changing your network password. If the procedures described here don't work, consult your network administrator.*

TIP

Case-sensitive. *Passwords in Windows 2000 are case-sensitive, so use the correct capitalization, and verify that the Caps Lock key isn't turned on.*

Change Your Password

1. Log on to the computer or domain where you want to change your password, and press Ctrl+Alt+Delete.

2. Click the Change Password button.

3. Specify where you log on (your domain or your local computer).

4. Type your old password.

5. Type a new password.

6. Type the new password again to confirm it, making sure to use the same capitalization.

7. Click OK.

8. Click OK to confirm the change, and then click Cancel to close the Windows Security dialog box.

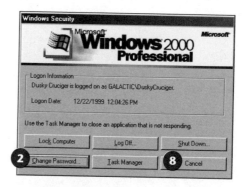

Adding Fonts to Your System

Fonts, or typefaces, are styles of lettering whose different designs add personality and feeling to our words. Windows 2000 installs some fonts automatically, and other programs often install additional fonts too. Sometimes more fonts are available, either on a program's CD or on a network drive. Windows 2000 makes it easy to install fonts and to view them on your screen. If you want to, you can print very nice sample sheets and store them in a binder—a handy reference tool when you're trying to decide which fonts to use.

Fonts

Add a Font

1 Click the Start button, point to Settings, and choose Control Panel from the submenu.

2 Double-click the Fonts icon to open the Fonts folder.

3 Choose Install New Font from the File menu.

4 Navigate to the drive and folder that contain the font to be installed. (If there are many fonts in the folder, you might need to wait a few seconds until all the font names have been retrieved.)

5 Select the font or fonts. (To select several fonts, hold down the Ctrl key and click each font.)

6 Click OK.

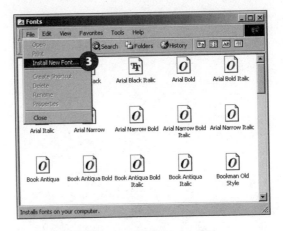

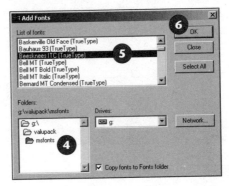

TIP

Installing fonts. *Some programs require you to use their own Setup to install the fonts that come with the program.*

SEE ALSO

For information about the different types of fonts you can install, see "Hooked on Fonts" on page 264.

TIP

Managing and using fonts. *Windows 2000 takes care of all the basic chores that are usually done by a type manager, so you can install, view, and print Type 1 fonts from the Fonts folder. If you're using a Type 1 font on a non-PostScript printer, Windows 2000 will rasterize (convert) the font information so that the printer can print the characters.*

View and Print a Font

1 Double-click the font name to view a font sample.

2 Click the Print button to print a font sample sheet.

3 Click the Done button.

4 Repeat steps 1 through 3 to view and print additional font samples.

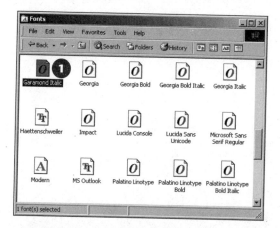

Hooked on Fonts

When you open a Font drop-down list, you might be surprised to see how many fonts you have! Windows 2000 Professional comes with quite a few fonts, and if you've installed any other programs, you've probably installed their font collections too. There are usually three *classes* of fonts—*outline, raster,* and *vector*—installed on your computer.

Outline fonts produce clear, fully scalable characters that can be rotated for landscape or portrait printing. They are usually WYSIWYG (what-you-see-is-what-you-get) fonts: that is, the printed output looks exactly the same as what you see on your screen. Until recently there were two competing formats for outline fonts: TrueType fonts and Type 1 (PostScript) fonts. These formats are now being merged into the single OpenType format, but, because the fonts must be upgraded, some older TrueType and Type 1 fonts are not yet integrated into the OpenType format. Windows 2000 uses mostly outline fonts but provides a few raster fonts and vector fonts for compatibility with some older or specialized programs. Vector fonts are used almost exclusively for printing with a plotter.

When you select a font, you'll often see an icon that identifies the font's format. Unfortunately, different programs classify the formats differently. Some programs don't recognize OpenType fonts and classify them based on their original TrueType or Type 1 format. Some programs display raster and vector fonts without any icon, or don't display them at all.

O **OpenType fonts** are composed of TrueType fonts and Type 1 PostScript fonts that have been upgraded to the OpenType standard. OpenType fonts are designed to print well at any size on almost any printer, and they provide a high level of compatibility among different programs and different web page designs.

TT **TrueType fonts** reside only on your computer, and they send information to the printer as "soft," or downloaded, fonts. Most TrueType fonts have been upgraded to the OpenType standard.

a **Type 1 fonts** use PostScript instructions to form the characters, which can be extensively manipulated when used on a PostScript printer. Type 1 fonts can reside on the printer or can be downloaded from the computer. When you're using a non-PostScript printer, Windows 2000 *rasterizes* (transforms) the instructions so that the printer can print the characters.

Printer fonts are fonts that Windows 2000 doesn't manage. They might be installed on the printer instead of on the computer, but some programs classify any non-TrueType font as a printer font. If you're using a printer font, what you see on your screen might not exactly match your printed output—sometimes you'll see a look-alike font instead.

A **Raster fonts** send a bitmap image of each character to the printer. This often produces jagged edges in the printed output, especially when the font is scaled.

What these rather dry facts don't tell you is what a delight it is to be able to transform the look and the personality of your text with a few mouse-clicks. Try it! Select some text, open your Font drop-down list, click a font name, and see what you get. Open the Font Size list and click to change the size. For a real surprise, try one of the picture fonts. Your words will change into little pictures (called *dingbats*), and you can enlarge them, italicize them, and so on, just as you can with words.

If you feel like a kid with a new toy, just keep in mind that you *can* have too much of a good thing. A document with too many different fonts can be very difficult to read and instantly marks you as an amateur in the world of graphic design. Keep things simple.

Professional designers seldom use more than two or three different fonts in a document—a *display font* for headlines or anything that's meant to attract attention, a *text font* for the body of the document, and perhaps a third font for elements such as captions, pull quotes, sidebars, and so on. A discussion about the best fonts to use for display or text is beyond the scope of this book, but you won't go wrong if you use a big, bold font for display and a plain, readable font for text.

There are literally *thousands* of fonts, and new ones are being created all the time. To learn more about fonts and their history, check the shelves of your local library or bookstore—they're overflowing with books about this fascinating art form.

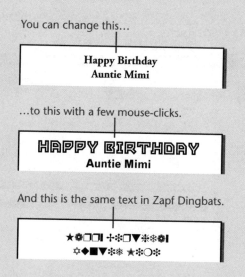

You can change this…

Happy Birthday
Auntie Mimi

…to this with a few mouse-clicks.

HAPPY BIRTHDAY
Auntie Mimi

And this is the same text in Zapf Dingbats.

★✪□❏ ✣✴☐▽✳❄❀❶
✿◆■▼✳✳ ★✳○✳

Three different looks created with display and text fonts

Stormy Night
It was a dark and stormy night. The wind howled through the broken windows. Moldy shutters banged relentlessly against the dank walls. "Why

STORMY NIGHT
It was a dark and stormy night. The wind howled through the broken windows. Moldy shutters banged relentlessly against

Stormy Night
It was a dark and stormy night. The wind howled through the broken windows. Moldy shutters banged relentlessly against the dank walls.

12

Updating Your System

When you're using Windows 2000, you might encounter little inconsistencies or incompatibility issues once in a while. This is the downside of rapidly changing technology. The upside, though, is that continuous improvements and new features are constantly being made available. By connecting to Windows Update over the Internet, you can determine what fixes, patches, and updates are available and which of them you can use, and then you can simply let Windows Update walk you through the installation process.

TIP

Service releases. *Microsoft periodically releases substantial updates for Windows. You'll often need these updates to install new features or recently released software. Go to* http://www.microsoft.com/windows *to find the release information you want.*

Start the Wizard

1. Click the Start button, and choose Windows Update from the menu.

2. Follow the web page links to Product Updates.

3. If necessary, install the Active Installation control.

4. Wait for a catalog to be built on your computer.

5. Scroll through the page, turning on the check boxes for any items you want to install.

6. Click the Download button.

7. Follow the instructions on the web page to install the software.

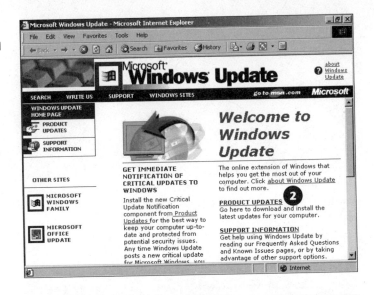

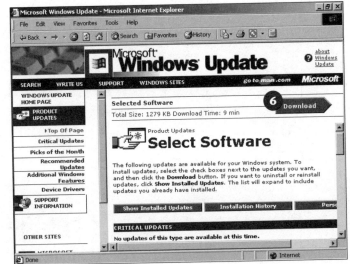

Maintaining the Drives

As the information stored in your computer gets used, moved, copied, added to, or deleted, the computer's drives can become cluttered with useless or inefficiently organized files. Windows 2000 provides a group of maintenance tools whose occasional use can make your computer run more smoothly, more efficiently, and—usually—faster.

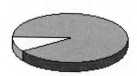

Maintain a Drive

1. Open the My Computer window.

2. Right-click the drive that needs attention, and choose Properties from the shortcut menu.

3. Click the appropriate button to use the tool you need:

   ◆ On the General tab, click the Disk Cleanup button.

   ◆ On the Tools tab, under Error-Checking, click the Check Now button.

   ◆ On the Tools tab, under Defragmentation, click the Defragment Now button.

4. Follow the instructions provided by the program.

5. When you've finished, close the program.

6. In the Properties dialog box for the drive, open and use another tool if desired. Close the dialog box when you've finished.

DISK-MAINTENANCE TOOLS	
Tool	**What it does**
Disk Cleanup	Checks the disk for unused files that can be deleted.
Error-Checking	Scans the disk to see whether there are disk errors in any files or folders. Optionally, fixes file-system errors and attempts to recover bad sectors on the hard disk. If the disk is in use, error-checking will be scheduled for the next time you log on. For NTFS formatted disks, records all file-transaction information.
Defragmentation	Analyzes the disk to see whether defragmentation is necessary. Re-orders the items on your disk so that files aren't separated into several noncontiguous parts. Can take a long time to run but speeds up disk performance.

12

Diagnosing Problems

Wouldn't it be nice if your computer could not only tell you that it isn't feeling good but also let you know exactly what ails it? Well, sometimes it can. You just have to know how to look and listen.

TIP

Dr. Watson. *When a program creates an error, information about the error is automatically recorded by Dr. Watson, the debugging program in the file drwtsn32.log. This file is useful only for those who thrive on hexadecimal numbers and memory addresses, so (unless you fit that description) the only time you'll need the file will be to send it to any support personnel who request it. To see or change the settings for Dr. Watson, click the Start button, choose Run, and type drwtsn32 in the Open box.*

View the Logs

1. Right-click the My Computer icon on your Desktop, and choose Manage from the shortcut menu.

2. Click the plus sign to expand the Event Viewer folder.

3. Click the log you want to review.

4. Double-click an event for more information.

5. Click the arrow buttons to view other events.

6. Choose another log to review.

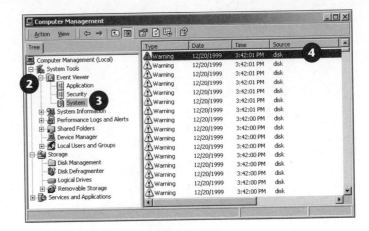

Click to copy the message text to the Windows 2000 Clipboard.

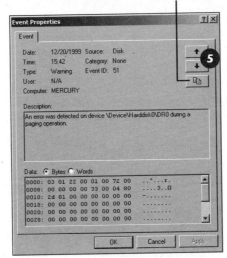

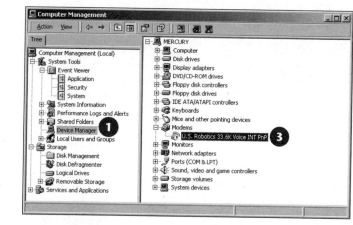

TIP

Update the drivers. *Use the Driver tab to manually change or update the drivers for the device. To automatically update the drivers, use Windows Update.*

SEE ALSO

For information about Windows Update, see "Updating Your System" on page 266.

Diagnose Hardware Problems

1 In the Computer Management window, click Device Manager.

2 Display the information for the type of device you suspect might be causing a problem. Look for symbols that indicate the device isn't working or is in conflict with a resource.

3 Double-click the device.

4 Review the status information.

5 Review the information on the other tabs.

6 If you can't identify the problem, click the Troubleshooter button on the General tab (if available), and step through the wizard to obtain additional diagnostic help.

7 Make changes to the settings only if you're authorized to make changes and you know what you're doing.

8 Click OK to save any changes or Cancel to discard them. Close the Computer Management window when you've finished.

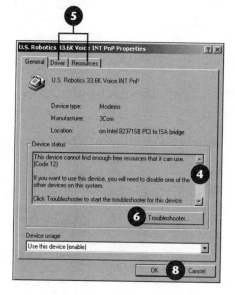

12

Documenting the System Configuration

When you record the configuration of your computer, you'll never be at a loss for words during one of those awkward pauses in conversation! Of course, the ability to fascinate your friends by using technical terms, arcane names, and all sorts of numbers is just a little bonus; the real reason you need to arm yourself with this information is because you'll need it if you call for technical support or when you plan to modify the system.

System
Information

Record the Configuration

1 Right-click the My Computer icon, and choose Manage from the shortcut menu.

2 Click the plus sign to expand the items under System Information.

3 Click an item to display the information.

4 To save the information, do any of the following:

◆ Right-click the folder, and choose Print from the shortcut menu.

◆ Right-click the folder, and choose Save As Text File from the shortcut menu.

◆ Right-click the System Information icon, and choose Save As Text File from the shortcut menu to save all the system information.

5 Copy any text files containing system information to a floppy disk in case you need the information in an emergency.

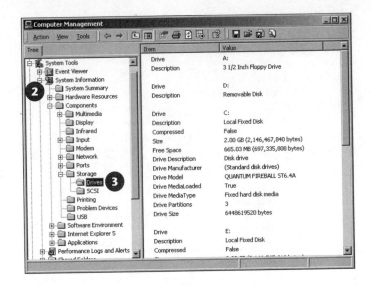

Creating an Emergency Repair Disk

Your computer shouldn't crash, but if it does, you'll be prepared if you have previously created an emergency repair disk that will let you repair your Windows 2000 installation using the Windows 2000 Professional CD. Your emergency disk contains information about your setup and the files that have been installed. Windows 2000 Setup will use the information from your emergency repair disk to reinstall any missing or damaged files.

> **TIP**
>
> **Update your disk.** *Create a new emergency repair disk whenever you make substantial changes to your system.*

Create the Disk

1. Click the Start button, point your way through Programs, Accessories, and System Tools, and choose Backup from the submenu.

2. On the Welcome tab, click the Emergency Repair Disk button.

3. Turn on the check box to back up the registry.

4. Click OK.

5. After the disk has been created, remove it, label it *Windows 2000 Emergency Repair Disk,* and include the current date and the computer name or your name. Store the disk where you'll remember to find it if you need it.

6. Close the Backup program.

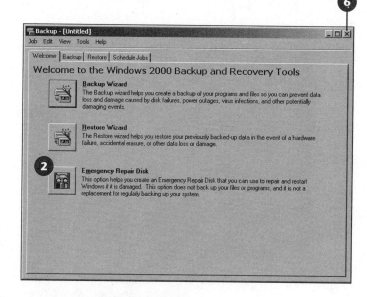

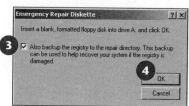

Starting Up When There's a Problem

If you can't get Windows 2000 to start up correctly, there are special modes you can use that either help you diagnose what's wrong or give you access to the system so that you can correct the settings or replace any incorrect, missing, or corrupted drivers. If none of these modes fixes the problem, you can start your computer from the Windows 2000 Professional CD or the boot disks and then repair your Windows 2000 installation using your emergency repair disk and the Windows 2000 Professional CD.

SEE ALSO

For information about creating an emergency repair disk, see "Creating an Emergency Repair Disk" on page 271.

Control the Startup

1. Turn on your computer.

2. As the computer starts up, wait for the message that tells you to select the operating system, or until you first see the "Starting Windows" message, and then press the F8 key.

3. Use the Up or Down arrow key to select the startup mode.

4. Make changes to your system to eliminate the problem.

5. Shut down Windows 2000, and restart the computer to see whether it starts correctly.

STARTUP OPTIONS

Option	What it does
Safe Mode	Starts with no network connections and without most of its drivers.
Safe Mode With Networking	Starts with network connections but without most of its drivers.
Safe Mode With Command Prompt	Starts without network connections, without most of its drivers, and with the command prompt only.
Enable Boot Logging	Starts normally; records startup information to the *ntbtlog.txt* file (in the WINNT folder).
Enable VGA Mode	Starts normally but uses only the basic VGA video driver.
Last Known Good Configuration	Starts normally using the settings stored in the registry when the computer was last shut down properly.
Directory Services Restore Mode	Not available for Windows 2000 Professional (server option only).
Debugging Mode	Starts normally but sends the debugging information to another computer over a serial cable.

TIP

Emergency repairs. *The emergency repair process requires that the hard disk be readable and that the Repair folder and its contents (in the WINNT folder) not be damaged. If this process fails, someone very knowledgeable about Windows 2000 can use the Recovery Console option to fix disk problems and other problems.*

TIP

Create new boot disks. *If you have the Windows 2000 Professional CD and you need but can't find the boot disks to start the computer, you can create a new set of disks. To do so, the Windows 2000 CD and a formatted floppy disk must both be in place. At the command prompt, change to the Bootdisk folder on the Windows 2000 CD, and type makeboot.exe a: (where a: is the floppy disk drive). You'll need four formatted disks.*

TIP

Boot directly from the CD. *Many of the newer computers can boot directly from the Windows 2000 Professional CD. Older computers generally require floppy boot disks to start the computer.*

Repair the System

1. Use the Windows 2000 Professional Setup disks, or, if your computer supports booting from a CD, the Windows 2000 Professional CD, to start Windows 2000 Setup.

2. Step through the setup process, and, in the Welcome To Setup section, press *R* to use the repair option.

3. Insert the Windows 2000 Professional CD into your computer's CD drive if it's not already there.

4. In the Windows 2000 Repair Options section, press *R* to use the emergency repair process.

5. Press *M* to use the manual repair process or *A* to use the automatic repair process.

6. Step through the repair process. When prompted, press Enter to use the emergency repair disk (ERD).

7. Insert the emergency repair disk, press Enter, and complete the repair process.

WINDOWS 2000 REPAIR OPTIONS	
Option	**What it does**
ERD, manual repair	Interactive; select to replace corrupted or deleted system files, to repair a dual-boot or multi-boot setup, or to repair the partition boot sector.
ERD, automatic repair	Automatic; select to replace corrupted or deleted system files, to repair a dual-boot or multi-boot setup, to repair the partition boot sector, and to use a backup copy of the registry.
Repair, no ERD	Uses data in the Repair folder only. Many of the settings that were made and any updated files that were installed after the original installation have probably been lost.
Recovery Console	Provides command-line access to the hardware, the software services, and the registry. Powerful and dangerous.
Reinstall	Conducts a full installation of Windows 2000 over the existing copy. Any changes that were made since the last installation will be lost. Use only if all other repair options fail.

12

Taking Control

IN THIS SECTION

Adding or Removing Windows 2000 Components

Installing, Modifying, or Removing a Software Program

Starting a Program with Full Access Rights

Adding New Users; Defining Custom Access and Access Rights

Hosting a Web Site

Scheduling Programs

Editing Windows 2000 Settings

Creating a New Hardware Profile

Changing Your Disk Format

Controlling the Startup

When you need to take control of one or more computers, you'll find that you can modify Microsoft Windows 2000 Professional settings in an almost limitless number of ways. Whatever you want to do—add, remove, or modify software or hardware components; provide additional security for files, folders, or computers; set up a local web server; or change the way you're connected to a network or to the Internet—Windows 2000 provides the appropriate tools. Of course, you also need the proper permission to make specific changes, and some basic knowledge about your computer and about Windows 2000 in order to be able to work your way through the technical aspects of the fairly advanced procedures in this section.

Taking control, however, means taking only as much control of your computer as you are *allowed*. Almost all the procedures described in this section require, at the very least, that you be a member of the Power Users group; many require that you be a member of the Administrators group. If you're not a member of either group, you won't be able to find or access the items that are discussed. Remember, too, that network policies can override any local settings you make on a computer, and a network administrator can specify access and settings for almost every aspect of your computer.

Adding or Removing Windows 2000 Components

When Windows 2000 is installed on your computer, many of its components are included in the installation. You'll need most of them, but if there are components you never use, you can remove them from your system to save disk space. By the same token, if any components you *do* need haven't been installed, you can add them.

SEE ALSO

For information about updating existing Windows 2000 components or adding components that have recently been released, see "Updating Your System" on page 266.

Add or Remove a Component Group

1 Save the documents you're working on and close all your running programs.

2 Click the Start button, point to Settings, and choose Control Panel from the submenu.

3 Double-click the Add/Remove Programs icon.

4 In the Add/Remove Programs dialog box, click the Add/Remove Windows Components button at the left of the dialog box to start the Windows Components Wizard.

5 On the Windows Components page of the wizard, turn check boxes on or off to add or remove all the items in a component group.

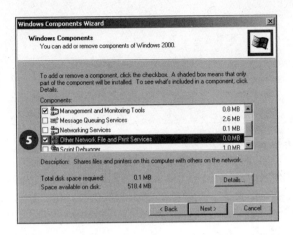

TIP

The Details button. *Some-times an item in a component group contains some additional items that you can select individually. If, when you select an item, the Details button becomes available (not grayed), you can click it and then select items to include or exclude.*

TIP

Shaded box. *A shaded check box indicates that only some of the items in the group will be installed. Use the Details button to modify which items are to be installed.*

Add or Remove an Item in a Component Group

1 Select the component group that contains the item you want to add or remove.

2 Click the Details button.

3 Click a checked box to remove the item, or click an unchecked box to add the item.

4 Continue checking or clearing check boxes until you've specified all the items you want to add or remove.

5 Click OK.

6 Repeat steps 1 through 5 for each component group you want to change. Click Next when you've finished.

7 If prompted, insert the Windows 2000 Professional CD into its drive, or specify the location of the installation folder.

8 Click Finish to close the Windows Components Wizard.

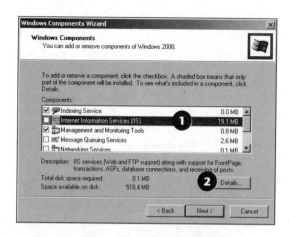

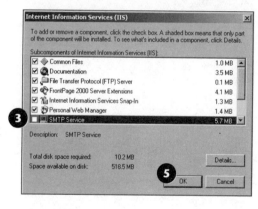

Installing a Software Program

Most software programs contain their own installation program, which copies the required files to the computer's hard disk and tells Windows 2000 which files are installed, where they are, and what they do. Most network installations based on group policies are automatic, so the procedure described here details an installation only from a CD, from floppy disks, or from a network folder.

TIP

Partial installation. *Some programs are only partially installed until you use them for the first time. When you first choose one of these programs from the Start menu, you'll be asked whether you want to install it. You'll see this request either if the network administrator assigned the program to you or to your computer or if you chose Install On First Use when you installed the program yourself.*

Install a Program

1. Close all your running programs. If you're installing from a CD, place the CD in its drive, follow the instructions that appear on the screen, and skip steps 2 through 5.

2. If the CD didn't start, or if you're installing from a different drive or from a network location, click the Start button, point to Settings, choose Control Panel from the submenu, and then double-click the Add/Remove Programs icon.

3. Click Add New Programs.

4. Click the CD Or Floppy button. Place the CD or the installation disk in its drive, and click Next.

5. If the Setup or installation program is found, click Finish. If not, click Browse, locate the Setup or installation program on a different drive or in a network folder, and click Finish.

6. Follow the Setup or installation program's instructions, and close the Add/Remove dialog box when the installation is complete.

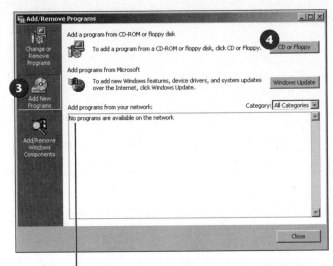

You'll see programs listed here only if a network administrator has published programs that can be installed from the server.

Modifying a Program's Installation

Some large programs and program suites that contain multiple components let you specify which components are installed. Windows 2000 Professional delegates the addition or removal of individual components to the program's Setup or installation program to ensure that all the components are properly registered.

> **TIP**
>
> **Windows Installer.** *Programs that display separate Change and Remove buttons use Windows Installer to control the installation. Windows Installer offers more options than do traditional Setup or other installation programs.*

> **TIP**
>
> **Not listed?** *If an installed program isn't listed, review the documentation to see whether there is a separate program to uninstall or modify it.*

Modify the Installation

1. Close all your running programs. Click the Start button, point to Settings, and choose Control Panel from the submenu.

2. Double-click the Add/Remove Programs icon.

3. Click Change Or Remove Programs.

4. Select the program you want to modify.

5. Click the Change/Remove or the Change button.

6. If the Application Removal dialog box appears, choose No to cancel removal. (In this case, the selected program doesn't allow you to modify the installation.)

7. Follow the instructions that appear. If prompted, insert the program CD or specify the installation folder.

8. Close the Add/Remove Programs dialog box.

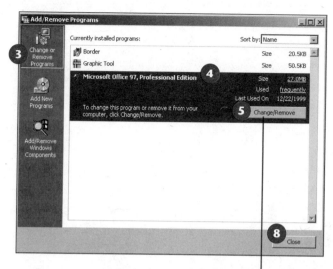

Some programs display a single Change/Remove button...

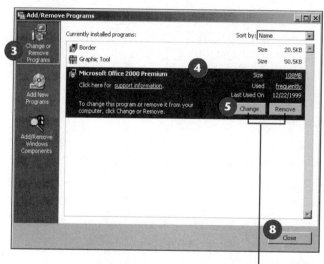

...and others display both a Change and a Remove button.

Removing a Software Program

Most programs are *registered* with Windows 2000 when you install them. You can—and should—use Windows tools to remove a program. If you simply delete the files, you might leave accessory files you don't need, or delete files you need for other programs. When you uninstall a program using Windows tools, Windows 2000 keeps track of the files, and only when a file is no longer needed by any of your programs does Windows 2000 delete the file.

SEE ALSO

For more information about registered programs, see "File Associations, File Extensions, and Registered Programs" on page 34.

For information about removing programs, see "Adding or Removing Windows 2000 Components" on page 276.

Uninstall a Program

1. Close all your running programs. Click the Start button, point to Settings, and choose Control Panel from the submenu.

2. Double-click the Add/Remove Programs icon.

3. Click Change Or Remove Programs.

4. Select the program you want to remove.

5. Click either of the following:

   ◆ Remove to remove the entire program (or suite of programs) for a program that uses Windows Installer

   ◆ Change/Remove to run the program's Setup or Uninstall program

6. Confirm that you want to remove the selected program. If another program starts and offers you a selection of actions, use it to remove the selected program.

7. Close the Add/Remove Programs dialog box when you've finished.

Uses Windows Installer to remove the program.

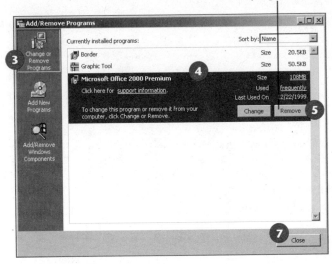

Uses the program's own Setup or Uninstall program to remove the program.

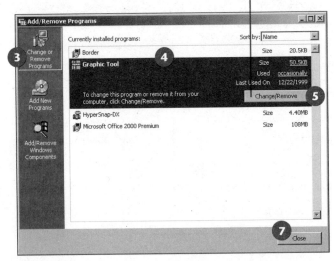

Starting a Program with Full Access Rights

When you log on, you have specific access rights. If you need different access rights, you can log on to individual programs as a different user—a useful ability when you're not logged on as an Administrator but you need administrative rights to make system changes.

TIP

Safer logon. *To make your computer less vulnerable to damage from viruses, hackers, and your own mistakes, don't routinely log on as an Administrator. Log on as a Power User instead, and use the Run As command to start a program as an Administrator when you need administrative rights.*

SEE ALSO

For information about creating user accounts and assigning access rights, see "Adding New Users" on page 284.

Run with Administrative Rights

1. Provide yourself with two user accounts—one as a Power User and one as an Administrator—and when you log on, log on as a Power User.

2. Hold down the Shift key and right-click a program, a tool, a Start-menu item, or a shortcut, and choose Run As from the shortcut menu.

3. In the Run As Other User dialog box, enter your user name and password, and, if necessary, the domain or the local computer name, for your Administrator account.

4. Click OK.

5. To use the Run command on the Start menu, precede the program name with *runas /user: domain\accountname* (where *domain* is the domain or local computer name and *accountname* is the Administrator account), and press Enter. When the command prompt appears, type the password, and press Enter.

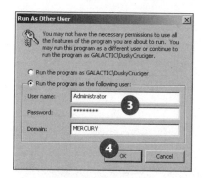

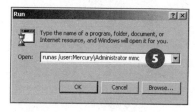

Protecting Individual Files and Folders

When a hard disk is formatted with the NTFS file system, any folder or file can have its own security settings that allow only certain individuals or members of specific groups to access those folders or files. This useful feature lets you protect not only specific files and folders on a shared computer but also those that are contained in a folder that's shared on a network.

TIP

"Inheritable" permissions?
This decidedly obscure term simply means that anyone who has permission to access a "parent" folder automatically has permission to access any of that folder's subfolders.

Set General Permissions

1. Right-click the file or folder, and choose Properties from the shortcut menu.

2. On the Security tab, turn off the check box to allow "inheritable" permissions if you want to remove anyone who already has permission to access the file or folder.

3. If prompted, click the Remove button to delete all the previous settings.

4. Click the Add button. In the Select Users, Computers, Or Groups dialog box, select the individuals, computers, or groups who may access the file or folder, click Add, and then click OK.

5. Select an individual or a group, and turn on the check boxes to specify access permissions.

6. Repeat step 5 to set permissions for all those listed.

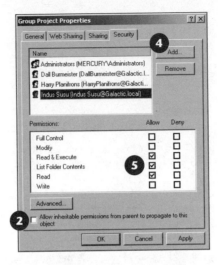

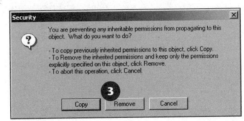

Add yourself! *When you're adding specific users to your permissions list, don't forget to include yourself! If your name isn't in the list, you won't have access to the file or folder.*

"Child objects"? *The check box in the Access Control Settings dialog box for resetting permissions on all "child objects" and "enabling propagation" and so on is displayed only if you're setting permissions for a folder and not for individual files. What this tortured language really means is that by turning off this check box, the individual permission settings for the files and folders (the "child objects") contained in the parent folder will be removed, and the permission settings of the parent folder will be applied to the child objects.*

Set Specific Permissions

1 Click the Advanced button on the Security tab of the Properties dialog box.

2 Select an individual or a group for whom you want to specify permissions.

3 Click the View/Edit button.

4 Specify the items to which these permissions will apply.

5 Turn on or clear the check boxes to specify the permissions.

6 Click OK.

7 Repeat steps 2 through 6 to specify permissions for other users.

8 Turn on the check box to reset permissions on all child objects if these permissions are to apply to all subfolders and files contained in this folder.

9 Click OK, and then click OK again in the file's or the folder's Properties dialog box.

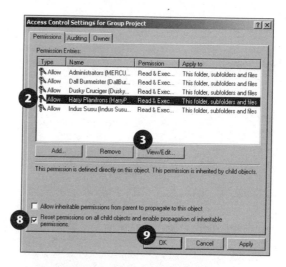

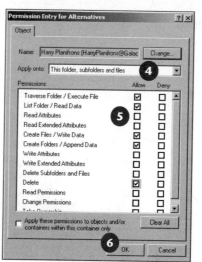

Adding New Users

When you're the administrator of a computer, you can grant other people access to the computer, and, if they're part of a workgroup, access to shared content on other computers in the workgroup. You do this by adding individuals to a group. Each group has specific access rights, so you assign individuals to a group based on the rights you want to grant them as new users.

Local Users and Groups

Create a New User

1. Right-click the My Computer icon on the Desktop, and choose Manage from the shortcut menu.

2. Click the plus sign to expand the Local Users And Groups item.

3. Right-click Users, and choose New User from the shortcut menu.

4. Enter a unique user name (up to 20 characters long, using letters and/or numbers).

5. Complete the other personal information.

6. Type and then retype a password (up to 14 characters long).

7. Specify whether the user may change his or her password and, if so, when.

8. Click the Create button, and then pass the information on to the new user.

9. Repeat steps 4 through 8 for any additional new users. Click Close when you've finished.

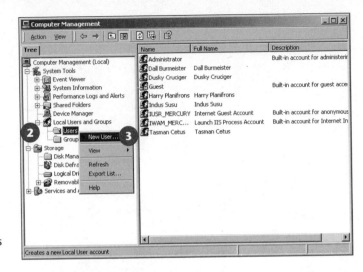

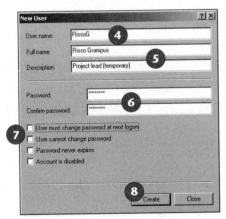

SEE ALSO

For information about creating custom groups, see "Defining Custom Access" on page 286.

For information about defining the access rights of each group, see "Defining Access Rights" on page 287.

TIP

Network restrictions. *In a typical client-server network (where a domain exists), the system administrator adds new users and sets access rights to the network. This information resides on a server instead of on the local computer. Adding local users to a computer allows the users to log on only to the computer and not to the network.*

Add a User to a Group

1. Double-click the user's name.

2. On the Member Of tab, click the Add button.

3. Select the group to which you want to add the user.

4. Click the Add button.

5. Repeat steps 3 and 4 if you want to add the same user to other groups.

6. Click OK.

7. Click OK.

8. Repeat steps 1 through 7 to add other users to the groups.

9. Close the Computer Management console when you've finished.

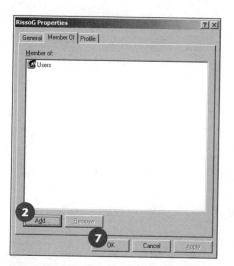

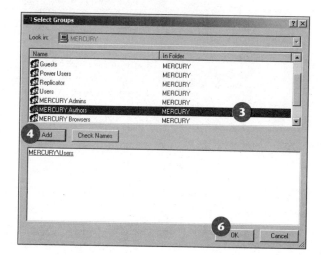

Defining Custom Access

By default, Windows 2000 creates certain groups and assigns specific access rights to each group. By creating new groups and assigning users to these groups, you can define your own set of access rights. After you've created the new groups, you'll need to edit the security settings to define the access rights for each group.

SEE ALSO

For information about modifying the security settings, see "Defining Access Rights" on the facing page.

TIP

Client-server policies. *On a client-server network, the groups and group policies set by the network administrator override any local groups and group policies for network access.*

Create a New Group

1. Right-click the My Computer icon on the Desktop, and choose Manage from the shortcut menu.

2. Click the plus sign to expand the Local Users And Groups item.

3. Click Groups, and review the existing groups.

4. Right-click Groups, and choose New Group from the shortcut menu.

5. Enter a unique group name and a description of the group.

6. Click the Add button. In the Select Users Or Groups dialog box, select the members of the group, click Add, and then click OK.

7. Click Create.

8. Create additional groups if you want, and then click Close.

9. Close the Computer Management window when you've finished.

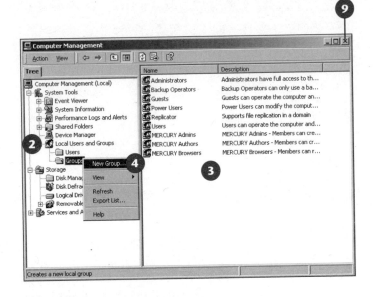

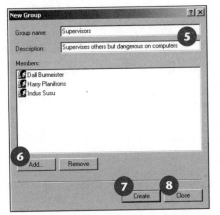

Defining Access Rights

Permissions to access resources and modify the computer environment are set by assigning individuals to groups that contain pre-defined access rights. To change the rights assigned to a group, you change the security settings on the computer.

Local Security Policy

TIP

Network policies. *On a client-server network, any security policies you create locally can be overridden by network policies.*

SEE ALSO

For information about adding the administrative tools to the Start menu, see "Change What's Displayed" on page 71.

Change the Security Settings

1 Click the Start button, point to Settings, and choose Control Panel from the submenu.

2 Double-click the Administrative Tools icon.

3 In the Administrative Tools window, double-click Local Security Policy.

4 Click the plus sign to expand the Local Policies item, and click User Rights Assignment.

5 Double-click the right you want to change.

6 Modify the listing to assign or revoke rights:

◆ Turn off a check box to revoke this right for a group.

◆ Turn on a check box to restore this right to a group.

◆ Click the Add button to add a group to the list.

7 Click OK.

8 Repeat steps 5 through 7 to change any other rights, and close the console when you've finished.

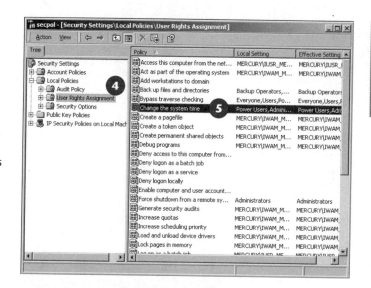

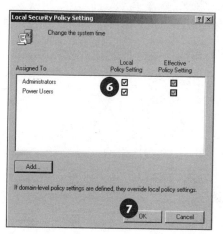

Hosting a Web Site

When Internet Information Services (IIS) is installed on your computer, you can host your own web site. You can create a custom home page, publish information on an intranet or an *extranet* (an intranet to which you have given individuals outside your company limited access), make specific files available to others, or test and modify web pages before they're posted on the main web server.

TIP

FTP. *Use the* ftproot *folder (in your Web Publishing folder) to hold the documents you want to make available for downloading using FTP.*

SEE ALSO

For information about using FTP, see "Downloading Files over the Internet" on page 212.

Set Up the Service

1 If Internet Information Services (IIS) isn't installed on your computer, use the Add/Remove Programs tool in the Control Panel to install it.

2 In the Control Panel, double-click the Administrative Tools icon.

3 In the Administrative Tools window, double-click the Personal Web Manager icon.

4 If the Start button is displayed, click it to start Web Publishing.

5 Note the address of your home page.

6 Click the address of your home directory.

7 Add your web pages to this folder. Make sure you have a start page named *Default.htm* or *Default.asp.*

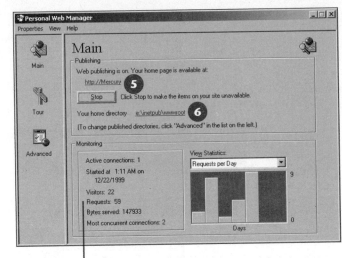

Shows how many connections have been made to your web site.

Web Sharing tab. *When you install IIS on your computer, Windows 2000 adds a Web Sharing tab to every folder's Properties dialog box. You can use that tab to specify whether the folder is accessible on the intranet, and to list its alias and its sharing properties. Turning on web sharing from this tab achieves the same result as using the Add button in the Personal Web Manager.*

Use an alias. *The use of an alias for a folder lets you create a virtual file structure that simplifies the administration of the web site, provides easier access to files, and provides security by not displaying the true folder structure of your computer to those visiting the web site.*

Document access. *To access a document in a folder that's set for web sharing, include the folder name (the alias) and the document name in the web address.*

Customize the Site

1. In the Personal Web Manager, click the Advanced button.

2. Specify the names of the default web pages to be used in each folder.

3. Select a folder, and click the Edit Properties button.

4. Make any changes to the folder's properties, and click OK.

5. To add web access to an existing folder, click the Add button.

6. Use the Browse button to specify the location of the folder to be accessed.

7. Specify a name (the alias) for the folder.

8. Set the access settings for the folder, and click OK.

9. Use a browser on a different computer to view and test your site.

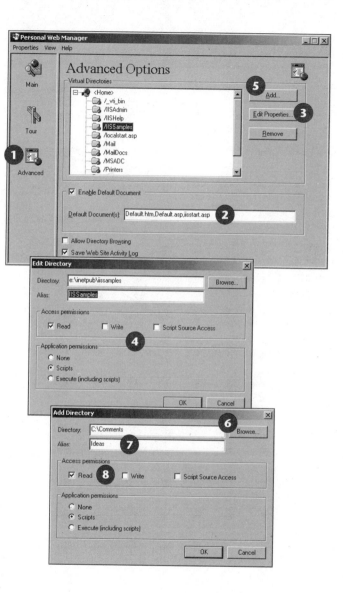

Scheduling Programs

If you use a program regularly, you can schedule it to start automatically. The use of this feature is usually very specialized—running a program unattended in the evening when you're not using the computer, for example, or having a document appear that must be completed each day before you can go home—so you'll need to adapt these processes to your own environment.

Scheduled Tasks

SEE ALSO

For information about scheduling periodic backups of your data, see "Backing Up Your Files" on page 250.

Schedule a Program to Run

1 Click the Start button, point to Settings, and choose Control Panel from the submenu.

2 Double-click the Scheduled Tasks icon.

3 Double-click Add Scheduled Task. Click the Next button to run the Scheduled Task Wizard.

4 Select the program or click the Browse button to locate the program. Click Next.

5 Specify when you want the program to run, and click Next.

6 If necessary, provide additional scheduling information. Click Next.

7 Enter your user name and password, and click Next.

8 Review the information, and then click Finish.

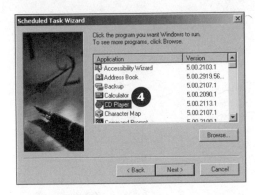

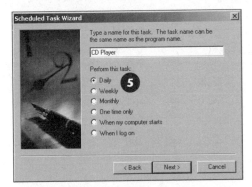

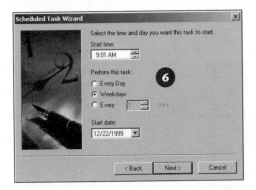

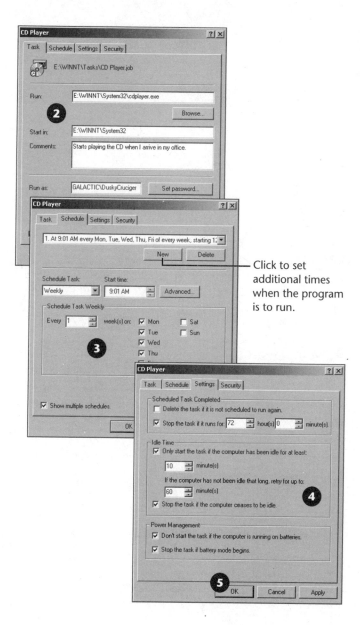

TIP

Use command switches.
To customize the way a program is executed, use command switches in the Run box on the Task tab. See the program's documentation for allowable command switches.

TRY THIS

Start a document. *Use the Add Scheduled Task Wizard to create a task whose purpose is to run WordPad at a specific time each day. (Use the Browse button to locate the program.) Right-click the WordPad task, and choose Properties from the shortcut menu. In the Run box on the Task tab, move to the end of the text, add a space, and type the path and name (enclosed in quotation marks) of a WordPad document. Close the dialog box, right-click the task again, and choose Run to test the setup. WordPad should start with the document loaded. You can do this with many different programs.*

Customize the Execution

1. Double-click the task.

2. On the Task tab, modify any program information.

3. On the Schedule tab:

   ◆ Modify the current settings for frequency, date, and time.

   ◆ Click the Advanced button to set an end date or to specify whether the program is to run repeatedly each time it's executed.

   ◆ Turn on the Show Multiple Schedules check box to set a new schedule.

4. On the Settings tab, specify whether the program is to run only when the computer is idle, and whether it's to run when the computer is using battery power.

5. Click OK.

6. Close the Scheduled Tasks folder when you've finished.

Click to set additional times when the program is to run.

Creating Custom Management Tools

The Microsoft Management Console (MMC) is a powerful tool that you can use to manage multiple items on your computer. By adding other "Snap-In" tools to the console, you can create a custom tool that will enable you to manage all the items you need to manage in one location. Of course, you need administrative permission to make changes, as well as a good working knowledge of the advanced features, or you could severely damage the system's configuration.

TIP

MMC. *No, this isn't the tool you've often wanted to use on your computer! It's the Microsoft Management Console icon.*

mmc

Create a Console

1. Click the Start button, and choose Run from the menu.

2. Type *mmc* in the Open box, and click OK.

3. Choose Add/Remove Snap-In from the Console menu.

4. In the Add/Remove Snap-In dialog box, click the Add button.

5. In the console, select the tool you want, and click Add. Complete the steps of any wizard that might appear. Repeat to add other tools.

6. Click Close.

7. Click OK.

8. Use the Save command on the Console menu to save the console for future use.

9. Use the console, and close it when you've finished.

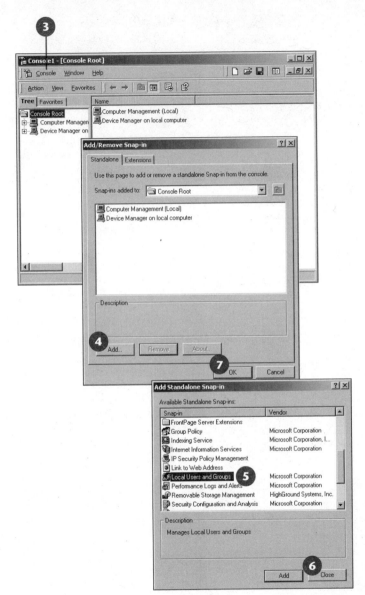

Editing Windows 2000 Settings

Windows 2000 uses a database called the *registry* to keep track of all its settings, including all the programs that are installed on the system. Occasionally—if there's a problem with your system or with a program, or if you simply want to customize the system—you'll need to modify the contents of the registry. Because any modifications to the registry can cause system-wide problems, you should do this only if you have detailed instructions from a reliable source, and—as everyone will warn you—at your own risk and only after you've backed up the registry.

> **TIP**
>
> **AutoComplete.** *The registry edit shown on this page enables the AutoComplete feature at the command prompt when you press the Tab key.*

Edit the Registry

1. Click the Start button, and choose Run from the menu.

2. Type *regedt32* in the Open box, and click OK.

3. Choose Find Key from the View menu. (The key is an identifier for a record or group of records in the database.)

4. Type the name of the key you're looking for, and click Find Next.

5. Check the directory structure to verify that you have the correct key. If so, click Cancel. If it's not the correct key, click Find Next until you've located the correct key, and then click Cancel.

6. Double-click the item you want to change.

7. Make your changes, and click OK.

8. Close the Registry Editor, and see whether the change works as expected.

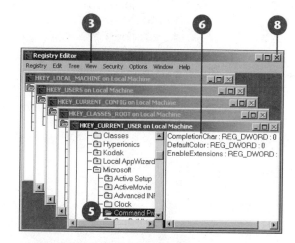

Sharing an Internet Connection

When only one computer on a network has an Internet connection, the connection can be shared with other computers on the network by having the computer with the Internet connection *host* the other computers. Because the host computer assigns new addresses to all the computers on the network, in most cases Internet connection-sharing should be used only in small workgroups and not on networks using domains, gateways, DNS (Domain Name System) or DHCP (Dynamic Host Configuration Protocol) servers, or static IP addresses.

Enable Connection Sharing

1. Make sure no one is working on documents on the network, in case the network is disrupted.

2. On the computer that will share its connection, right-click the My Network Places icon, and choose Properties from the shortcut menu.

3. Right-click the connection to be shared, and choose Properties from the shortcut menu.

4. On the Sharing tab, turn on the check box to enable sharing.

5. If the connection is a dial-up connection, turn on the Enable On-Demand Dialing check box if you want other computers to be able to initiate the connection.

6. Click OK.

7. Restart the computer.

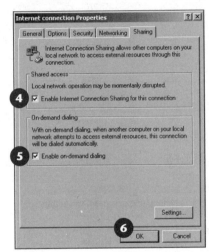

Use the Connection

1. On a computer that will use the shared connection, right-click My Network Places, and choose Properties from the shortcut menu.

2. Right-click Local Area Connection, and choose Properties from the shortcut menu.

3. Select Internet Protocol (TCP/IP), and click the Properties button.

4. Verify that the options for obtaining IP and DNS server addresses are selected, and click OK. Click OK to close the Local Area Connection Properties dialog box, and then restart the computer if you made any changes.

5. If you have an existing dial-up Internet connection, right-click Internet Explorer, and choose Properties from the shortcut menu. On the Connections tab, select an option to disable the connection, and click OK.

6. Repeat steps 1 through 5 for the other computers, and then connect to the Internet from one of them to confirm the connection.

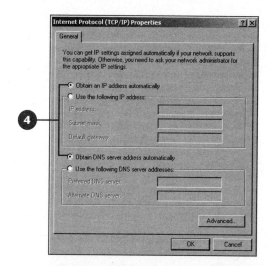

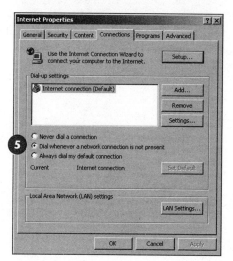

Joining a Domain or a Workgroup

When you're adding a computer to a network or a workgroup, you must identify the computer and specify the domain or workgroup. If you're connecting to a domain—unless you've been granted permission to add a computer to the network—an account for the computer and the user must already have been established on the network before you can connect.

SEE ALSO

For information about running a Control Panel tool as an Administrator, see "Starting a Program with Full Access Rights" on page 281.

TIP

Wizard help. *If you have any problems when naming or adding a computer, click the Network ID button instead of the Properties button, and use the wizard to step through the process.*

Identify the Computer and the Network

1 Right-click the My Computer icon, and choose Properties from the shortcut menu.

2 On the Network Identification tab, click the Properties button.

3 If the computer hasn't already been named, enter a name for it.

4 Specify whether you're joining a domain or a workgroup, and enter the name of the domain or workgroup.

5 Click OK.

6 Close the System Properties dialog box, and restart the computer.

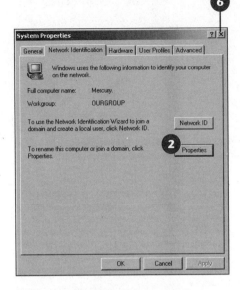

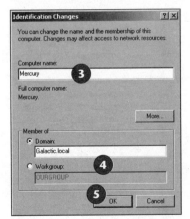

Creating a New Hardware Profile

A hardware profile tells Windows 2000 how your computer is configured, and, if it's configured differently at different times, you notify Windows 2000 by selecting the appropriate profile at startup. This feature is designed primarily for portable computers using docking stations, but it's useful for any computer that uses different hardware setups.

TIP

Laptop profiles. *On a laptop computer using a docking station, Docked and Undocked profiles are created automatically. The laptop detects the docking state and uses the correct profile.*

SEE ALSO

For information about changing hardware configurations, see "Changing a Hardware Profile" on page 298.

Create a New Hardware Profile

1 With the computer running in its normal configuration, right-click the My Computer icon, and choose Properties from the shortcut menu.

2 On the Hardware tab, click Hardware Profiles.

3 With the current profile selected, click the Copy button.

4 Type a descriptive name for the new profile, and click OK.

5 Specify how you want Windows 2000 to select the profiles when the computer starts.

6 Click OK, and then shut down Windows 2000.

7 Attach or remove any removable components that are to be used in the new profile. Restart Windows 2000 and, when prompted, select the new profile. Modify any hardware settings to properly configure your computer.

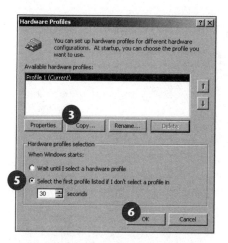

Changing a Hardware Profile

Windows 2000 can properly detect most of the hardware components that are part of your computer. Sometimes, however, you might have to correct a problem by making some settings manually—to specify a similar-but-different device, for example, or to resolve a hardware conflict. Manual hardware settings can also be used to enable or disable a device for a specific hardware profile.

> **TIP**
>
> **Make a copy.** *Before you make any substantial changes to your computer's hardware settings, copy the existing profile. That way, if the changes cause problems, you can revert to the original hardware profile when you restart Windows 2000. Once you're sure the settings are correct, delete the copy so that you don't have to select a profile each time you start the computer.*

Change the Settings

1. Right-click My Computer, and choose Properties from the shortcut menu.

2. On the Hardware tab, click Device Manager.

3. Expand a classification to display a device, and double-click the device.

4. Do any of the following:

   ◆ On the General tab, specify whether the device is enabled or disabled for this or all hardware profiles.

   ◆ On the Driver tab, click Update Driver to find an updated driver or to list all devices so that you can select a different device or driver if the correct one isn't currently listed.

   ◆ On the Resources tab, select a different configuration, select a resource, and click Change Setting to change the Input/Output Range or the Interrupt Request.

5. Click OK when you've finished.

6. Close Device Manager, and then close the System Properties dialog box.

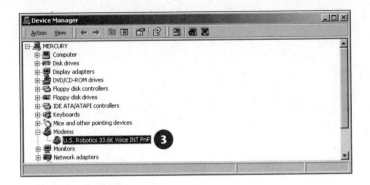

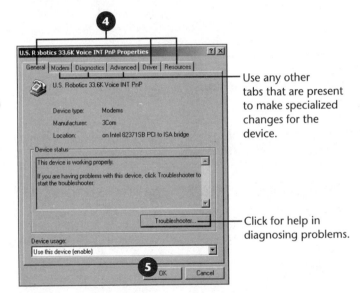

Use any other tabs that are present to make specialized changes for the device.

Click for help in diagnosing problems.

Changing Your Disk Format

Windows 2000 supports three disk formats—FAT, FAT32, and NTFS. The NTFS format provides the speed, resources, and security that aren't available with FAT or FAT32, while FAT and FAT32 provide compatibility with other operating systems (dual-boot or multi-boot configuration) running on your computer. If your hard disk uses FAT or FAT32, and if you're certain that compatibility won't be an issue, you can convert the disk to the NTFS format.

TIP

Convert to FAT32. *To convert from NTFS to FAT32, first back up all the data on the disk (because everything will be deleted in the conversion process). Then format the disk for FAT32, and restore the data.*

Check Your File System

1 Open the My Computer window.

2 Right-click the disk you want to check, and choose Properties from the shortcut menu.

3 Note the file system.

4 Click OK.

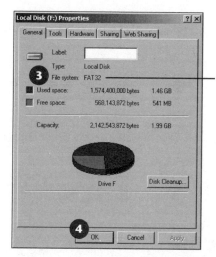

The disk is formatted for FAT32 and can be converted to NTFS.

Convert the Disk

1 Back up your work, and then close all the files and folders on the disk you're going to convert.

2 Click the Start button, point to Programs and then Accessories, and choose Command Prompt from the submenu.

3 At the command prompt, type *Convert drive: /FS: NTFS /v* (where *drive* is the drive letter of the drive to be converted), and press Enter. Wait for the files and the drive to be converted. Close the Command Prompt window when you've finished.

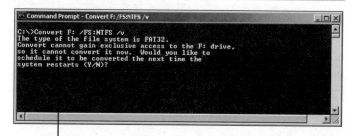

If the converter can't take exclusive access control of the drive, the conversion will be set to take place the next time you start the computer.

Controlling the Startup

If your computer has more than one operating system as a startup option, you can specify which one is the default, the order of the startup options, and the length of time the system waits for your response. If you want to use Windows 2000 exclusively, you can specify that it start by default and that other startup options not be displayed. Once the system starts, you can specify whether anyone else who uses your computer needs to press a key combination to log on.

TIP

Delay the restart. *If you make changes in the Recovery section of the Startup And Recovery dialog box, you'll need to restart the computer to implement the changes. However, if you delay the restart until you've made the changes necessary to implement the secure logon, you'll need to restart only once instead of twice.*

Change the Startup Options

1 Right-click the My Computer icon, and choose Properties from the shortcut menu.

2 On the Advanced tab, click the Startup And Recovery button.

3 Select the operating system that will start if you don't specify otherwise at startup.

4 Turn off the check box for displaying a list of operating systems if you always want the default operating system to start.

5 Specify the actions to be taken if the operating system fails and stops.

6 Click OK. Click OK again if you're told that you need to restart your computer.

7 Click OK to close the System Properties dialog box, and click No if you're prompted to restart your computer but you want to make additional system changes. Click Yes to reboot if you're not making any further system changes.

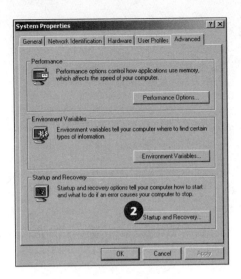

If you want to see the list of operating systems, specify how long it will be displayed before the default system starts.

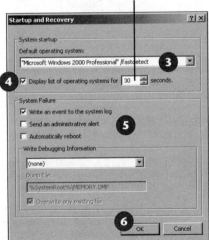

TIP

Overridden. *Any local logon settings can be overridden by network group policies and security settings.*

TIP

Secure logon. *Using a secure logon reduces the possibility that a malicious program known as a "Trojan horse," often used by hackers, might record your user name and password. When you press Ctrl+Alt+Delete, the operating system checks to make sure that no programs are running, thereby disabling the Trojan horse when you log on.*

TIP

Ctrl-Alt-Delete? *Yes, we know you're used to seeing plus signs in key combinations. In Windows 2000, for some unknown reason, the familiar Ctrl+Alt+Delete key combination is sometimes strung together with minus signs (or hyphens). Don't worry about it. Do what you've always done— press the keys simultaneously.*

Require a Secure Logon

1 Save any files you're using, and close all your open programs.

2 In the Control Panel, double-click the Users And Passwords icon.

3 On the Advanced tab, turn on the Require Users To Press Ctrl-Alt-Delete Before Logging On check box to require the key combination, or turn the check box off to skip the key combination and immediately display the Log On To Windows dialog box at startup.

4 Click OK.

5 When prompted, click Yes to restart the computer.

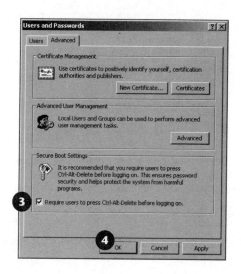

Creating More Disk Space

When a disk is formatted for NTFS, you can compress its files and folders—and even the entire drive—so that you can store even more information in the same location. The cost of compression can be a slightly longer time to access files, which must be decompressed before you can use them. This delay is usually so minor, however, that you won't even notice it on most systems.

SEE ALSO

For information about determining which file system you have and then converting the disk format to NTFS, see "Changing Your Disk Format" on page 299.

Compress a File or Folder

1. Right-click the file or folder, and choose Properties from the shortcut menu.

2. On the General tab, click the Advanced button.

3. In the Advanced Attributes dialog box, turn on the Compress Contents To Save Disk Space check box.

4. Click OK, and then click OK again to close the file's or the folder's Properties dialog box.

5. In the Confirm Attribute Changes dialog box that appears, specify whether to apply the changes to the folder only or to all the subfolders and files in the folder.

6. Click OK. Wait for the files and folders to be compressed.

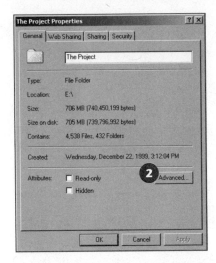

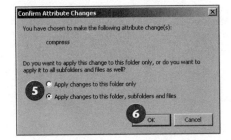

13

Not compressed. *If, in the Confirm Attribute Changes dialog box, you chose to compress only the folder, any items that are already in the folder will not be compressed.*

Move or copy. *Any files that you copy to a compressed folder, or files that you move from another drive to a compressed folder, will be compressed. However, any files that reside on the same drive as the compressed folder, but which are in a different folder that you then move into the compressed folder, will not be compressed (unless they were compressed before you moved them).*

Different colors. *To display the names of compressed files, folders, or drives in a different color, open the My Computer window or another folder window, choose Folder Options from the Tools menu, and, on the View tab, turn on the Display Compressed Files And Folders In An Alternate Color check box.*

Compress a Drive

1. Open the My Computer window.

2. Right-click the drive you want to compress, and choose Properties from the shortcut menu.

3. On the General tab, turn on the check box to compress the drive.

4. Click OK.

5. In the Confirm Attribute Changes dialog box, specify whether to compress only the root directory of the drive or all the folders and files on the drive.

6. Click OK.

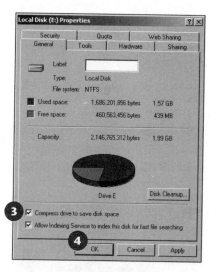

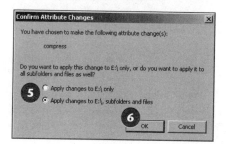

Allocating Disk Space

Disk space is a valuable resource on most computers. When a disk is formatted for NTFS, you can specify the amount of data, or the *quota*, each user can store on a disk. The ability to set a quota is a powerful tool on a computer that's used by more than one person, but it's even more useful when you share folders over your network and allow others to place files in those folders.

TIP

No quota? *If you don't see the Quota tab, either the disk isn't formatted for NTFS or you don't have the administrative rights to set quotas.*

SEE ALSO

For information about formatting a disk for NTFS, see "Changing Your Disk Format" on page 299.

Set the Quota

1. Open the My Computer window, right-click the drive for which you want to set a quota, and choose Properties from the shortcut menu.

2. On the Quota tab, turn on the Enable Quota Management check box.

3. Turn on the check box to deny disk space to stop others from exceeding the quota.

4. Set the maximum usage allowed and the usage that will generate a warning.

5. Turn on check boxes for any logs you want to generate.

6. Click OK. When prompted, confirm that you want to enable quotas.

7. Right-click the drive, choose Properties from the shortcut menu, click the Quota Entries button on the Quota tab, and then close the Properties dialog box.

8. Review the entries.

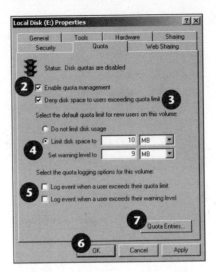

To change a quota, double-click the user's name, and change the settings in the Quota Settings dialog box.

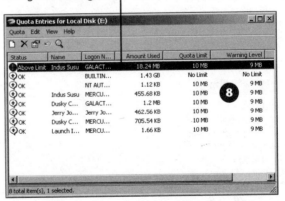

Index

Italicized page numbers refer you to information you'll find in a Tip or a "Try This" entry.

...(ellipsis) in menu
    commands, 123
* (asterisk) wildcards, 61, 212
>> (greater-than signs), *118*
? button (Help button), 15
+ (plus sign) icons in Outlook
    Express, 161
? (question mark) wildcards,
    61, 212
" "(quotation marks) with
    filenames, *61*

accessibility options, 94, *236*,
    238–39, *239*, 240-241
Accessibility Wizard, 240
accessing computers. *See*
    connecting to networks
    or other computers
access rights. *See* permissions
accounts
    Administrator rights, 202, 281
    computer, 284–85
    domain or workgroup, 296
    e-mail and news, 150–51, *151*
    Power Users, 275, 281
    user, 8, *63*, *82*, 281-85
    workgroup, 296
ACPI, 255, *255*

Active Desktop
    arranging, 215
    backgrounds, 220–21, *221*, 222
    displaying pictures on, *221*
    hiding icons, 223
    illustration, 7
Active Directory
    adding users, *187*
    listing printers in, 90
    searching for printers or
        people, *23*, *42*, 126, *126*
active windows, 97
Add Printer Wizard, 122, 130
Address Bar, 43, 45, *46*, *47*, 49, 74
Address Book
    adding addresses, *166*, *167*
    adding groups, 167
    addressing messages, 152, 163
    contact information in, 94
    Contacts list and, 166–67
    digital signatures, 173
    finding addresses, 42, 184
    identities and, *168*
    importing addresses into, *167*
    Internet e-mail addresses, 150
    Phone Dialer, 186
    sharing addresses, *168*, 169
    vCards, *167*, 171, *171*, 173
addresses
    e-mail or contacts (*see* Address
        Book; Contacts list)

    servers, 295, *295*
    web sites, 45, *45*, 288, *289*
Address toolbar, *22*, 40, *45*, 74
Administrators group
    changing printer
        functions, *129*
    network administrators, 24
    permissions, 79, 275
    remote control of
        computers, 202
    running programs with
        administrative
        rights, 281
    safer logons, *281*
Advanced Configuration And
    Power Interface (ACPI),
    255, *255*
Advanced Power Management
    (APM), 9, 255, *255*
alerts
    battery alerts, 255
    disk space quotas, 304
    sound alerts, 154, 238
    special key usage, 236
aliases for groups, 167
aligning
    columnar data, 117
    icons on Desktop, 67
    items on fax cover pages, 183
allocating disk-space quotas, 304
allowing access. *See* permissions

alternative input devices, 236
animated Desktop items, 222, 242
annotating. *See* notes
APM, 9, 255, *255*
applications. *See* programs and
    program windows
archiving files. *See* backing up files
area codes, *178*, 195, 197
arranging
    icons in folders, 55
    icons on Desktop, 67, *67*
    items on Favorites menu, 73
    items on Start menu, 67–68
    items on toolbars, 40, 47,
      47, 224
    taskbar and toolbars, 216–17
    windows on Desktop, 66,
      97, 225
ASCII text files, 102–3
asterisk (*) wildcards, 61, 212
attachments, 62–63, 156, *156*,
    157. See also e-mail
audio files. *See* sound files
AutoComplete feature, *293*

Background folder, 221
backgrounds. *See also* Desktop;
    wallpaper
    Desktop, 220–21, 222
    e-mail background colors, 153
    folder windows, 226, 227
    icon text and contrast, 227
backing up files
    Backup Operators group, 79
    Backup program, 94
    Backup Wizard, 250
    catalogs, *252*
    before converting hard-disk
      file system, 299
    daily backups, *251*
    emergency repair disks, 271
    network warnings, *78*
    Normal backups, *250*

procedures, *250*, 250–51
registry file, 271
restoring backed-up files, 252
schedule changes, *251*
bandwidth for streaming media,
    142, *143*
batch files, 119
battery-power status, 255, 291
beep sounds, 238. *See also* alerts
billing codes for faxes, *175*
binary-mode file transfers, 212
bitmaps. *See also* pictures
    creating in Paint, 106–7
    defined, *106*
    editing in Paint, 94, 108–9
    file extensions and icons, 35
    special font characters, 111
    as wallpaper or on Desktop,
      221, *221*
blinking rate of cursors, *259*
boot disks or CDs, *273*
Briefcase, 190–91, *191*
buffering in downloads, 140,
    143, *143*
bulletin boards, 204–5
business cards (vCards), *167*,
    171, *171, 173*
buttons on mouse, 234
buttons on toolbars, 40, 47

cable connections, *205*,
    208–9, *209*
caching shared files or programs
    on hard drives, 86–87
Calculator, 94, *112*, 112–13, *113*
calling cards, dialing with, 195
calling computers. *See* connecting
    to networks or other
    computers; outgoing
    phone calls
canceling. *See* deleting; stopping
    or canceling
capitalization in passwords, *261*

capturing screen images, *109*
cascading Desktop windows, 66
CD Player, 94, *138*, 138–39, *139*
CDs and CD drives
    downloading album
      information, 138,
      138, 139
    exploring CD contents, 21
    installing programs, 278
    playing CDs, 138–39
    Windows 2000 CD, 272, *273*
certificates, 172, 173
Character Map program, 94,
    105, 111
characters, 105, 111. *See also*
    keyboards
Chat feature (NetMeeting), *89*, 184
checking for new e-mail, 154
child objects in permissions, *283*
classic folder windows, 229
clearing
    Calculator data, 113
    command prompt window, 114
    lists of recently used items, 74
clicking. *See* mouse actions
client-server networks, 3,
    24–25, *285*
Clipboard, 98, *105*
clocks, 218, 256–60
closing
    command prompt window, 114
    dialog boxes, 104
    folders, 20, 225
    programs or Windows
      2000, 120
    windows, *10*, 10–11, *66*
CODECs, 145
collating print jobs, 123
color
    compressed folders or files, *303*
    e-mail backgrounds, 153
    fonts, 244
    icons, *221*, 227, 242, *244*
    monitor color-resolution
      settings and palette,
      242, 245

monitor color schemes, 240,
    241, 244
mouse pointers, *233*
Paint color choices, 106–7
command prompt
    changing folders, *51*
    changing settings
      permanently, *115*
    climbing directory trees, *118*
    copying text, 117
    displaying just-executed
      command, *116*
    FTP commands, 212
    listing commands, 116
    MS-DOS program behavior, 119
    multiple monitors and, *247*
    network printers and, 133
    renaming multiple files, 61
    repairing computers, 273
    repeating commands, 115
    running commands, 114–15
    sending output to files, 118
    sending print files to
      printers, *131*
    starting command prompt, 51
    starting computer with, 272
    switches, *114, 115*
commands
    … (ellipsis) in menu
      commands, *123*
    listing available commands,
      13, 116
    listing for FTP servers, 212
    listing of MS-DOS
      commands, 114
    shortcut menus, 13
command switches. *See* switches
comments in windows, 226
compatibility issues, *211*, 245,
    246, 266
components
    of programs, 279
    of Windows 2000, 6–7, 276,
      277 (*see also names of
      specific components*)
compression, 210, *211*, 251, 302–3

Computer Management console, 85, *85*, 269, 270, 284, 286,
computers
 connecting to
  directly by name, *22*
  from other locations, 196–97
  over Internet, 200–201
  with terminals, 204–5
 hardware profiles, *8*, 297–98
 local (*see* local computers)
 locking, 253
 logging on or off, 8, 9
 multiple operating systems on, *8, 63, 300*
 My Computer folder, 21
 in networks (*see* networks)
 power management, 254–55
 security issues, 77
 shutting down, 9
 Windows 2000 startup, 8
 in workgroups, 8, 296
Computers Near Me icon and window, 22
conferencing, *185, 187*
configuration
 dial-in access, 198, 199
 disk-maintenance tools, 267
 documenting, 270
 dual-boot, *8, 63, 299, 300*
 hard-drive efficiency, 267
 hardware profiles, 297–98
 last known good configuration, 272
 MMC and, 292
 network impacts, *78*, 79
 restarting after changes, *9*
conflicts between devices, 269, 298
connecting by phone, 186–87
connecting to e-mail or news accounts
 adding accounts, 150–51
 adding addresses to Contacts list, 166–67
 attachments, 156

 automatically after new e-mail arrives, 154
 customizing Outlook Express, 170
 downloading news messages, 162
 encrypted messages, 172–73
 identities, 168
 mail messages, formats, and servers, 164
 managing messages, 158–59
 newsgroup subscriptions, 160
 reading messages, 154–55, 161
 replying to or forwarding messages, 157
 sending messages, 152–53, 163
 sending vCards, 171
 signatures on messages, 165
connecting to fax modems
 receiving faxes, 180–81
 sending faxes, 178–79
 setup, 174–75, 176–77
connecting to Internet, 43, 184–85, 200–201, 294–95
connecting to networks or other computers
 cable connections, *205*, 208–9
 from different locations, *99*, 195
 host computers, 197
 by modem, 198, 206, 207
 NetMeeting, 184, 202–3
 network printers, 126
 shared folders, 27
 terminal connections, 204–5
 VPN connections, *201*
consoles, 292
Console Tree, *85*
contacts in Address Book, 94
Contacts list
 adding addresses, 166–67
 choosing e-mail recipients, 152
 identities and, 168, *168*, 169
 illustrated, 170
 importing addresses into Address Book, *167*

controlling
 access (*see* permissions)
 computers remotely with NetMeeting, 202–3
 shared programs, 88
Control Panel, *18, 56, 79*
converting
 disks to other formats, *299, 299*
 numbers, 112–13
copies
 number to print, 123
 of e-mail messages, sending, 152
copying addresses
 from History Explorer Bar, *33*
 importing, *167*
 into Shared Contents folder, *168*
 web site addresses, *45*, 49
copying command prompt text, 117, *117*
copying files
 into Briefcase, 190–91, *191*
 in command prompt, 114
 into compressed folders, *303*
 entire documents, 99
 from Internet, 212
 to other computers, 190–91
 to removable disks, 211
 sending by modem, 196–97, 206–7
 with Send To submenu, 62–63
 to use off site, 192–93
copying floppy disks, 211
copying folders, 57, 62–63
copying hardware profiles, *297, 298*
copying information
 to Clipboard, *105*
 Copy command unavailable, *99*
 displaying icons instead of information, 100
 by dragging items, *99*
 editing copied material, 101

 e-mail and news account information, *151*
 embedding or linking, *99, 100, 101*
 to NetMeeting Whiteboard, 89
 to other programs, 98–99
 pasted object formats, 99
 portions of images, 109, *109*, 110
 results from Calculator, 112
 saving items as scraps, *65*
 special characters, 105, 111
copyrights to sound files, *147*
corrupted drivers, 272–73
country-specific settings, 258–59
cover pages
 for faxes, *175*, 178, 183, *183*
 for print jobs, 127
crashing, 120, 271. *See also* problem solving
Create Shortcut Wizard, *63*
creation dates for files, 37, 55
CSID numbers, *176*
currency display settings, 258–59
cursors
 blinking rate, *259*
 enlarging, *233*, 240
 NetMeeting Remote Pointer, 89
 pointer schemes, 232–33
 shapes of, 16
 pointing with mouse, 16
 snapping to default buttons, 235
 using with Narrator, 239
 for window resizing, *11*
Customize This Folder Wizard, 226, 227, 228
customizing Desktop, 49, 214–15, 220–21, 222, 223
customizing display settings, 240–47
customizing e-mail or news accounts, *158, 159*, 171
customizing fax cover pages, 175, *175, 183*

customizing folders
  backgrounds, 227
  classic folder display, 229
  comments in folders, 226
  file-listing display, 54–55
  folder filing structure, 57
  folder windows, 227
  opening folders, 225
  pictures in folders, 228
  problems with, *227*
customizing menus or toolbars
  Favorites menu, 73
  hiding taskbar or toolbars, 218–19
  rearranging toolbar links, 47, *47*
  rearranging taskbar and toolbars, 216–17
  Send To submenu, *62*
  Start menu, 68–71
  toolbars, *40*, 41, 224
customizing mouse or keyboard actions, 16, 232–37
customizing programs
  computer management tools, 292
  Outlook Express, 170
  program installation, 279
  scheduled tasks, 291
  startup behavior, 96
customizing sharing privileges, 82, 286
customizing sounds, *147*, 238–39

D

daily backups, 251, *251*
dates
  date display formats, 256–57
  date stamps on faxes, *182*
  displaying
    in documents, *257*
    over taskbar, *256*
  finding files by, 32, 33, 37

international settings, 258–59
  scheduled tasks and, 291
  sorting files by, 55, 67
  system dates and times, 260
daylight saving time, 260
debugging programs, *269, 272*
decimal numbers, converting, 112–13
defining
  access rights (*see* permissions)
  identities in Outlook Express, 168–69
Defragmentation utility, 267
delaying
  print jobs, *91*, 132
  restart process, *300*
deleting
  Calculator entries, 113
  CD play list tracks, 139
  command prompt text, 115
  customized toolbars, *41*
  Desktop items, 223
  fax cover pages, 175
  files or folders, 59
  folder window pictures, *227*
  group permissions, 82
  links, 26, 47
  menu items, *63, 73, 74*
  NetMeeting items, 89
  parts of images, 109, 110
  print jobs, 128
  programs or components, 279, 280
  recovering deleted files or folders, 60
  Start-menu items, 70, *70*
  text in WordPad, 102
  toolbar items, 224
  unwanted e-mail, 164
  users or groups from printer permissions, 91
  vCards from messages, *171*
  Windows 2000 components, 276–77
denying access. *See* permissions
deselecting files, *58*

deselecting items in groups, 17
Desktop
  accessing icons, *66*
  accessing with toolbars, 40
  arranging
    icons, 67, 243
    windows, 66
  backgrounds, 220–21, 222
  buttons in Save As dialog box, *65*
  color of icon text, *221*
  color schemes, 244
  computers (*see* computers; local computers)
  customizing, 214–15, 220–21
  display scale and resolution, 243
  files and folders, 6, 31, 64–65
  hiding icons, 223
  icons (*see* icons in windows or on Desktop)
  illustration, 6–7
  links, *47*, 49, 50
  multiple monitors and, 246
  saving files to, 65
  toolbar, 40, *66, 223*
  wallpaper, 7, *107*
Device Manager, 269, 298
devices
  device conflicts, 298
  diagnosing problems, 298
  displaying information, 298
  fax modems, 174, 176–77
  hardware profiles, 297–98
  updating device drivers, *269*
  volume controls, 148
diagnosing problems, 268–69, 298.
    See also problem solving
dial-in connections
  connecting to networks, 195, *195*, 197, 198, 199
  HyperTerminal, 204–5
  logging on, 8
  on-demand dialing, 294
  shared Internet connections, 294, *295*

starting connection before opening Internet Explorer, 43
  transferring files, 196–97
dialing phone calls, 186
dialing rules, 178, *178*, 197
dialog boxes, 104
digital
  IDs, 172–73
  recordings, 146
  signatures, 153, 165
dimensions
  for wallpaper, *107*
  in Paint window, 106
dingbats, 265
Direct Connection icon, 209
directories. *See* folders and folder windows
directory services
  Active Directory, 3, 90, *187*
  finding printers or people, *23, 42*, 90, 126, *126*
  importing addresses into Address Book, *167*
  incoming calls, *184*
  NetMeeting calls, *185*
  Outlook Express, 94
  Phone Dialer and, 186, 187
Directory Services Restore Mode, 272
directory trees. *See* file structures; folders and folder windows
disconnecting
  after newsgroup sessions, 162
  FTP server connections, 212
  host computer connections, 197
  HyperTerminal, 204, 207
  NetMeeting sessions, *203*
  Phone Dialer connections, 186
  users from shared folders, *84*
Disk Cleanup utility, 267
disks. *See* floppy disks; hard drives; removable disks and disk drives
disk space, *191*, 302–3, 304

display. *See* monitors
displaying closed captions on
video clips, 141
displaying command prompt
commands, 114, *116*
displaying dates and times,
256–57, *260*
displaying e-mail, news, or
contact information
Contacts list, 152
lists of newsgroups, 160
logs of phone calls, *186*
messages, 155, 161, *163*
displaying faxes, 181, *181*, 182
displaying files or folder structure
classic file-folder display, 229
compressed folders or files, *303*
Console Tree, *85*
copies of offline files, 193
expanded folder structure, 57
file extensions and paths, 75
file structure, 54
folder contents in command
prompt, 114
hidden files or folders, 63, 75
listing files, 54–55
messages in folders, 158–59
recently used documents,
32, 33
displaying fonts or text, 105, 111,
111, 242, 263
displaying hidden icons or links,
49, 223
displaying images or pictures
Imaging program, 94
magnifying images, 110
Paint's grid feature, 108
thumbnail pictures, 108, *108*,
110, *110*
displaying memory
configuration, 114
displaying print queues, 128
displaying toolbars or taskbar
Address Bar, 45
buttons on toolbars, 40
dates and times, 256–57, *260*

hiding or displaying, 218–19
list of toolbars, 40
stacking or resizing, *217*
volume controls, 148
displaying web pages, 43, 222
docking stations, 297–98
docking taskbar and toolbars, 216
documenting system
configuration, 270
documents. *See* files
Documents menu, *74*
domains, 8, 24, *294, 296*
DOS. *See* MS-DOS commands
double-clicking. *See* mouse actions
downloading
CD information, 138, *138, 139*
CODECs, 145
files or media from Internet,
137, 142–43, 212
files via FTP, *288*
fixes and updates, 266, *266*
news messages, 161, 162, *162*
radio broadcasts, 140
Dr. Watson, *269*
draft e-mail messages, *152*
dragging actions with mouse, 17
dragging Briefcase to another
computer, 190–91
dragging dialog boxes, 104
dragging files or folders
onto Desktop, 64–65
files into Briefcase, 190
files into folders, 58
files into Startup menu, 95
files onto printers, 124
folders onto command
prompt, 51
folders to new locations, *57*
web site shortcuts into
folders, 50
dragging items on Desktop
items onto toolbars, 41, 47
printer icons into Printers
folder, 126
resizing list of Desktop
links, 49

scraps onto Desktop, 65
taskbar or toolbars, 216
web site shortcuts onto
Desktop, 50
window borders, 11
windows and display
effects, 242
windows on multiple
monitors, 247
WordPad text onto
Desktop, 65
dragging items to copy, *65, 99, 99*
dragging menu items, 67, 68, 73
dragging messages into
folders, 158
dragging text to new
location, 103
drawing on Whiteboard, 89
drawings. *See* pictures
drawing tools, 106–7, 183
drivers
printer, 90, 122, *131*
starting without, 272–73
updating, *269*, 298
drives. *See* CDs and CD drives;
floppy disks; hard drives;
removable disks and
disk drives
dual-boot computers, *8, 63,*
299, 300
duplicating. *See* backing up
files; *entries beginning*
with copying

editing command prompt
commands, 115
editing faxes and cover pages, 181,
181, 182, 183
editing files
embedded objects, 101, *101*
keeping copies of original files
before editing, *102*
MS-DOS text files, 102–3

Notepad or WordPad, 94,
102–3
web pages on multiple
monitors, *247*
editing group permissions, 286
editing pictures, 94, 108–9, 110
editing play list for CDs, 139
editing registry, 34, 293
ellipsis (…) in menu
commands, *123*
e-mail
accounts, 150–51, *151*
addresses, 150, 152, 166,
167, *173*
alerts for new mail, 154
attachments, 62–63, 156,
156, 157
downloaded *vs.* stored, *159*
encryption, priority, and
digital signatures,
153, 165, 172–73
faxes, e-mailing, *177*
fields don't display, *152*
filtering, rules for, 159
fonts and sizes, *154*
formats, *153*, 164
headers on messages, 170
high- or low-priority, 153
identities and, 168–69
IMAP mail folders, *159*
NetMeeting, 184
organizing, 155, *158*, 158–59
Outlook Express, 94, 170
reading messages, 154–55
sending and receiving
attachments, 156
receiving e-mail, 154–55
replying to or forwarding
messages, 157
saving draft copies without
sending, *152*
secure messages, 172–73
sending messages,
152–53, *154*
Send To submenu, 62–63
writing e-mail off line, *153*

e-mail, *continued*
  servers and downloaded
    mail, 164
  stationery, 153
  styled text in, *153, 165*
  vCards, *167,* 171, *171, 173*
  web site shortcuts in, 50
embedding objects, *99,* 100, *100,*
    101. *See also* pictures
emergencies, 252, 271, *271,*
    272–273, *273*
enclosures (attachments),
    62–63, 156, *156, 157.*
    See also e-mail
encryption, 153, 172–73, 194
enlarging. *See* resizing
erasing
  disks, *210*
  items on Whiteboard, 89
ERDs (emergency repair disks),
    271, 273
Error-Checking utility, 267
errors in file transfer, *207*
events in Windows 2000,
    144, *144,* 233
Everyone group, 82
Excel, *33*
exchanging digital IDs, *173*
exiting
  command prompt sessions, 114
  crashed programs, 120
  FTP sessions, 212
  Magnifier, 241
  Narrator, 239
  NetMeeting, 203
  remote sharing, *203*
  shared Internet
    connections, *295*
  tasks and shutting down,
    9, 120
  Windows 2000, 9, 120
Explorer Bar, 6
exploring
  history of recently used
    documents, 32–33
  Internet sites, 43

My Computer folder, 21
My Documents folder, 20
networks, 21–22
exporting e-mail and news
    account information, *151*
extensions on files, 34–35, 75, *137*
extranets, 288

FAT and FAT32 formats, *83,*
    211, 299
Favorites Explorer Bar, 48, *48*
Favorites menu, 72–73, *73*
Favorites pane, *47*
faxes
  annotating faxes, 181, 182
  area codes, *178*
  cover pages, 175, *175,* 183, *183*
  CSID numbers, *176*
  dialing rules, *178*
  displaying as thumbnails, 182
  e-mailing, *177*
  Fax Cover Page Editor, 183
  fax modems, 174–75, 176–77
  Fax Queue window, 178
  Fax Service Management
    console, 174, 176–77
  fax wizards in programs, *178*
  identifying sender and
    recipient, *179*
  Microsoft Fax, 94
  monitoring, 180
  opening and editing, 110,
    181, *181*
  paging through, 181
  Print dialog box
    unavailable, *179*
  printing, *174, 175,* 179, 181
  receiving, 180–81
  reviewing status, 178
  sending, 178–79, *179*
  setting up to send or receive,
    174–75, *175,* 176–77
  stamping dates on, *182*

storing fax numbers, 174
  TSID numbers, *174*
fax modems, 174–75, 176–77
fax printers, *174, 175,* 179, 181
Fax Queue window, 178
fields missing in e-mail, *152*
file extensions, 34–35, 75, *137*
file formats
  arranging icons by type, 67
  audio files, *136,* 137
  Desktop pictures, *221*
  multimedia files, 145
  searching for files by, 37
  sorting by, 55
filenames
  arranging icons by, 67
  finding files by name, 36
  print job files, 130
  renaming multiple files, 61
  sorting files by, 55
  space characters in, *61*
files
  accessing with toolbars, 40
  adding to Desktop, 64–65
  adding to Startup menu, 95
  addresses in History Explorer
    Bar, *33*
  associating programs with,
    29, 34–35, *103*
  attachments, 156, *156, 157*
  backing up, 94, 250–51, *252*
  batch, 119
  compressing, 302, *303*
  copying
    into Briefcase, 190
    in command prompt
      window, 114
    into compressed
      folders, *303*
    information into other
      programs, 98–99
    inserting entire
      documents, 99
    from networks to use off
      site, 192–93
    to other computers, 190–91

to removable disks, 211
  with Send To
    submenu, 62–63
deleting, 59, 60
descriptions of, 20
digital signature, *165*
downloading from
    Internet, 212
editing
  dragging items into, *99*
  embedded objects, 101
  image files, 110
  keeping copies of
    originals, *102*
  protecting shared
    documents, *81*
  updating after changes, 191
  updating linked
    information, 100
  in WordPad, 102–3
embedding or linking,
    100, 101
encryption and protection, *81,*
    194, 282–83
extensions and formats, 34–35,
    75, *137*
Favorites menu list of,
    72–73, *73*
faxing, 179
filenames, *61,* 130
file size (*see* file size)
frequently used document
    links, 31
hidden files or folders,
    63, 75
initialization, 119
locations of, 75
manually synchronizing, *193*
My Documents folder, 20
opening, 28, 30, *33,* 95
orphaned in Briefcase, *191*
print files, sending to
    printer, *131*
printing, 124, 128, 130–31
properties of, 39
read-only, *81*

recently changed or recently
used, 74, 190–91
renaming, 59, 61, 114
saving, 65, *65*, 191, 210–11
searching for, 32–33, 36–37, 38
selecting and deselecting, *58*
sending command prompt
output to, 118
sharing, 80–81, 85, 86–87
system, 75
Thumbnail previews, *54, 55*
transferring
by incoming calls, 196–97
by modem, 206–7
with NetMeeting, *185*
to print shops, *131*
versions of, 190–91
web site shortcuts in, 50
working off line with, 193
file size
arranging icons by, 67
fitting on removable
disks, *191*
searching for files by, 37
sorting files by, 55
wave files, *146*
file structures
aliases for folders, *289*
listing folder contents, *118*
organizing folders, 54–55,
56, 58
organizing list of favorites, *48*
overview, 12
refreshing lists, *54*
reorganizing, 57
sorting listings, 55, *55*
Start-menu lists, 70
file systems for hard drives, 210,
211, 299, 299
File Transfer Protocol (FTP), 212,
212, 288
file types. *See* file formats
filters
for GIF or JPEG files, *107*
rules for e-mail, 159
for sound files, 145

finding
digital IDs or public keys, *173*
documents
copies of offline files, 193
in History view, 33
Indexing Service, 38
narrowing searches for, 37
recent documents, 30,
32–33
Search command, 36–37
source documents
for linked
information, *100*
e-mail addresses, 152, 184
Help topics, 15
hidden taskbar, *218*
Internet radio stations, 140
Internet sites, 43, 44
keys in registry, 293
networked computers, *23*
people, *23*, 42, *42*, 184, *185*
printers, 23, *23*, 91, 123,
126, *126*
special characters, 105
fixes to system files, 266
flickering screen display, *242*
floating taskbar and toolbars,
215, 216
floppy disks
copying to, 62–63
deleting files from, *59*
duplicating, 211
formatting cautions, *210*
installation of programs, 278
Folder Bar, 158, 170
folders and folder windows
accessing with toolbars, 40
adding to Desktop, 64–65
aliases for, *289*
animating on screen, 242
arranging, 225
child objects in, *283*
classic folder windows, 229
closing, 20, 225
in command prompt, 51,
114, *118*

comments displayed in, 226
compressed folders, 302, *303*
copying, 62–63, 190,
192–93, 211
deleting, 59, 60
Desktop folders, 6, 65
drive letters for, 27
e-mail folders, 158, *158, 159*
Favorites menu or list, 48,
72–73
FTP connections, 212
hidden folders, 63
leaving windows open for
quick access, *192*
listing contents, *54, 55*, 114,
118, 212
locations, displaying full, 75
more space for icon
display, 229
moving and dragging, *57*, 242
My Computer folder, 21
My Documents folder, 20
My Pictures folder, 228
new folders, 56
opening
files in folder windows, *33*
folders in own
windows, 225
My Documents folder, 20
organizing filing systems, 12,
54–55, 56, 57, 58
pictures in backgrounds, 227
previewing pictures in, *60,
110*, 228, *228*
problems customizing, *227*
properties of folders, 39
protecting, 282–83
renaming, 56, 59
restoring entire folders, *60*
scraps in, *65*
searching for, 36, *36*, 37
Send To folder, 63
shared folders (*see* sharing
files or folders)
single or multiple
windows, *225*

sorting files in, 55, *55*
Start-menu submenu
relationships, 70
subfolders, *56*
toolbar customizing, 224
user profile folder, 63
web content option, *110*
web pages in servers, 92
web site shortcuts in, 50
Folders Explorer Bar, *57*
fonts
adding to system, 262
Character Map program, 94
colors, 244, *244*
creating characters, 111
in e-mail messages, *154*
font managers, *263*
Fonts folder, 262
installing with programs, *263*
locations of font files, *263*
On-Screen Keyboard and, 237
overview, 264–65
Private Character Editor, 111
rasterizing, *263*
resizing and changing, 18, 265
smoothing on screen, 242
special characters, 94, 105, *111*
types of, *263*, 264–65
viewing and printing, 263
in windows, 107, 119, *170, 205*
formats of files. *See* file formats
formatting
digital signatures, *165*
disks, cautions, *210*
in e-mail, 153, *153*, 164
lost in WordPad, 102
pasted information format, 99
removable disks, 210
testing removable disks, *211*
forwarding
e-mail messages, 157, *157*
faxes to e-mail Inbox, *177*
Found New Hardware Wizard, 122
frequently used items, 31, 64–65
frozen programs, 120
FTP, 212, *212, 288*

full access rights, 281
Full Control permission, 81
full-screen video clips, 141
full-screen mode for
    programs, *119*

G

garbled keystrokes, 236
garbled text in terminal
    connections, 205
GIF files, *107, 221*
graphics. *See* pictures
grayed options in dialog boxes,
    104, *277*
grid, displaying in Paint, 108
groups (network or workgroup)
    adding computers to, 296
    adding users to, 284–85
    aliases, 167
    assigning access, 83, 283, 286
    changing security access,
        283, 287
    Contacts list, 166
    creating, 167, 286
    file and folder permissions, 282
    limiting access to shared
        folders, 82–83
    logging on to, 8
    monitoring sharing, 84–85
    network policies overriding
        local-access policies,
        286, 287
    peer-to-peer networks, 24
    permissions overview, 79
    setting up network sharing,
        80–81
    shared Internet connections,
        294–95
    shared printers, 91
    workgroups defined, 3
groups of Windows 2000
    components, 276, 277
guest computers, 208, *209*
Guests group permissions, 79

H

hammer icon, 292
hanging up. *See* disconnecting
hard drives
    compressing, 302–3
    disk-format systems, 210, *211,
        299, 299*
    disk-maintenance
        tools, 267
    disk-space quotas, 304
    exploring contents of, 21
    identifying drive with
        Windows 2000
        installation, *63*
    letters for drives, 27
    switching in command
        prompt, *51*, 114
    virtual drives, *27*
hardware
    compatibility list, *246*
    diagnosing problems, 269
    memory configuration
        display, 114
    multimedia requirements, 135
    profiles, *8*, 297–98, *298*
    sound acceleration, 146
headers on messages, 170
hearing screen contents with
    Narrator, 94, 238–39, *239*
Help
    Calculator button
        functions, *113*
    command prompt
        commands, 116
    Dialog Box Help, 15, 104
    FTP commands, 212
    hiding window
        panes in, *15*
    online manual, *14*
    printing topics, *15*
    waiting for first-time
        loading, *15*
hibernation (standby mode), 9,
    254, 255

H

hiding
    Desktop icons, 223, *223*
    files or folders, 63, 75, 223
    Help window panes, *15*
    items in NetMeeting, 89
    links in Desktop list, *49*
    Magnifier, *241*
    read e-mail messages, 161
    shortcut-key underlines, 242
    Start menu, 215
    taskbar and toolbars, 215,
        217, 218, 219
    web pages on Desktop, 222
High Color setting, 242
high-contrast color schemes,
    240, *241, 244*
highlighting text in
    NetMeeting, 89
high-priority e-mail, 153
History Explorer Bar,
    32, 33, 46
history
    of NetMeeting calls, *185*
    of recently used documents,
        32–33
home pages, 288. *See also*
    start pages
host computers, 196–97, 200–201,
    208, *209*
hosting
    Internet connections, 294–95
    web pages, 92, 288–89
Hotmail, *150,* 150–51
hours, displaying, 257, 260
hovering mouse actions, 231, 237
HTML
    digital signatures, *165*
    file extensions and icons, 35
    folder-window templates, 228
    formatting in e-mail, *153*
    hosting web sites, 288–89
    web pages on Desktop, 222
HTTP protocol, 45, *159,* 164
hyperlinks. *See* links
HyperTerminal, 204–5, *205,*
    206–7

I

icons in windows or on Desktop
    accessing on Desktop, *66*
    arranging, 55, 67, 215
    customizing size and display,
        54, *217,* 240
    for different program files,
        20, 28, 34–35
    displaying instead of linked
        files, 100
    dithering on, 242
    drive icons, 21
    file-listing display, 54–55
    frequently used documents, 31
    hammer icon, 292
    hidden icons, 223, *223*
    icon text, *217, 221,* 227,
        244, 264
    more space for display of, 229
    selecting, 16, 214
    underline options, 231
    Word *vs.* WordPad icons, *103*
icons on toolbars or taskbar,
    218, 224
identities in Outlook Express,
    168, 168–69, *169*
IDs, digital or network, *172,*
    172–73
ignored messages, 161, *162*
IIS, 92, 288–89
image quality for fax
    printers, *175*
images. *See* pictures
Imaging Preview program, 35,
    181, *181,* 182
Imaging program, 94, 110, *181*
IMAP protocol and mail, *159,* 164
importing
    account information, *151*
    contact information, *167*
Inbox (Outlook Express), 155
incoming phone calls
    alerts, 180, 185
    directory services, *184*

fax calls, 177, 180
incoming connections, 196
Internet phone calls, *187*
NetMeeting calls, 184, *184,*
    185, 203
phone access to networks, 195
setting modem to answer, 177
transferring files, 196–97,
    206, 207
voice phone calls, 187, *187*
incoming mail servers, 150
increasing screen area, 243
Incremental file backup
    option, 251
Indexing Service, *37,* 38, *38*
infrared ports, *209*
inheritable permissions, *282*
initialization files, 119
in-place editing of embedded
    information, 101, *101*
input devices and options for
    accessibility, 236–37
Input Locales settings for
    keyboards, 259
inserting
    attachments in e-mail, 156
    fields in fax cover pages, 183
    information (embedding or
        linking), 98–99, *99,* 100
    sound files into Sound
        Recorder, *147*
    text in WordPad, 102
installing
    CODECs, 145
    digital IDs, 172
    file and printer sharing, 78
    fonts, 262, *263*
    printers, 78, 122, *122, 130, 131*
installing programs
    installation programs, 278,
        279, 280
    installing procedures, 278
    partial installations, 277,
        278, 279
    permissions for adding or
        deleting programs, 79

registry and, 293
Setup programs, 278, 279, 280
uninstalling programs, 280
installing Windows 2000
    additions to registry, 34
    components, 276–77, *277*
    fixes, updates, and
        patches, 266
    identifying drive with
        Windows 2000
        installation, *63*
    Windows 2000, 2
IntelliPoint software, *18, 235*
international display settings,
    258–59
Internet connections and sites
    accessing with toolbars, 40
    CD information, *138,* 139
    connecting to other
        computers, 200–201
    copying Internet look to
        Desktop, 214
    downloading files, 212
    e-mail addresses, 150
    exploring and browsing, 43
    file extensions and icons, 35
    finding items or people,
        42, 44
    going to specific sites, 45
    hosting web sites, 288
    Internet phone calls, 186, *187*
    Microsoft NetMeeting, 184–85
    newsgroups (*see* newsgroups)
    radio broadcasts, 140
    sharing connections, 294–95
    shortcuts to, 48, 50
    start pages, 46, *46*
    storing pages off line for
        later viewing, *50*
    streaming media, 142–43
Internet Connection Wizard,
    150, 151, 168
Internet Directory, *185*
Internet Explorer
    accessing with toolbars, 40
    clearing History folder, 74

customizing toolbars, 224
exploring and browsing, 43
finding web sites, 44
going to web sites, 45
links, 48, 49, 50, *231*
Narrator and, *239*
overview, 94
radio broadcasts, 140
shared Internet
    connections, *295*
single-clicking, 231, *231*
starting, 43
start pages, *43,* 46
storing pages off line for
    later viewing, *50*
Internet Information Services
    (IIS), 92, 288–89
Internet newsgroups. *See*
    newsgroups
Internet Protocol addresses,
    92, 200–201, *295*
Internet Service Providers
    (ISPs), *46, 151*
intranets
    accessing with toolbars, 40
    going to specific sites, 45
    Microsoft NetMeeting,
        184–85
    posting web pages, 92,
        288–89
    start pages, 46
    Web Sharing tab, *289*
inverted faxes, rotating, 181
inverting color schemes, *241*
IP addresses, 92, 200–201, *295*
IRQ settings, 298
ISPs, *46, 151*

Japanese characters, 127
joysticks, 237
JPEG files, *107,* 221, *221*
jumps. *See* links

keeping copies of original
    files, *102*
keyboards, 94, 236–37, *237,*
    258–259, *259*
keyboard shortcuts
    assigning for programs, 96
    compared with using
        mouse, 16
    copying and pasting, *99*
    creating subfolders, *56*
    ending tasks or shutting
        down, 120
    key commands, 301, *301*
    magnifying Paint pictures, *108*
    quickly turning off sound, *137*
    speeding up calculations, *112*
    typing special characters, 105
keypad (numeric), *112*
keys
    keyboard (*see* keyboard
        shortcuts)
    public and private, *173*
    registry, 293

labels on icons, *217*
languages, installing for display
    settings, 258
laptops, 190–91, 254–55, 297–98
large icon display, 54, 224, 240
large mouse pointers, *233*
large window display, 240
Last Known Good Configuration
    mode, 272
left-handed mouse settings, 234
letters for drives or network
    folders, 27
limiting access. *See* permissions
lines, drawing, 89, 107
linking and embedding, *99,* 100,
    100, 101. *See also* pictures

links
  Address Bar, 47
  creating your own list of, *49*
  deleting, 47
  to documents, 31, 40
  dragging and rearranging, *47*
  fonts and special
      characters, *111*
  hyperlinks illustrated, 7
  linking files to programs,
      34–35
  on Desktop, 48, 49, *49*, 215
  on toolbars, 40, 47, *47*
  Links toolbar, 40, 47, *47*
  renaming on buttons, 47
  to shared folders, 26
  shortcuts for, 50
  underlining and selecting, *231*
  to web sites, 43, 45
listing
  commands, 116, 212
  e-mail folders, *159*
  e-mail messages, 154
  operating systems on
      computers, 300
  radio stations, 140
listing files
  cached files, 87
  contents of FTP
      directories, 212
  folder contents, 114, *118*
  List view, 54
  recent documents and
      activities, 32–33, 74
loading programs. *See*
      opening programs
local computers
  caching shared programs
      on, 86–87
  Fax Service properties, 174
  hosting extranets on, 288
  hosting web sites on, 288
  logging on to, 8, *197*
  network policies overriding
      local access policies,
      285, *286, 287, 301*

protecting folders, 282–83
security settings, 287
sharing Internet connections,
    294–95
storing shared documents
    on, 86–87
locales, regional, 259
local printers, 122
Local Users And Groups item,
    284, 286
locations
  displaying
    file locations, 75
    folder locations, *20*
  dragging folders to new
      locations, *57*
  of fonts, *263*
  My Documents folder, *20*
  off site or remote (*see* working
      off site)
  pixels in Paint window, 106
  shared printers, *91*
  tracking Briefcase files, 191
locking computers, 253
locking files, 81
logging off, *9, 71*
logging on
  changing passwords, 261
  domains defined, 24
  logon names, *63*, 150, 151
  multiple operating systems
      and, *8, 300*
  to NetMeeting directories, 184
  to networks, 198, 199, *301*
  permissions and, 79, *285*
  as Power User, 281
  reestablishing connections
      to shared folders, 27
  required key commands, 301
  secure logons, *281, 301, 301*
  types of access rights, 281
  to Windows 2000, 8, 199
logos with special fonts, 111
logs of computer events, 269
logs of phone calls, 186
low-priority e-mail, 153

M

Magnifier program, 94,
    240–41, *241*
magnifying. *See* Magnifier
    program; resizing
mail accounts or messages.
    See e-mail
Main Identity in Outlook
    Express, *169*
maintenance tools, 267
managing power usage, 254–55
manual for Windows 2000, *14*
manually
  adding links to shared
      folders, *26*
  answering NetMeeting
      calls, 185
  downloading CD
      information, 138
  receiving faxes, 177, 180
  repairing problems, 273
  synchronizing files, *193*
MAPI mail clients, *177*
mapping network drives, 27
marking news messages for
    retrieval, *162*
matching case of characters
    in searches, 37
mathematical calculations,
    94, *112*, 112–13, *113*
maximizing
  toolbars, *40*
  windows, 10–11, 96, *97, 247*
media. *See* multimedia
Media folder, *144*
Media Player
  customizing, 137
  description, 94
  file formats, *137*, 145
  playing sound files, 136–37
  previewing video clips, *141*
  streaming media, 142–43
  typical documents for, 35
meetings software. *See* NetMeeting

members of groups, 167, 285.
    See also groups (network
    or workgroup)
memory configuration, 114
memory requirements for
    programs, 119
menu bars, 6, 240
menu items on taskbar, 218
menus, 6, 13, 16, 242. *See also*
    names of specific menus
message bar (status bar), 6
messages. *See* e-mail; newsgroups
Microsoft Excel 2000, 33
Microsoft Fax. *See* faxes
Microsoft hardware compatibility
    list, *246*
Microsoft IntelliPoint software,
    18, 235
Microsoft Internet Directory, *185*
Microsoft Internet Explorer. *See*
    Internet Explorer
Microsoft Magnifier, 94,
    240–41, *241*
Microsoft Management Console
    (MMC), 292
Microsoft NetMeeting. *See*
    NetMeeting
Microsoft Notepad, 35, 94,
    118, *239*
Microsoft Outlook Express. *See*
    Outlook Express
Microsoft Paint. *See* Paint
Microsoft Windows 2000. *See*
    Windows 2000 Professional
Microsoft Word 2000. *See*
    Word 2000
Microsoft WordPad. *See* WordPad
Microsoft Write, 102–3
minimizing
  CD Player to taskbar
      icon, *139*
  windows, 10–11, *66*, 96,
      97, 225
minutes, displaying, 257, 260
misbehaving programs, 120
MMC, 292

modems
connecting to networks by, 198
connecting with terminals,
204–5
fax modems, 174, 176–77
transferring files by, 206–7
monitoring for faxes, 177
monitors
capturing screen images, *109*
clearing screen in command
prompt, 114
describing screen contents
with Narrator, 94,
238–39
dimensions for wallpaper, *107*
displaying valid settings
for, *243*
flickering screen display, *242*
full-screen display for
programs, 119
High Color or True Color, 242
magnifying elements, 94,
240–41
multiple monitors, *219*, 246–47
refresh rate, *242*
resolution and color, 242,
243, 245
shutting down to save
power, 254
smoothing fonts
on screen, 242
video-card compatibility
list, *246*
months, changing display,
256, 260
mouse actions
accessibility options, 236–37
basics of mouse devices, 16–17
behavior in dialog boxes, 235
changing cursors, 232–33
clicking options, 231
cursors for window resizing, *11*
cursor speed on screen, 235
double-click speed
settings, 234
IntelliPoint software, *18, 235*

MS-DOS program defaults, 119
On-Screen Keyboard and, *237*
right-clicking, 6, 13, *13*
single- or double-clicking,
214, 231
snapping to default
buttons, 235
switching buttons, 234
wheel functionality, 18, *235*
mouse pointers. *See* cursors
mouse wheel, 18, *235*
moving
ahead in print queues, *129*
Desktop list of links, 49
dialog boxes, 104
e-mail into folders, 158
items on menus, 68, 73
notes on faxes, *182*
taskbar and toolbars, 216–17,
219, 224
text, 103
through pages on
Whiteboard, 89
windows, 11, 242
moving files or folders
in Briefcase, *191*
into compressed folders, *303*
linked documents, *100*
into Favorites menu folders, 72
folders or subfolders, 57
items into subfolders, 58
MS-DOS commands
copying text, 117
listing, 116
modifying ways programs
run, 119
navigating in folders, 51
printing to network
printers, 133
renaming multiple files, 61
running, 114–15
MS-DOS programs, multiple
monitors and, *247*
MS-DOS text files, editing, 102–3
multi-boot configurations, *8, 63,
299, 300*

multimedia. *See also* Media Player
audio files, 136–37, 145,
146–47
file formats and CODECs, 145
hardware requirements, 135
Internet media, 142–43, 145
music CDs, 138–39
playing sounds for events, 144
radio, 140
video clips, 141
volume control, 148
multiple
monitors, 246–47, *247*
operating systems, *8, 63,
299, 300*
programs, switching
between, 97
users in Outlook Express
(identities), *168,*
168–69, *169*
multitasking, *97*
music files, 94, 136–37, 139, *139,
147. See also* sound files
My Computer window, 21, *27,* 28
My Documents folder, 20, *20,* 28,
62–63, 223
My Network Directory, *187*
My Network Places window, 22,
23, 26, 27, 126
My Pictures folder, 228

names
of Briefcases, 190
of computers, *22,* 92, 296
of disks, 210
of files (*see* filenames)
of folders, 56, 289
of items on Start menu, 67, *69*
of newsgroups, *160*
of people or contacts, 94, 152,
166, *166, 167*
of users or groups, *8, 63,
82, 198*

Narrator program, 94, 238–39, *239*
NetMeeting
Chat feature, *89*
connection requirements, *184*
history of calls, *185*
as meeting software, 184–85
overview, 184–85
Phone Dialer vs., *185*
re-calling people, *185*
remote control feature,
202–3, *203*
saving session information, *89*
Setup Wizard, 184
sharing programs, 88–89
Whiteboard activities, 89
Net Phone calls, 187
network administrators. *See*
Administrators group
Network Connection Wizard,
196, 198, 200, 208
network folders. *See* sharing files
or folders
Network ID Wizard, *296*
Network Neighborhood icon, 22
network printers. *See* sharing
printers
network protocols. *See* protocols
networks
adding computers to, 296
backing up files to, *250*
caching shared documents on
hard drives, 86–87, *87*
client-server, 24–25
copying files to use off site,
192–93
disconnecting users from, 84
domains, 24
e-mail protocols and
servers, 164
exploring, 21–22
groups, 79
locked computers, 253
logging on, *8,* 199, *301*
monitoring connections,
84–85
NetMeeting connections, 185

networks, *continued*
   network IDs, *172*
   overriding local policies or
      logon, *286, 287, 301*
   overview, 24
   passwords, changing, *261*
   peer-to-peer, 24–25
   permissions, 79, *285*
   personal fax cover pages
      and, *175*
   program installation, 278
   searching for connected
      computers, *23*
   security, 79
   shared
      files and folders, 26, 78,
         80–81, *81*, 82–83
      Internet connections, *294*
      printers, 90–91, *91*
      programs, 88–89
   starting with or without
      connections, 272
   synchronizing files, *193*
   types of, 24–25
newsgroups
   adding accounts, 150–51, *151*
   customizing window, 170
   digital signatures, 165
   full names of, *160*
   identities and, 168–69
   messages
      downloading, 162, *162*
      reading, 94, 161, *161*
      replying to, 163, *163*
      sending, 163
      subscribing to, 160
      synchronizing, 162
      watching or ignoring, *162*
   news server names and
      addresses, 151
   Outlook Express and, *96*
   threads, *161*
   vCards, 171
   working off line, 162
non-PostScript printers, *263*
Normal backups, *250*, 251

notebook computers. *See* laptops
Notepad, 35, 94, 118, *239*
notes
   annotating folder
      windows, 226
   in NetMeeting, *185*
   on faxes, 178, 181, 182
   on images, 110
notifications
   of fax reception, *175*
   of new e-mail, 154
NTFS format
   changing or choosing, *211, 299*
   disk-space quotas, 304
   file compression, 302–3
   file encryption, 194
   removable disks, 210
   security settings, 80, *83*, 282
numeric keypad, *112*

O

objects, 98–99, *99*, 100. *See also*
   pictures
Offline Files icon, 193
Offline Files Wizard, 192
online help. *See* Help
on/off buttons on computers, 255
On-Screen Keyboard, 94, 237, *259*
opening faxes, 175, 181, *181*,
   182, 183
opening files
   attached files, 156
   basics, 28
   in folder windows, *33*
   in Imaging program, 110
   in Paint, *107*, 108–9
   recently used files, 30, 32
   in WordPad, 102
opening folders, 20, 33, 225
opening programs
   accessing with toolbars, 40
   automatically, 95, 290–91
   command prompt
      commands, 114–15

on Desktop, 7
by double-clicking files, 28
with full access rights, 281
full-screen startup mode, *119*
Internet Explorer, 43
methods in Windows 2000, 94
MS-DOS, 119
multiple, 97
Paint, 106
restarting after closing, *95*
startup behavior of programs,
   96, 119
when Windows 2000 starts, 95
Windows 2000 procedures, 94
opening Recycle Bin, 60
opening windows, 10–11, 51, 61,
   66, *66*
OpenType fonts, 264
operating systems
   choosing at startup, 300–301
   disk formats and, 299
   multiple, *8, 63, 300*
options in dialog boxes, 104
organizing
   e-mail messages in folders, 158
   files in folders, 54–55, 56, 58
   hard drives, 267
   menu items, *48*, 67–68, *69*,
      72–73
   scraps in folders, *65*
orientation of fax pages, *175*
orphaned files in Briefcase, *191*
outgoing fax calls, 178–79
outgoing mail servers, 150
outgoing NetMeeting calls,
   184–85, 203
outgoing phone calls, 184, 185,
   186–87, 195, 203
outline fonts, 264
Outlook Express
   accessing with toolbars, 40
   adding accounts, 150–51
   attachments, 156
   Contacts list, 166–67
   customizing, 170, 224
   digital IDs or public keys, *173*

downloading and working
   off line, 162
identities, *168*, 168–69
launching, 150
mail protocols and, 164
messages
   managing, 158–59
   reading, 154–55, 161
   replying to or
      forwarding, 157
   sending, 152–53
   signatures on, 165
   opening as news reader, *96*
   subscribing to newsgroups, 160
out-of-town connections. *See*
   working off site
output files, 118, 130–31
overlapping icons, 67
overlapping windows, 66, *97*
overriding local access
   permissions, *286, 287, 301*

P

padlock icon, 173
page orientation for faxes, *175*
pages
   choosing number to print, 123
   in faxes, 181
   in Imaging program files, *110*
   on Whiteboard, 89
Paint, 35, 106–109, *107, 108, 109*
Paint-type pictures, *221*
parallel ports, 133, *209*
Parallel Technologies
   web site, *209*
parent folders, 225, *282, 283*
parts of documents. *See also*
   embedding objects
   copying parts of images, 109,
      109, 110
   saving on Desktop, 65
   saving as scraps, *65*
password-protected screen savers,
   203, 230

passwords
case-sensitivity, *261*
changing, 261
dialing in to networks, *198*
e-mail, 150
FTP connections, 212
identities, 168
logging on with, 8
new computer users, 284
news servers, 151
power-management settings
and, 255
screen savers, *203,* 230
unlocking computers, 253
pasting. *See also entries beginning*
with copying
from Clipboard, *105*
command prompt text, 117
Copy or Paste command
unavailable, *99*
editing copied material, 101
embedding or linking objects,
99, 100
icons instead of
information, 100
items onto Whiteboard, 89
into other programs, 98–99
pasted information formats, 99
portions of files, *65, 109,* 110
results from Calculator, 112
special characters, 105, 111
web site addresses, *45,* 49
patches for system files, 266
paths
command prompt commands,
51, 114, *115*
displaying for files, 75
for print-job files, 130
working-folder paths, 119
patterns on Desktop, 220, *221*
pausing
audio file playback, 136
CD playback, 138
print jobs, 128
in streaming media, *143*
video-clip playback, 141

PCL printing, 127
peer-to-peer networks, 24–25
performance
caching shared documents, *87*
disk-maintenance tools, 267
file compression and, 302
slow network site
compilation, *23*
slow performance with
sharing, *80*
slow file transfers, *207*
speeding up
calculations, *112*
folder display, 229
hard drives, 267
streaming media
downloads, 143
permissions
adding users, *82,* 282, 283,
284–85
Administrators group, 79, 275
allowing NetMeeting
control, 88
allowing or denying access,
81, 83, 85, 282–83
child objects, *283*
connecting by modem, 198
group access rights, 79, 81,
82, 83, 286
including self in lists, *283*
inheritable permissions, *282*
MMC and, 292
network policies overriding
local access policies,
285, 286, 287
NTFS file system, *83*
parent and subfolder
permissions, *282*
Power Users group, 79, 275
Run As command, *281*
security settings on local
computers, 287
shared printers, 91
shared programs, 88
starting programs with full
access rights, 281

personal fax cover pages, *175*
Personal Web Manager, 288, 289
phone calls. *See* incoming phone
calls; outgoing phone calls
Phone Dialer, *185, 186,*
186–87, *187*
phone lines, 176–77, 180, 186–87
phone numbers. *See also* Address
Book; Contacts list
area codes in fax numbers, *178*
calling with Phone Dialer, 186
dial-in connections, 197
pictures
adding text to, *107*
bitmaps defined, *106*
capturing screen images, *109*
creating in Paint, 106–7
Desktop, 221, *221*
editing, 94, 108–9, 110
in e-mail, 153
of file contents, *54, 55,*
108, 110
in folder backgrounds, 227
Imaging program, 94, 110
My Pictures folder, 228
picture fonts, 265
special characters for
fonts, 111
thumbnails, *54, 55, 108, 110,*
182, *228*
wallpaper effects, *221*
placing calls, 184, 185, 186–87,
195, 203
Plain Text formatting, *153*
playing multimedia files
audio files, 136–37, *143*
CDs, 138–39
quickly turning off sound, *137*
radio broadcasts, 140
streaming media, 142–43
video clips, 141
play list for CDs, 139
plug-and-play printers, 122
pointing to items. *See* cursors;
mouse actions; selecting
items on screen

POP3 mail protocol, 164
portable computers. *See* laptops
portions of documents. *See* parts
of documents
ports, 133, *209*
posting newsgroup messages,
161, 163
posting web pages, 92, 288–89
PostScript fonts, 264
PostScript printing, 127
power buttons on computers, 255
power management, 9, 254–55
Power Users group, 79, 275,
281, *281*
pressing mouse buttons, 16–17, 18
preventing changes. *See*
permissions; security
preventing problems
backing up files, 250–51
boot disks, *273*
disk-maintenance tools, 267
documenting system
configuration, 270
emergency repair disks, 271
restoring backed-up files, 252
previewing
Desktop patterns, 220
event sounds, 144
file contents, *54, 55*
pictures, 228, *228*
screen savers, 230
tracks on CDs, 138
video clips, *141*
preview pane for e-mail, 155, 170
printer fonts, 264
Printers folder, 56, 125
printing and printers
Active Directory listing,
90, *126*
command prompt
printing, 133
default printers, *124,* 125, *125*
different printers' dialog
boxes, *123*
directly from Windows
2000, 124

printing and printers, *continued*
  faxes, *175,* 179, *179,* 180–81
  to files, 130–31, *131*
  finding printers, *23, 91,* 123,
    126, *126*
  font sample printouts, 263
  Help topic printing, 14, *15*
  installing local printers, 122
  plug-and-play printers, 122
  printer drivers, 122, *131*
  print jobs
    canceling, 128
    delaying, *91,* 132
    multiple copies of, 123
    pausing or restarting, 128
    priority of, 129
    separating, 127
  print queues, 128, *129, 132*
  print servers, 126
  from programs, 123
  selecting printers, 104
  sending print files to
    printers, *131*
  serial printers, *122*
  service bureaus, *131*
  shared or network printers,
    25, 90–91, *91,* 126
  unlisted printers, *126*
  without a printer attached, 132
  WordPad documents, 103
print shops, *131*
priority e-mail settings, 153
priority of print jobs, 129
privacy, 194, 230. *See also* security
private and public keys, *173*
Private Character Editor, 111
private networks, 198, 200–201
problem solving
  ACPI option missing, *255*
  BCC field in e-mail
    missing, *152*
  Briefcase has orphaned
    files, *191*
  calculations are slow, *112*
  cannot add sender to
    Address Book, 166

cannot arrange icons as
  desired, *67*
cannot create subfolders, *56*
changes made to online and
  offline files, 193
clock not on taskbar, *260*
command prompt text
  copying, *117*
commands not on shortcut
  menu, 13
Copy or Paste commands
  unavailable, *99*
cursor won't snap to default
  buttons, *235*
deleted files need to be
  recovered, *59, 60*
device conflicts, 298
dialog-box options are
  grayed, 104
disk-space quota problems, *304*
drivers for devices need
  updating, *269*
editing in-place not
  working, *101*
embedded information
  can't be edited, 101
fax printer sharing, *174*
File And Printer Sharing
  option missing, 78
file sharing is slow, *80*
files opening in window
  without toolbars, *33*
file transfer errors, *207*
file transfer slow, *207*
finding files and folders, *64*
finding hidden taskbar, *218*
finding people's addresses, *42*
finding source files for linked
  information, *100*
folders can't be
  customized, *227*
garbled streaming media, *143*
help sources
  diagnosing problems,
    268–69
  Dr. Watson, *269*

getting ideas from shortcut
  menu commands, *13*
Help, 14–15
  online manual, *14*
  repairing systems, 273
  system updates, 266
  Troubleshooter Wizard, 269
hidden folders, 63
high resolution slows
  computer, *242*
icons are cluttered, 67
network asks for user name
  and password, *198*
network is down and I need
  shared files, 87
network policies and local
  access policies, *286, 287*
Print dialog box missing,
  123, 179
printers shared by too many
  users, 90
printer wasn't detected, 122
programs not listed in
  Add/Remove Programs
  dialog box, *279*
quitting programs and
  shutting down, 120
reconnecting to networks, *197*
reinstalling Windows
  2000, 273
screen is flickering, *242*
searching for text is slow, *37*
Sharing command
  unavailable, *81*
starting up in special
  modes, 272–73
Start menu is disorganized, *69*
Stop button grayed in Sound
  Recorder, *147*
synchronizing files, *87, 193*
terminal-connection
  problems, 205
undoing actions, *60*
viruses in attached files, *156*
wrong program opens
  files, 34

Product Updates web site, 266
profiles
  hardware, 8, 297–98, *298*
  user, 63, *63*
programs and program windows.
  See also names of specific
  Windows 2000 programs
  active windows, 97
  arranging open programs
    on Desktop, 11, 66
  command prompt, 114–15,
    116, 117, 118
  copying information
    between, 98–99
  fax wizards, *178*
  file type associations, 29, *29,*
    34–35, *103*
  full names on taskbar, 97
  installing or removing (*see*
    entries beginning with
    installing)
  maximizing and minimizing
    windows, 10–11, *66*
  MS-DOS program behavior, 119
  opening and closing windows,
    10, 10–11
  printing from, 123
  quitting, 120
  registry and, 34
  related files and folders, 96
  resizing windows, 10–11, *11*
  running programs (*see* opening
    programs)
  shared programs, 86–87,
    88–89, *185*
  on Start menu, 67–68, 69
  startup size of windows, 96
  switching between multiple
    programs, 97
  Windows 2000 programs
    list, *94*
prompts in command prompt
  window, 114
properties
  of documents, 38, 39
  of shortcuts, *20*

protecting files and documents. *See* permissions; security
protecting your work. *See* preventing problems
protocols
 FTP, 212, *212*
 HTTP, 45, *159*, 164
 IMAP, 164
 network, *208*
 POP3 mail, 164
public and private keys, *173*
public folders, *159*
publishing web pages, 92

queries
 Indexing Service, 38
 searching Internet, 44
question mark button (Help button), 15
question mark wildcards, 61, 212
queues, print, 128–29, *129*, 132
quick keys. *See* keyboard shortcuts
quickly opening files or programs, 6, 31, 40, *47*
quitting. *See* exiting
quotas, allocating disk space, 304
quotation marks, *61*

radio broadcasts, 140, *140*
radio buttons in dialog boxes, 104
random play for CDs, 138
raster fonts, 264
reading
 messages, *154*, 154–55, 161, *162*
 screen contents aloud (Narrator), 94, 238–39, *239*
read-only documents, *81*
Read permission, 81

rearranging. *See* arranging
receiving
 e-mail, *154*, 154–55, 156
 faxes, 176–77, 180–81
 files by modem, 206–7
 incoming calls (*see* incoming phone calls)
 text over terminal connections, 205
recently changed files, 190–91
recently used files, 30, 32, 55, 74
recipients
 of e-mail messages, 152
 of faxes, 178, *179*
reconnecting
 to computers with dial-in access, *197*
 to networks, 193 (*see also* synchronizing files)
 to shared folders, 27, *84*
recording sound files, 94, 146–47
recovering deleted files or folders, 60
Recycle Bin, 60
reducing text size, *170, 217*
reestablishing connections to shared folders, 84
refreshing
 folder window display, 226
 lists of files, *54*
 web pages on Desktop, 222
refresh rate for monitors, *242*
regaining control of shared programs, 88
regional settings, *237*, 256, 257, 258–59
registry, 34, 271, 272, 280, 293
reinstalling Windows 2000 or components, 271, 273, 276–77
reloading Windows 2000, 9
remote access. *See* working off site
remote control in NetMeeting, 202–3
Remote Desktop Sharing Wizard, 202

Remote Pointer (Whiteboard), 89
removable disks and disk drives
 compressing files, 210
 copying items to, 62–63
 duplicating floppy disks, 211
 exploring disk contents, 21
 formatting, 210, *210*
 hardware profiles and, 297
 saving files on, 210–11
 space on, *191*
 testing disks, *211*
renaming
 files, 59, *100*, 114
 folders, 59
 items on Start menu, 67
 links, 47
 multiple files, 61
 tracks on CD play list, 139
reopening documents, 30, 32
reorganizing filing structure, 57
repair disks, 271, *271*
repairing systems, 271, *271*, 273
repeating
 characters or keystrokes too quickly, 236
 command prompt commands, 115, *115*
 tracks on CDs, 138
replacing
 file backups completely, 251
 folder window contents, 225
 text, 103, *103*
Replicator And Backup Operators group permissions, 79
replying to messages, 157, *157, 161*, 163, *167*
requesting control in NetMeeting, 88
rerouting printer output, 133
resizing
 cursors, 240
 fax contents, 181
 icons on toolbars, 224
 icon text, 217
 list of Desktop links, 49
 pictures, 108, *108*, 109, 110

screen elements, 240–41
 taskbar and toolbars, *40*, 217, *217*
 text in Outlook Express, *170*
 text in programs, *240*, 265
 video-clip playback, 141
 view of special characters, 105
 windows, 10–11, *11*
resolution
 color settings, 242, 245
 Desktop display, 240–41, 243
 fax printers, *175*
 slow performance and, *242*
 wallpaper, *107*
resource settings, 298
restarting computers
 after configuration changes, 9, 245
 delaying restart process, *300*
 key commands for logging on, 301
 restarting Windows 2000, 9
restarting print jobs, 128
restarting programs, *95*
resting states (hibernation or standby), 9, 254, 255
Restore Wizard, 252
restoring
 backed-up files, 252
 deleted files or folders, 60
 permissions (*see* permissions)
 toolbars to original settings, *224*
restricting users or access. *See* permissions
resuming
 audio-file playback, 136
 print jobs, 128
returning
 to favorite web sites, 48
 to start pages, 43, *46*
reversing guest and host computers, *209*
Rich Text Format
 digital signatures in messages, *165*

Rich Text Format, *continued*
  editing files in WordPad, 102–3
  e-mail formatting, *153*
  file extensions and icons, 35
  files associated with
    Word, *103*
right-clicking. *See* mouse actions
right-handed mouse settings, 234
rights for sound files, *147*
rights of users (*see* permissions)
rings, number of before
    answering, 176
rotating
  fax contents, 181
  images in Paint, 109
  mouse wheel, 18
  portions of images, 110
rules
  for area codes, 195
  for filtering e-mail, 159
running
  command prompt
    commands, 114–15
  programs (*see* opening
    programs)

S

Safe Modes for running
    Windows 2000, 272
sample sheets of fonts, 263
sampling rates for sound
    files, 146
saving
  fax cover pages, 183
  Help topics, 14
  links to favorite sites, 48
  NetMeeting sessions, *89*
  power, 254
  print jobs, 130–31, 132
  special characters, 111
  system configuration
    information, 270
  web pages for offline
    viewing, *50*

saving files
  attached files, 156
  in Briefcase, 191
  to Desktop, 65, *65*
  event sound files, *144*
  image files, *107,* 108, *109,* 110
  keeping copies of
    originals, *102*
  pieces of files, *65, 109*
  print jobs as files, 130–31
  on removable disks, 210–11
  sound recordings, 147
  Thumbnail previews, *55*
  Word files in WordPad, *102*
  WordPad files, 103
scaling of display, 243
scanned images, 110
scanning
  attachments for viruses, *156*
  CD tracks, 138
  drives for errors, 267
Scheduled Task Wizard, 290–91
scheduling
  backups, *251*
  programs to start
    automatically, 290–91
scraps, *65*
screen area, increasing, 243
screen captures in Paint, *109*
screen savers, *203,* 230
ScreenTips (tooltips), 33, 97
scrolling and scroll bars
  adding bars to Start-menu
    submenus, 71
  enlarging bar size, 240
  in Folders Explorer Bar, *57*
  in open folders, 20
  scrolling text on Desktop, 222
  scrolling with mouse wheel, 18
searching. *See* finding
seconds, displaying, 257, 260
sections of documents. *See* parts
    of documents
security. *See also* permissions
  backing up files, 250–51
  changing passwords, 261

disk formats and, 299
encryption, 153, 194
folder aliases and, *289*
locking computers, 253
network IDs, *172*
network security issues, 79
NTFS file system, 80, *211,* 282
private and public keys, *173*
protecting information, 77
screen savers, *203,* 230
secure logons, *281,* 301, *301*
secure messages, 172–73
securing computers, 77
security settings on local
    computers, 287
sharing Internet connections
    and IP addresses, *295*
sharing programs, *89*
Seek Bar, 136
selecting
  files to move or copy, *58*
  members of groups, 167
  printers, 104
  program components to
    install, 277
  text, 102, 110
  web site addresses, 49
selecting items on screen
  by dragging, 17
  elements on fax cover
    pages, 183
  multiple items, 17
  on Whiteboard, 89
  by pointing and clicking,
    16, 231
selections, saving as scraps, *65*
Send Fax Wizard, *178,* 179
sending
  faxes, 174–75, *178,* 178–79, *179*
  files, 205, 206–7, 212
  newsgroup messages, 163
  print files to printers, *131,* 132
  web site address to
    shortcuts, 50
sending command prompt
    output to files, 118

sending debugging information
    to other computers, 272
sending e-mail
  attachments, 156
  to groups of people, 167
  overview, 152–53
  replying to or forwarding
    messages, 157
  sending instantly, *154*
  vCards, 171, 173
Send To command, 31, 211
Send To folder, 63
Send To submenu, *62,* 63, *63*
separating print jobs, 127
SerialKey devices, 236
serial port connections,
    208, *209*
serial printers, *122*
servers
  addresses, 294
  in client-server networks, 24
  e-mail servers, 164
  FTP servers, 212
  in peer-to-peer networks, 24
  print servers, 90
service bureaus, printing at, *131*
service releases for Windows
    2000, *266*
Setup programs, 278, 279, 280
shaded boxes in installation
    process, *277*
Shared Contacts folder, *167,
    168,* 169
sharing addresses in Outlook
    Express, *168,* 169
sharing computers
  assigning type of access, 83
  disconnecting users, 84
  disk-space quotas, 304
  monitoring sharing, 84–85
  NetMeeting remote control,
    202–3
  overview, 78
  reconnecting users, *84*
  Sharing command
    unavailable, *81*

sharing files or folders
    assigning drive letters to
        folders, 27
    cable connections, 208–9
    caching shared documents
        on hard drives, 86–87
    controlling item sharing, 85
    deleting shared files, 59
    disconnecting users, 84
    disk-space quotas, 304
    enabling sharing, 78
    groups, permissions, and
        security, 79
    HyperTerminal access,
        204–5
    limiting access, 82–83
    linking to shared
        folders, 26
    logging off and folder
        sharing, 9
    making files always
        available, 86–87
    modem connections, 198
    monitoring sharing, 84–85
    NTFS file system and, 83
    opening shared files or
        folders, 22, 23
    overview, 80–81
    permissions, 81
    problems when creating
        subfolders, 56
    protecting shared files, 81
    reconnecting users, 84
    restricting numbers of
        users, 80
    Sharing command
        unavailable, 81
    slow computer
        performance, 80
    transferring files by phone
        line, 196–97
    turning off sharing for
        items, 85
    Web Sharing tab, 289
sharing Internet connections,
    294–95, 295

sharing printers
    after-hours print sharing, 91
    command prompt
        printing, 133
    fax printers, 174
    locating shared printers, 91
    network printers, 90–91,
        126, 127, 133
    separating print jobs, 127
sharing programs, 85, 88–89,
    89, 185
sharing web pages, 92
shortcut keys. See keyboard
    shortcuts
shortcut menus, 6, 13, 13
shortcuts. See also keyboard
    shortcuts
    for closing open windows, 225
    for copying and pasting, 99
    for creating subfolders, 56
    on Desktop, 49, 64–65
    for finding hidden taskbar, 218
    to frequently used files, 31
    hiding shortcut key
        underline, 242
    key command notations, 301
    mouse-wheel shortcuts, 18
    My Documents folder
        location, 20
    pressing one key at a time, 236
    for printing, 124
    for program startup
        behavior, 96
    for reconnecting to computers
        with dial-in access, 197
    in Send To folder, 63
    on Start menu, 67
    on toolbars, 40, 41
    for turning off sound, 137
    to web sites, 45, 50
showing. See entries beginning
    with displaying
shutting down, 8, 9, 71, 120
sideways faxes, rotating, 181
signatures in e-mail, 153, 165, 173
single-clicking. See mouse actions

sites. See web pages and web sites
sizes
    of disks, 210, 211
    of files (see file size)
    of icons, 54, 217, 218, 224
    of mouse pointers, 233
    of taskbar and toolbars, 217
    of text, 265
    of windows, 10–11, 11
skips in streaming media, 143
slow performance. See
    performance
small icons, 54, 224
smoothing fonts on screen, 242
Snap-In tools, 292
snapping cursors to default
    buttons, 235
sorting
    e-mail messages, 155
    file listings in folders, 55
    folders to top in listings, 55
    history by categories, 32, 33
    items on menus, 69, 70, 73
sound cards, 136, 146
sound features
    in e-mail, 153, 154
    event sounds, 144, 144
    Narrator, 94, 238–39, 239
    sound controls, 148, 238
    special alert key sounds, 236
sound files
    associating with events,
        144, 144
    browsing for, 137
    copyrights, 147
    creating, 94, 146–47
    creating sound effects, 147
    default media player, 145
    downloading from
        Internet, 137
    file extensions and icons, 137
    file formats, 35, 137, 145
    Media Player, 94
    playback devices, 143
    playing CDs, 138–39
    playing, 136–37, 137

radio broadcasts, 140
recording, 94
sound effects, 147
streaming audio, 142–43
volume control, 141, 148
Sound Recorder, 94, 146–47, 147
sound systems, 94, 238–39
source documents, 100, 100
space characters in filenames, 61
speakers, 136, 137, 143, 148,
    148, 187
special characters, 94, 105,
    111, 111
special modes for startup, 272–73
speed
    of double-clicking, 234
    of mouse on screen, 235
    of sound files, 147
    of streaming media, 142, 143
    of text readback, 239
speeding up operations.
    See performance
stacking taskbar or toolbars,
    214, 217
stand-alone computers. See
    computers; local computers
Standard Buttons toolbar, 224
standby mode (hibernation),
    9, 254, 255
Start button, 6, 31, 94
starting programs. See opening
    programs
starting up computers, 8, 27,
    272–73, 300–301
Start menu
    adding items to, 31, 95
    display options, 71
    full menu display, 71
    hiding, 215
    illustration, 7
    moving, 214
    organizing items, 67–68, 69, 70
    personal items on, 71
    scroll bars on submenus, 71
    shortcuts on, 67
    submenus, 70, 70

start pages, 43, *43*, 46, *46*, 288
startup identities, 168
startup window size, 119
stationery in e-mail, 153
statistical calculations, 94, *112*, 112–13, *113*
status bar, 6
stopping or canceling
    audio file playback, 136, *137*
    CD playback, 138
    command prompt commands, 115
    decisions in dialog boxes, 104
    print jobs, 128
    program sharing, 88
    shared Internet connections, *295*
    sharing for items, 85
    sound recording, 147
    video-clip playback, 141
streaming media, *142*, 142–43
stretching pictures on Desktop, 221
styled text in e-mail, *153, 165*
subfolders
    in compressed folders, 302
    creating, 56, *56*
    dragging to move or copy, *57*
    in Favorites list, 48
    naming, 56
    narrowing searches, 37
    organizing files in, 57, 58
    permissions, *282*, 283
    recovering deleted, 60
    renaming or deleting, 59
    sorting to top in listings, *55*
    on Start menu, 70, *70*
submenus, 7, 13, 67
subscribing to newsgroups, 160
suspending Windows 2000, 9
switches
    command prompt commands, *114*
    program behavior and, 96, *119*
    scheduled tasks and, *291*
    trying out switches, *115*

switching
    CDs in multiple CD players, 138
    CD tracks, 138
    drives or folders in command prompt, 51, 114
    folder window display, 229
    identities, 168–69
    keyboard layouts, 259
    mouse buttons, 234–35
    programs, 97
    windows, 21
    window sizes, 10
symbols, 105, 111, *111*
synchronizing files
    from Briefcase, 191
    cached files, 87
    network files, 192, *193*
    versions of files, 190–91
synchronizing newsgroup messages, 162
system configuration. *See* configuration
system files, showing or hiding, 75
System Tools, 84, *85*

tabs in dialog boxes, 104
targeting printers, 124, 125
taskbar
    date display on, *256*
    displaying or hiding, 215, *217*, 218–19
    full names of programs on, 97
    icons on, *217*, 218, 255
    illustration, 7
    keyboard locales on, 259
    menu items on, 218
    minimized window names on, 10
    on multiple monitors, *219*
    rearranging or resizing, 216–17
    time display on, 218, *260*
    toolbars and, 40, 217

Task Manager, 120
TCP/IP networks, 164
technical support
    Dr. Watson files, *269*
    system configuration information, 270
telephone calls. *See* incoming phone calls; outgoing phone calls
telephone numbers. *See* phone numbers
Telnet terminals, *204*
templates, fax cover page, 183
terminals, 204–5, 206–7
terminology for Windows 2000, 6–7
testing removable disks, *211*
text. *See also* text files
    aligning columnar data, 117
    in command prompt window, 114, 115, 117, *117*, 118
    digital signatures, 165
    displaying text instead of sounds, 238
    e-mail formatting, *153, 165*
    fax and cover page notes, 182, 183
    folder window comments, 226
    fonts (*see* fonts)
    icon text, 47, *217, 221*, 224, 227, *244*
    magnifying in programs, *240*
    moving within documents, 103
    NetMeeting notes, 89
    Outlook Express text, *170*
    picture notations, *107*, 110
    reading aloud with Narrator, 94, 238–39, *239*
    replacing, 103, *103*
    scrolling across Desktop, 222
    searching for in documents, *37*
    size, 18, *170*, 240–41, 265
    special characters and symbols, 111
    working in WordPad, 102

text files, 35, 94, 102–3, 205
text-mode file transfers, 212
threads in newsgroups, *161*
thumbnail fax views, 182
thumbnail Paint pictures, *108*
Thumbnails view of files, *54, 55, 110*
TIF files, 35, *110, 181*
tiling
    pictures on Desktop, 221
    windows, 66, *97*
times and dates
    changing, 260
    daylight saving time, 260
    display formats, 256–57
    displaying in documents, *257*
    displaying on taskbar, 218, 260
    finding files by date used, 32, 33
    international settings, 258–59
    scheduled tasks and, 291
    time zones, 260
title bars, 6, 10, 11, 104, 240
toolbars
    always on top, 218
    arranging, 214, 216–17, 247
    customizing, 41, 170, 224
    deleting links from, 47
    deleting, *41*
    displaying or hiding, 40, *217, 218*, 218–19
    floating, 215
    icons on, *217*
    illustration, 6
    on multiple monitors, *219*, 247
    overview, 40
    rearranging items on, 40, *47*
    resizing, *40*, 217
    restoring to original settings, *224*
    stacking, 217
tooltips, 33, 97
tracks on CDs, 138, 139, *139*

transferring files
downloading from
Internet, 212
by modem, 196–97, 206–7
with NetMeeting, *185*
to print shops, *131*
to removable disks, 210–11
traveling. *See* working off site
Troubleshooter Wizard, 269
troubleshooting problems.
See problem solving
True Color setting, 242
TrueType fonts, 264
"Try This" exercises
addresses on History Explorer
Bar, *33*
browsing for audio files, *137*
closing windows, *11*
command prompt
switches, *115*
daily backups, *251*
date and time formats, *257*
digital IDs and public keys, *173*
e-mail and news accounts on
multiple computers, *151*
e-mail message fonts and
sizes, *154*
fax date stamps, *182*
keyboard locales, *259*
logoff options, *71*
navigating in command
prompt, *118*
opaque and transparent
images in Paint, *109*
Outlook Express as news
reader, *96*
phone-call logs, *186*
preventing changes to shared
documents, *81*
previews of files, *55*
printing from files, *131*
print separator pages with
messages, *127*
programs associated with
documents, *29*
projects on Favorites menu, *73*

removable disk formatting, *211*
resizing toolbars, *40*
scheduled tasks, *291*
scraps, *65*
showing or hiding toolbars
and taskbar, *217*
sound effects, *147*
subfolders, *56*
wallpaper, *107*
watching or ignoring news
messages, *162*
web pages on multiple
monitors, *247*
TSID numbers, *174*
turning off. *See* exiting
turning on computers. *See*
starting up computers
two-monitor setups, 246–47
Type 1 PostScript fonts, *263*, 264
typefaces. *See* fonts
type manager programs, *263*
types of files. *See* file formats
typing
accessibility options, 236–37
adding text to pictures, *107*
addresses for web sites, *45*
command-line
instructions, 114
in command prompt, 115
input settings, 236–37
On-Screen Keyboard, 237
over text, 103
repeated characters or rapid
keystrokes, 236
special characters, 105
text in WordPad, 102
text on NetMeeting
Whiteboard, 89

unavailable options in dialog
boxes, 104
underlining, *231*, 242
undoing actions, *60*, 106

uninstalling programs or
components, 276–77,
279, 280
unlisted printers, *126*
unlocking computers, 253
unread messages, 161
Update Driver Wizard, 298
updating
Computer Management
window, *85*
drivers or system, 266,
269, 298
embedded or linked objects,
100, 101
files, *54*, 87, 191
folder window display, 226
Media Player, *136*, 145
repair disks, *271*
web pages on Desktop, 222
upside-down faxes,
rotating, 181
URLs, *45*. *See also* addresses for
web sites
user groups. *See* groups
(network or workgroup)
users
access to shared
folders, 82–83
access to shared
printers, 91
adding addresses, 166–67, *167*
adding to Active Directory, *187*
assigning type of access, 83
calling with Phone Dialer, 186
choosing e-mail recipients, 152
Contacts list, 152, 170
creating accounts, *82*, 196,
283, 284–85
dial-in access, 196, *198*
digital IDs or public keys, *173*
disk-space quotas, 304
file and folder permissions,
82–83, 282, 287
in groups, 79, 167
identities and, 168, *168*, 169
local logons, *197*

monitoring sharing, 84–85
restricting numbers of, 80
searching for, *23*, 42
setting up two accounts, 281
user names, 8, 212
user profiles, 63, *63*
Users group permissions, 79

vCards, *167*, 171, *171*, *173*
vector fonts, 264
versions of files, *102*, 190–91
VGA video drivers, 272
video
cards, 246, *246*
clips, 94, 141, 142–43, 145
conferences, 184, *187*
drivers, startup modes
and, 272
viewing. *See entries beginning
with* displaying
Views toolbar, 170
virtual drives, 27
Virtual Private Network
connections, 196, 199, *200*,
200–201, *201*
viruses, *156*, *301*
visibility
color schemes, *244*
enlarging screen, 240–41
mouse pointer, *233*
visual glossary, 6–7
voice-enabled software (Narrator),
94, 238–39, *239*
volume controls
computer settings, 148
quickly turning off sound, *137*
recording sound files, 146, 147
for sound files, 136
for speakers, *148*
of text readback, 239
for video-clip playback, 141
VPN connections, 196, 199, *200*,
200–201, *201*

wallpaper, 7, *107, 221*
warnings. *See* alerts
watching for news messages, *162*
wave sounds. *See also* sound files
  creating sound effects, *147*
  file extensions and icons,
    35, *137*
  file sizes, *146*
  sound file formats and
    CODECs, 145
  storing, *144*
web-based radio stations, 140
web browsers, 94. *See also*
    Internet Explorer
web content
  on Active Desktop, 215
  comments in folder
    windows, 226
  My Pictures folder
    previews, 228
  option for folders, *110*
  pictures in folder
    windows, 227
  removing from folder
    windows, 229
  web-style icons, 16
Web Events (Media Player), *137*
web pages and web sites
  aliases for folders, *289*
  Desktop backgrounds, 215, 222
  editing on multiple
    monitors, *247*
  exploring, 43
  Favorites menu list, 72–73
  going to specific sites, 45
  hosting, 288–89
  illustration, 7
  IIS, 92
  links and shortcuts to, 48,
    49, 50, 215

recently used addresses, 74
  searching for, 44
  start pages, 46
  storing off line for later
    reading, *50*
  streaming media, 142–43
  Web Sharing tab, 80
wheel mouse, 18, *235*
Whiteboard (NetMeeting), 89, *89*
wildcard characters, 61, 212
windows
  active, 97
  animating on screen, 242
  arranging, moving, and
    dragging, 11, 66,
    242, 247
  cascading or tiling, 66
  command prompt, 114
  comments in, 226
  default size for programs,
    96, *119*
  docked taskbar or toolbars, 216
  fonts used in, 119
  illustration, 7
  leaving open for quick
    access, *192*
  maximizing and minimizing,
    7, 10–11, *66, 247*
  messages in separate, 155, *161*
  multiple monitors, 247
  opening and closing, *10*,
    10–11, 222, 225, *225*
  pictures in backgrounds, 227
  resizing, 10–11, *11*
  selecting items in, 16–17
  switching to previous, 21
  thumbnails for images in, *110*
  visual glossary, 6–7
Windows Briefcase, 190–91, *191*
Windows Components Wizard,
    276–77
Windows Help. *See* Help
Windows Installer, *279,* 280

Windows Media Player. *See*
    Media Player
Windows 2000 Professional
  boot disks, *273*
  CDs, 272, *273*
  disk formats, 299
  identifying drive with installed
    files, *63*
  installing or removing
    components, 2, 276–77
  multiple operating
    systems, 300
  online manual, *14*
  registry, 293
  service releases, *266*
  shutting down, 120
  sounds for events, 144
  starting up, 8
  updating automatically, 266
  visual glossary, 6–7
Windows 2000 Server, 3
Windows Update Wizard, 266
wizards. *See names of specific*
    wizards
WordPad
  creating scraps with, *65*
  description, 94
  editing documents in, 102–3
  running automatically, *291*
  saving and printing, 103
  typical documents for, 35
  using Narrator with, *239*
Word 2000, *33, 102,* 102–3, *178*
workgroups. *See* groups
    (network or workgroup)
working folders, 119
working off line
  offline e-mail messages, *153*
  offline files, using, 87, 192–93
  offline printing, 132
  offline web sites, *50*
  working with news
    messages, 162

working off site
  connecting
    with cables, 208–9
    from different
      locations, 195
    by modem, 198
    over Internet, 200–201
    by phone, 196–97
    to terminals, 204–5
  controlling computers
    remotely, 202–3
  copying network files, 192–93
  disconnecting remote
    access, *203*
  downloading Internet files, 212
  encrypting files, 194
  logging on, 199
  NetMeeting sessions, 202–3
  removable-disk storage, 210–11
  tracking copied files, 190–91
  transferring files by modem,
    206–7
  working long distance, 189
Write program, 102–3
WYSIWYG fonts, 264

years, displaying, 256, 260

Zapf dingbats, 265
ZIP disks. *See* removable disks
    and disk drives
zooming
  enlarging
    fax contents, 181
    images, *108,* 110
  video-clip playback, 141
  zoom controls, *240*

Jerry Joyce has had a long-standing relationship with Microsoft: he was the technical editor on numerous books published by Microsoft Press, and he has written manuals, help files, and specifications for various Microsoft products. As a programmer, he has tried to make using a computer as simple as using any household appliance, but he has yet to succeed. Jerry's alter ego is that of a marine biologist; he has conducted research from the Arctic to the Antarctic and has published extensively on marine-mammal and fisheries issues. As antidotes to staring at his computer screen, he enjoys traveling, birding, boating, and wandering about beaches, wetlands, and mountains.

Marianne Moon has worked in the publishing world for many years as proofreader, editor, and writer—sometimes all three simultaneously. She has been editing and proofreading Microsoft Press books since 1984 and has written and edited documentation for Microsoft products such as Microsoft Works, Flight Simulator, Space Simulator, Golf, Publisher, the Microsoft Mouse, and Greetings Workshop. In another life, she was chief cook and bottlewasher for her own catering service and wrote cooking columns for several newspapers. When she's not chained to her computer, she likes gardening, cooking, traveling, writing poetry, and knitting sweaters for tiny dogs.

Marianne and **Jerry** own and operate **Moon Joyce Resources**, a small consulting company. They are coauthors of *Microsoft Word 97 At a Glance, Microsoft Windows 95 At a Glance, Microsoft Windows NT Workstation 4.0 At a Glance, Microsoft Windows 98 At a Glance,* and *Microsoft Word 2000 At a Glance*. They've had an 18-year working relationship and have been married for 8 years. If you have questions or comments about any of their books, you can reach them at moonjoyceresourc@hotmail.com.

The manuscript for this book was prepared and submitted to Microsoft Press in electronic form. Text files were prepared using Microsoft Word 2000. Pages were composed using QuarkXPress 3.32 for the Power Macintosh, with text in ITC Stone Serif and ITC Stone Sans, and display type in ITC Stone Sans Semibold. Composed pages were delivered to the printer as electronic prepress files.

Cover Design and Illustration
Girvin | Strategic Branding & Design

Interior Graphic Artist
Sue Cook Visuals

Interior Illustrator
s.bishop.design

Typographer
Blue Fescue Typography & Design

Proofreader/Copy Editor
Alice Copp Smith

Indexer
Wright Information Indexing Services